ZAGATSURVEY®

2001

SAN FRANCISCO BAY AREA RESTAURANTS

Editor: Catherine Bigwood

Local Editor: Meesha Halm

Local Coordinator: Maura Sell

Published and distributed by
ZAGAT SURVEY, LLC
4 Columbus Circle
New York, New York 10019
Tel: 212 977 6000
E-mail: sanfran@zagat.com
Web site: www.zagat.com

Acknowledgments

We'd like to thank the nearly 3,000 respondents who tirelessly ate their way through the Bay Area's top restaurants and then lived to tell us about it. Without their participation in the questionnaire, this *Survey* would not have been a success. Special thanks are due to Whole Foods Market Northern California stores for distributing the questionnaires, as well as Jon Fox, Conor and Vincent Logan, and Willow Waldeck. And of course, to the region's great chefs and restaurateurs whose talents and efforts continue to make the Bay Area arguably the best dining region in America.

This guide would not have been possible without the exacting work of our staff:

Phil Cardone, Erica Curtis, Liz Daleske, Laura du Pont, Jeff Freier, Sarah Kagan, Natalie Lebert, Mike Liao, Dave Makulec, Jefferson Martin, Andrew O'Neill, Bernard Onken, Benjamin Schmerler, Troy Segal, Robert Seixas, Zamira Skalkottas and LaShana Smith.

Contents

About This Survey

Here are the results of our *2001 San Francisco Bay Area Restaurant Survey* covering some 932 restaurants from the wine country in the north to the Monterey Peninsula in the south.

By regularly surveying large numbers of local restaurant-goers, we have achieved a uniquely current and reliable guide. Nearly 3,000 people participated. Since the surveyors dined out an average of 3.17 times per week, this *Survey* is based on about 488,000 meals per year.

We want to thank each of our participants. They are a widely diverse group in all respects but one – they are food lovers all. This book is really "theirs."

Of the surveyors, 55% are women, 45% are men; the break-down by age is 14% in their 20s, 28% in their 30s, 23% in their 40s, 22% in their 50s and 13% in their 60s or above.

To help guide our readers to The Bay Area's best meals and best buys, we have prepared a number of lists. See, for example, The Bay Area's Most Popular Restaurants (page 11), Top Ratings (pages 12–16) and Best Buys (page 17). On the assumption that most people want a quick fix on the places at which they are considering eating, we have provided handy indexes.

We are particularly grateful to our editor, Meesha Halm, a nationally published restaurant critic, Internet columnist and cookbook author, and our coordinator, Maura Sell, a professionally trained chef and consultant to the specialty food industry.

We invite you to be a reviewer in our next *Survey*. To do so, simply send a stamped, self-addressed, business-size envelope to ZAGAT SURVEY, 4 Columbus Circle, New York, NY 10019, or e-mail us at sanfran@zagat.com, so that we will be able to contact you. Each participant will receive a free copy of the next *San Francisco Bay Area Restaurant Survey* when it is published.

Your comments, suggestions and even criticisms of this *Survey* are also solicited. There is always room for improvement with your help.

New York, New York
October 6, 2000

Nina + Tim
Nina and Tim Zagat

What's New

This is a boom year for Bay Area restaurants, much of it fueled by money from the dot-com crowd, which upped eating-out traffic, drove the average meal price to $30.47, helped give rise to online reservations and shepherded in related debate over whether manners in the millennium can coexist with cell phones at the dining table. Note to Web heads: some start-ups like Venture Frogs Restaurant, a high-tech Pan-Asian funded by two twentysomething entrepreneurs, are gearing their entire menus to Internet-oriented items like 'Microsoft minced chicken in lettuce' and 'eBay eggplant.'

Not surprisingly, many of this year's highest-ranking rookies are expense-account establishments: Gary Danko's eponymous French–New American; the serene Elisabeth Daniel Restaurant (from the ex chef-owners of Sonoma's Babette's); and George Morrone's ultraluxe Fifth Floor. Bay Area foodies even forked over big bucks to dine at Don Johnson and Cheech Marin's lavish Vietnamese Ana Mandara, Jody Denton's French-Asian Azie, the opulent Chaya Brasserie, sib of the LA Franco-Japanese winner, and Roy Yamaguchi's Euro-Asian Roy's, despite easy access to far less expensive ethnic options.

Still, escalating restaurant rents haven't stunted the growth of neighborhood spots, they've just pushed them into some of the city's dicier 'hoods. The Mission continues to expand with hip venues like the Pacific Rim restaurant/jazz club, butterfly, and across town, the opening of the Giants' new stadium, Pacific Bell Park, revitalized the restaurant-barren China Basin; now the cry "take me out to the ball game" is augmented by "take me out to dinner while you're at it." Stepping up to the plate to fill the need are Livefire Grill & Smokehouse, Paragon and Twenty Four.

There were several significant losses this year: the legendary Washington Square Bar & Grill followed its famous client Herb Caen into immortality; Carlo Middione's Vivande Ristorante folded; and the revered Redwood Room in the Clift Hotel closed down for a complete, and hotly contested, renovation.

However, the good news is there are also a number of promising premieres. Among them: Eos Restaurant & Wine Bar chef-owner Arnold Eric Wong is scheduled to open the American brasserie, Bacar, in SoMa, and in Larkspur, foodies are looking forward to celeb chef Bradley Ogden's New England–inspired seafood shack, Yankee Pier, which is anticipated to open later this autumn.

There's also been a bumper crop of activity in the wine country. Notable Napa newcomers include the meat mecca, Cole's Chop House, and the jaunty trattoria, Tuscany, while Sonoma welcomes the seasonally driven Italian Santi (run by ex Jordan Winery chefs) and the American Mucca.

San Francisco, CA Meesha Halm
October 6, 2000

Dining Tips

Over our 20-plus years of surveying restaurant-goers, we've heard from hundreds of thousands of people about their dining-out experiences. Most of their reports are positive – proof of the ever-growing skill and dedication of the nation's chefs and restaurateurs. But inevitably, we also hear about problems.

Obviously, there are certain basics that everyone has the right to expect when dining out: 1. Courteous, hospitable, informative service; 2. Clean, sanitary facilities; 3. Fresh, healthful food; 4. Timely honoring of reservations; and 5. Smoke-free seating.

Sadly, if these conditions aren't met, many diners simply swallow their disappointment, assuming there's nothing they can do. However, the truth is that diners have far more power than they may realize. Every restaurateur worth his or her salt wants to satisfy customers, since happy clients equal a successful business. Rather than the adversaries they sometimes seem to be, diners and restaurateurs are natural allies – both want the same outcome, and each can help the other achieve it. Toward that end, here are a few simple but sometimes forgotten tips that every restaurant-goer should bear in mind:

1. Speak up: If dissatisfied by any aspect of your experience – from the handling of your reservation to the food, service or physical environment – tell the manager. Most problems are easy to resolve at the time they occur – but not if management doesn't know about them until afterward. The opposite is also true: if you're pleased, speak up.

2. Spell out your needs ahead of time: If you have specific dietary requests, wish to bring your own wine, want a smoke-free (or smoking) environment, or have any other special needs, you can avoid disappointment by calling ahead to make sure the restaurant can satisfy you.

3. Do your part: A restaurant's ability to honor reservations, for example, is largely dependent on diners honoring reservations and showing up on time. Make it a point to cancel reservations you're unable to use and be sure to notify the restaurant if you'll be late. The restaurant, in turn, should do its best to seat parties promptly, and, if there are delays, should keep diners informed (a free drink doesn't hurt either).

4. Vote with your dollars: Most people tip 15 to 19%, and often 20% or more at high-end restaurants. Obviously, you have the right not to tip at all if unhappy with the service; but in that case, many simply leave 10% to get the message across. If you like the restaurant, it's worth accompanying the low tip with a word to the management. Of course, the ultimate way to vote with your dollars is not to come back.

5. Put it in writing: Like it or not, all restaurants make mistakes. The best ones distinguish themselves by how well they acknowledge and handle mistakes. If you've expressed your complaints to the restaurant management but haven't gotten a satisfactory response, write to your local restaurant critic, with a copy to the restaurant, detailing the problem. That really gets the restaurateur's attention. Naturally, we also hope you'll express your feelings, pro and con, by voting on zagat.com.

Key to Ratings/Symbols

This sample entry identifies the various types of information contained in your Zagat Survey.

(1) Restaurant Name, Address & Phone Number

(2) Hours & Credit Cards

(3) ZAGAT Ratings

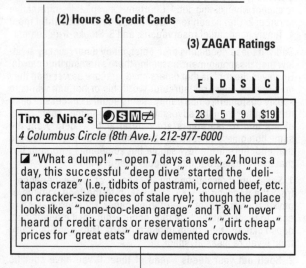

F	D	S	C
23	5	9	$19

Tim & Nina's ◐⑤Ⓜ⌀

4 Columbus Circle (8th Ave.), 212-977-6000

☑ "What a dump!" – open 7 days a week, 24 hours a day, this successful "deep dive" started the "deli-tapas craze" (i.e., tidbits of pastrami, corned beef, etc. on cracker-size pieces of stale rye); though the place looks like a "none-too-clean garage" and T & N "never heard of credit cards or reservations", "dirt cheap" prices for "great eats" draw demented crowds.

(4) Surveyors' Commentary

The names of restaurants with the highest overall ratings, greatest popularity and importance are printed in **CAPITAL LETTERS**. Address and phone numbers are printed in *italics*.

(2) Hours & Credit Cards

After each restaurant name you will find the following courtesy information:

◐	....	*serving after 11 PM, Monday–Thursday*
L	....	*open for lunch*
S	....	*open on Sunday*
M	....	*open on Monday*
⌀	....	*no credit cards accepted*

(3) ZAGAT Ratings

Food, **Decor** and **Service** are each rated on a scale of **0** to **30**:

F	D	S	C

F .... *Food*
D .... *Decor*
S .... *Service*
C .... *Cost*

23	5	9	$19

0 - 9	....	*poor to fair*
10 - 15	....	*fair to good*
16 - 19	....	*good to very good*
20 - 25	....	*very good to excellent*
26 - 30	....	*extraordinary to perfection*

▽ 23	5	9	$19

▽ .... *Low number of votes/less reliable*

The **Cost (C)** column reflects the estimated price of a dinner with one drink and tip. Lunch usually costs 25% less.

A restaurant listed without ratings is either an important **newcomer** or a popular **write-in**. The estimated cost, with one drink and tip, is indicated by the following symbols.

–	–	–	VE

I .... *$15 and below*
M .... *$16 to $30*
E .... *$31 to $50*
VE .... *$51 or more*

(4) Surveyors' Commentary

Surveyors' comments are summarized, with literal comments shown in quotation marks. The following symbols indicate whether responses were mixed or uniform.

◪ .... *mixed*
■ .... *uniform*

Most Popular

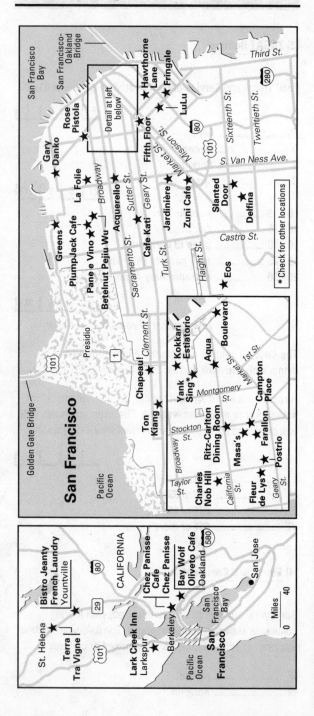

San Francisco

Golden Gate Bridge
San Francisco Bay
San Francisco-Oakland Bridge
Third St.
Pacific Ocean
Presidio

Gary Danko
Rose Pistola
Hawthorne Lane
Fringale
LuLu
Fifth Floor
La Folie
Acquerello
Betelnut Pejiu Wu
Greens
PlumpJack Cafe
Pane e Vino
Cafe Kati
Jardinière
Zuni Cafe
Slanted Door
Delfina
Eos
Chapeau!
Ton Kiang

Detail at left below

Broadway
Sutter St.
Geary St.
Market St.
Mission St.
Sixteenth St.
Twentieth St.
S. Van Ness Ave.
Castro St.
Turk St.
Haight St.
Sacramento St.
Clement St.

280
80
101
1

* Check for other locations

Kokkari Estiatorio
Aqua
Boulevard
Yank Sing*
Campton Place
Ritz-Carlton Dining Room
Masa's
Farallon
Postrio
Charles Nob Hill
Fleur de Lys

Montgomery St.
Stockton St.
Taylor St.
Broadway
California St.
Geary St.
Market St.
1st St.

CALIFORNIA
Bistro Jeanty
French Laundry
Yountville
Chez Panisse Cafe
Chez Panisse
Bay Wolf
Oliveto Cafe
Oakland
San Jose
Terra
Tra Vigne
St. Helena
Lark Creek Inn
Larkspur
Berkeley
San Francisco
San Francisco Bay
Pacific Ocean

580
80
29
101

Miles
0   40

10   www.zagat.com

Most Popular*

Each of our reviewers has been asked to name his or her five favorite restaurants. The 40 spots most frequently named, in order of their popularity, are:

1. Boulevard
2. French Laundry/N
3. Jardinière
4. Aqua
5. Gary Danko
6. Farallon
7. Fleur de Lys
8. Hawthorne Lane
9. Postrio
10. Chez Panisse/E
11. Fringale
12. Ritz-Carlton Din. Rm.
13. Slanted Door
14. Chez Panisse Cafe/E
15. Masa's
16. Fifth Floor
17. La Folie**
18. Tra Vigne/N
19. Bistro Jeanty/N
20. Chapeau!

21. Kokkari Estiatorio
22. Eos
23. Zuni Cafe
24. Charles Nob Hill
25. Delfina
26. Rose Pistola
27. Betelnut Pejiu Wu
28. Oliveto Cafe/E
29. Acquerello
30. Campton Place
31. PlumpJack Cafe
32. Terra/N
33. Pane e Vino
34. Greens
35. Cafe Kati
36. Lark Creek Inn/N
37. Bay Wolf/E
38. Ton Kiang
39. LuLu
40. Yank Sing

It's obvious that many of the restaurants on the above list are among the most expensive, but San Franciscans also love a bargain. Were popularity calibrated to price, we suspect that a number of other restaurants would join the above ranks. Thus, we have listed 80 Best Buys on page 17.

---

* All restaurants are in the City of San Francisco unless otherwise noted (E=East of San Francisco; N=North of San Francisco; and S=South of San Francisco).
** Tied with the restaurant listed directly above it.

Top Ratings*

Top 40 Food Ranking

29 French Laundry/N
28 Gary Danko
   Chez Panisse/E
   Masa's
   Ritz-Carlton Din. Rm.
   La Folie
   Elisabeth Daniel
27 Terra/N
   Fleur de Lys
   Erna's Elderberry/S
   Charles Nob Hill
   Boulevard
   Sent Sovi/S
   Le Papillon/S
   Cheeseboard/E
   Chez Panisse Cafe/E
   Aqua
26 Fifth Floor
   Jardinière
   Acquerello

   Postrio
   Bistro Jeanty/N
   Hawthorne Lane
   Mariposa/N
   Domaine Chandon/N
   Campton Place
   Fringale
   Rivoli/E
   Sushi Ran/N
   Pisces/S
   Slanted Door
   Emile's/S
   Emporio Rulli/N
   John Bentley's/S
   Fresh Cream/S
   Kirala/E
25 Delfina
   Pacific's Edge/S
   Woodward's Garden
   Ravenous/N

Top Spots by Cuisine

American (New)
29 French Laundry/N
28 Gary Danko
27 Boulevard
26 John Bentley's/S
25 Woodward's Gardens

Californian
28 Chez Panisse/E
27 Terra/N
   Erna's Elderberry/S
   Charles Nob Hill
26 Jardinière

American (Traditional)
23 House of Prime Rib
   Mama's/Washington Sq.
   Hayes St. Grill
22 Bix
   JoAnn's Cafe/S

Chinese
25 Tommy Toy's
   Ton Kiang
22 Harbor Village
   Eliza's
21 Shen Hua/E

Bakery/Deli
27 Cheeseboard/E
26 Emporio Rulli/N
25 Gayle's Bakery/S
24 Downtown Bakery/N
22 Vivande Porta Via

Continental
22 Ovation
21 Bella Vista/S
20 Caprice/N
19 Eulipia/S
   Rocco's Seafood

---

* Excluding restaurants with low voting; all restaurants are in the City
  of San Francisco unless otherwise noted (E=East of San Francisco;
  N=North of San Francisco; and S=South of San Francisco).

Dim Sum
25 Ton Kiang
24 Yank Sing
22 Harbor Village
   Fook Yuen/S
   Hong Kong Flower/S

Eclectic/International
25 Ravenous/N
   Café La Haye/N
24 Celadon/N
23 Wappo Bar Bistro/N
   Firefly

French (Bistro)
26 Bistro Jeanty/N
   Fringale
25 Chapeau!
24 Cafe Marcella/S
   L'Amie Donia/S

French (Classic)
28 Masa's
26 Campton Place
   Emile's/S
25 Le Mouton Noir/S
   Cafe Jacqueline

French (New)
28 Ritz-Carlton Din. Rm.
   La Folie
   Elisabeth Daniel
27 Fleur de Lys
   Sent Sovi/S

Fusion
25 Eos
   Ondine/N
   Roy's at Pebble Beach/S
24 Silks
   House

Indian
23 Amber India/S
   Shalimar
   Indian Oven
22 Breads of India/E
   Ajanta/E

Italian
26 Acquerello
25 Delfina
   Tra Vigne/N
24 Bistro Don Giovanni/N
   Oliveto Cafe/E

Japanese
26 Sushi Ran/N
   Kirala/E
24 Sanraku Four Seasons
   Ebisu
   Kyo-Ya

Mediterranean
26 Rivoli/E
25 PlumpJack Cafe
   Lalime's/E
   Bay Wolf/E
24 Zuni Cafe

Mexican/Tex-Mex
23 La Taqueria
22 Aqui Cal-Mex Grill/S
21 Pancho Villa Taqueria
   Maya
   Taqueria Cancun

Pizza
23 Zachary's/E
   L'Osteria Del Forno
   Tommaso's*
22 Pauline's Pizza
21 Vicolo

Seafood
27 Aqua
26 Pisces/S
25 Swan Oyster Depot
24 Farallon
22 Yabbies Coastal Kit.

Spanish/Tapas
23 Zarzuela
22 B44
20 César/E
19 Alegrias, Food From Spain
   Cha Cha Cha @ Original

Steakhouse
24 Harris'
23 Morton's of Chicago
21 Vic Stewart's/E
   Izzy's
20 Alfred's

Thai
25 Thep Phanom
22 Marnee Thai
   Royal Thai
   Manora's Thai
21 Neecha Thai

---

* Tied with the restaurant listed directly above it.

Top Food

Vegetarian
27 Fleur de Lys
23 Millennium
22 Greens
21 Valentine's Cafe
19 Joubert's

Vietnamese
26 Slanted Door
24 Thanh Long
22 Crustacean
   Le Cheval/E
   Tu Lan

Top Food by Special Feature

Breakfast*
23 Universal Cafe
   Mama's/Washington Sq.
22 Dottie's True Blue
   Cafe Fanny/E
   JoAnn's Cafe/S

Brunch
24 Wente Vineyards/E
   Lark Creek Inn/N
   Zuni Cafe
23 Insalata's/N
22 Mikayla/N

Hotel Dining
28 Masa's
      Hotel Vintage Ct.
   Ritz-Carlton Din. Rm.
      Ritz-Carlton Hotel
26 Fifth Floor
      Hotel Palomar
   Postrio
      Prescott Hotel
   Campton Place
      Campton Pl. Hotel

Late Night
23 Bouchon/N
22 Globe
21 Yuet Lee
   Great Eastern
18 Absinthe

Newcomers/Rated
28 Gary Danko
   Elisabeth Daniel
26 Fifth Floor
   Pisces/S
25 Ondine/N

Newcomers/Unrated
   Chez Nous
   Citizen Cake
   Jianna
   paul K
   Santi/N

People-Watching
26 Jardinière
   Postrio
   Hawthorne Lane
25 Tra Vigne/N
24 Spago Palo Alto/S

Worth a Trip
29 French Laundry/N
      Yountville
28 Chez Panisse/E
      Berkeley
27 Terra/N
      St. Helena
   Erna's Elderberry/S
      Oakhurst
   Sent Sovi/S
      Saratoga

---

* Other than hotels.

Top 40 Decor Ranking

28 Garden Court
Farallon
Auberge du Soleil/N
Ritz-Carlton Din. Rm.
Fifth Floor
27 Ondine/N
Club XIX/S
Gary Danko
Chateau Souverain/N
Pacific's Edge/S
Kokkari Estiatorio
Fleur de Lys
French Laundry/N
26 Erna's Elderberry/S
Jardinière
Domaine Chandon/N
Postrio
Top of the Mark
Ovation
Le Colonial

Caprice/N
Wente Vineyards/E
Mikayla/N
Cypress Club
Boulevard
Tra Vigne/N
St. Orres/N
Aqua
Roy's at Pebble Beach/S
25 Grand Cafe
El Paseo/N
Bix
Campton Place
Compass Rose
Hawthorne Lane
Chez Panisse/E
Manka's Inverness/N
Azie
Masa's
Carnelian Room

Outdoor

Auberge du Soleil/N
Bay Wolf/E
Bistro Don Giovanni/N
Bistro Jeanty/N
Brix/N
Chateau Souverain/N
Citron/E
Domaine Chandon/N
Foreign Cinema

Lark Creek Inn/N
Mariposa/N
Ritz-Carlton Terrace
Roy's at Pebble Beach/S
71 Saint Peter/S
Spago Palo Alto/S
Tra Vigne/N
Waterfront
Wente Vineyards/E

Romantic

Acquerello
Cafe Jacqueline
Elisabeth Daniel
El Paseo/N
Erna's Elderberry/S
Fleur de Lys
Gary Danko

John Bentley's/S
La Folie
Manka's Inverness/N
Ritz-Carlton Din. Rm.
Sent Sovi/S
Terra/N
Woodward's Garden

Room

Ana Mandara
Aqua
Azie
Bouchon/N
Boulevard
Campton Place
Chaya Brasserie
Cypress Club
Farallon
Fifth Floor
Fleur de Lys
Garden Court

Grand Cafe
Jardinière
Kokkari Estiatorio
Le Colonial
mc^2
Pisces/S
Postrio
Ritz-Carlton Din. Rm.
Silks
St. Orres/N
Wild Hare/S
Wine Spectator/N

View

Albion River Inn/N
Alta Mira/N
Auberge du Soleil/N
Beach Chalet Brewery
Bella Vista/S
Caprice/N
Carnelian Room
Cielo/S
Cliff House
Domaine Chandon/N
Gaylord India/S
Greens
Guaymas/N
John Ash & Co./N
Julius' Castle
Mandarin, The
Mikayla/N
Nepenthe/S
Pacific's Edge/S
Ondine/N
Rest. at Meadowood/N
Roy's at Pebble Beach/S
Waterfront
Wente Vineyards/E

Top 40 Service Ranking

28 Ritz-Carlton Din. Rm.
27 French Laundry/N
Gary Danko
Fifth Floor
Erna's Elderberry/S
Masa's
26 Fleur de Lys
Chez Panisse/E
Charles Nob Hill
La Folie
La Toque/N
25 Acquerello
Campton Place
Domaine Chandon/N
Terra/N
Elisabeth Daniel
Emile's/S*
Le Papillon/S
Auberge du Soleil/N
Ritz-Carlton Terrace
Silks
Boulevard
24 Fresh Cream/S
Rest. at Meadowood/N
Club XIX/S
Jardinière
John Bentley's/S
Chapeau!
Park Grill
Postrio
Tommy Toy's
Chez Panisse Cafe/E
Chez T.J./S
Aqua
Sent Sovi/S
Roy's at Pebble Beach/S
Pacific's Edge/S
Hawthorne Lane
Covey/S
Le Mouton Noir/S

---

* Tied with the restaurant listed directly above it.

40 Top Bangs for the Buck

This list reflects the best dining values in our *Survey*. It is produced by dividing the cost of a meal into the combined ratings for food, decor and service.

1. Cheeseboard/E
2. El Balazo
3. Taqueria Cancun
4. Pancho Villa Taqueria
5. La Cumbre Taqueria/S
6. La Taqueria/S
7. Downtown Bakery/N
8. Cactus Taqueria/E
9. Truly Mediterranean
10. Emporio Rulli/N
11. Gayle's Bakery/S
12. Aqui Cal-Mex Grill/S
13. Caffe Greco
14. Dottie's True Blue
15. Model Bakery/N
16. Picante Cocina/E
17. Pork Store Cafe
18. It's Tops Coffee Shop
19. Tomales Bay Foods/N
20. JoAnn's Cafe/S
21. Vi's/E
22. Mo's Burgers
23. Alice's
24. Cafe Fanny/E
25. Red Tractor Cafe/E/S
26. King of Thai
27. Mario's Bohemian
28. Joe's Taco/N
29. Mama's Royal Cafe/E
30. Bette's Oceanview Diner/E
31. Crescent City Cafe
32. Pluto's/S
33. Cafe Borrone/S
34. Zachary's/E
35. Herbivore
36. Juan's Place/E
37. Crepevine/E
38. Tu Lan
39. Mifune
40. Bill's Place

Additional Good Values

(A bit more expensive, but worth every penny)

Antica Trattoria
Baker Street Bistro
Belon
Betelnut Pejiu Wu
Bistro Aix
Cafe Marimba
Cha Cha Cha @ Original
Charanga
Chez Nous
Chez Panisse Cafe/E
Doña Tomás/E
Flea St. Cafe/S
Foothill Cafe/N
42°
House
Insalata's/N
Kabuto Sushi
Lalime's/E
Le Charm French Bistro
Left Bank/N

Liberty Cafe & Bakery
L'Osteria Del Forno
LuLu
Luna Park
Mariposa/N
Mazzini Trattoria/E
Mustards Grill/N
O Chamé/E
Pane e Vino
Pearl/N
Plouf
Soizic/E
Suppenküche
Sushi Groove
Swan Oyster Depot
Tokyo Go Go
Villa Poppi
Watergate
Zaré on Sacramento
Zinzino

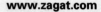

Alphabetical Directory of Restaurants

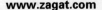

San Francisco

| F | D | S | C |

Absinthe ◐ⓁⓈ   18 | 22 | 18 | $37
398 Hayes St. (Gough St.), 415-551-1590
◪ "One of the stars in the up-and-coming Hayes Valley" dining scene, this buzzing "très French" brasserie blends "fabulous" vintage cocktails with the likes of steak frites in a "faux decadent" atmosphere that resembles a "Toulouse Lautrec painting"; detractors insist that the "setting surpasses the food and service" but concede that it's a "very good spot" for a late-night meal after the symphony.

Academy Grill ⓁⓂ   ▽ 18 | 14 | 16 | $26
(fka Tavern on the Tenderloin)
California Culinary Academy, 625 Polk St. (Turk St.), 415-292-8229
■ The most casual, least expensive dining option at the California Culinary Academy, this Civic Center American can be an "amazing deal"; however, food can be "hit-or-miss" and "service can be spotty", which is "hardly surprising since it's run by students."

Ace Wasabi's ⓈⓂ   21 | 14 | 14 | $26
3339 Steiner St. (bet. Chestnut & Lombard Sts.), 415-567-4903
■ "If you like [eating] your sushi among cell phones", this "crowded", "rowdy" Marina "scene", where the pricey, "inventive, shamelessly nontraditional rolls" are "almost as beautiful as the clientele", is the place; despite "long waits" devotees swear "bingo night is worth it."

ACQUERELLO   26 | 23 | 25 | $56
1722 Sacramento St. (bet. Polk St. & Van Ness Ave.), 415-567-5432
■ Fans feel this "romantic", "hidden gem" in Van Ness/Polk may be the "best" Italian in the city, with "food and service to suit a king" and a "superb (albeit expensive) wine list" to match; despite the "spare", some say "stuffy", interior, most maintain this "converted church" makes for a "divine restaurant."

Alamo Square ⓈⓂ   17 | 16 | 17 | $26
803 Fillmore St. (bet. Fulton & Grove Sts.), 415-440-2828
◪ "Cute" seafooder with a "French accent" in the Western Addition that lets locals "pick their fish, sauce and cooking method"; you may not shout 'remember the Alamo' (the fare's not "distinctive"), but its three-course prix fixe menu is an "excellent value."

Albona Ristorante Istriano   21 | 15 | 23 | $34
545 Francisco St. (bet. Mason & Taylor Sts.), 415-441-1040
■ "Exuberantly charming host Bruno Viscovi" greets guests
with the "warmest welcome in the city" at this North
Beach "hideaway", serving the "unusual", "wonderfully
spiced" cuisine of Istria (a peninsula in the north Adriatic
Sea), which is "like no Italian food you know"; there's "no
decor", but it's "like going to a favorite uncle's for dinner."

Alegrias, Food From Spain S M   19 | 15 | 19 | $27
2018 Lombard St. (Webster St.), 415-929-8888
■ Marina Iberian offering "tasty paella" and a "great
selection of tapas"; the "cozy setting" heats up on
weekends when a spirited flamenco guitarist performs.

Alfred's Steak House L S M   20 | 19 | 20 | $40
*659 Merchant St. (bet. Kearny & Montgomery Sts.),
415-781-7058*
☑ This "classic" is a "throwback to the good ole boy days",
but while loyalists "love the red leather booths", "good,
solid steaks" and "nurturing service", a few curmudgeons
complain that it has "slipped since moving" Downtown.

Alice's L S M   20 | 17 | 16 | $17
1599 Sanchez St. (29th St.), 415-282-8999
■ "You can have anything you want" at this Noe Valley
Chinese as long as you're in the mood for "excellent food
with a healthy California feel" wokked up in an "airy",
attractive setting featuring "awesome orchids" and elaborate
glass art; the "price is right" and "lunches are a real bargain."

Alioto's L S M   15 | 14 | 16 | $31
*8 Fisherman's Wharf (bet. Taylor St. & The Embarcadero),
415-673-0183*
☑ Cynics say this "tired" and "touristy" establishment run
by the Alioto clan serves up "so-so" seafood with a "salty
attitude"; still, its Fisherman's Wharf locale lures out-of-
towners looking for a "nice" Bay view, and some oenophiles
opine there's an "exceptional wine list."

Allegro S M   19 | 18 | 19 | $33
1701 Jones St. (Broadway), 415-928-4002
■ A "favorite political hangout" for San Francisco's "movers
and shakers", this "classy hideaway" atop Russian Hill
wins votes for its "consistent" "traditional" Italian fare
served in a "romantic", "intimate" atmosphere; just be
warned that "parking is an adventure."

Ana Mandara S M   ▽ 22 | 27 | 18 | $39
Ghirardelli Sq., 891 Beach St. (Polk St.), 415-771-6800
■ New Ghirardelli Square hot spot that's partly owned by
Don Johnson and Cheech Marin and filled with "gorgeous",
"authentic" Colonial Vietnamese appointments that make
for an "incredible interior" that "transports you" to "another
country"; fans also drool over the "excellent" food.

Angkor Borei L S M   ∇ 23 | 12 | 18 | $15
3471 Mission St. (Cortland Ave.), 415-550-8417
■ The few surveyors who frequent this "unassuming" hole-in-the-wall at the base of Bernal Heights swear that it serves "utterly reliable Cambodian food" with a "melody of delicate flavors that float on the tongue"; just don't expect much in the way of decor.

Angkor Wat L S M   21 | 16 | 19 | $21
4217 Geary Blvd. (bet. 6th & 7th Aves.), 415-221-7887
■ "Real gem" in the Inner Richmond (legend has it "the Pope ate here" and "what's good enough for him is good enough for me") featuring "fragrant" Cambodian fare (think "coconut chicken curry") at "great prices"; service is "friendly", and for a real treat, "be sure to go" on Friday or Saturday when native dancers perform.

Anjou   22 | 19 | 21 | $34
44 Campton Pl. (bet. Post & Sutter Sts.),
415-392-5373
■ This "low-key, authentic French bistro" in a "hidden alley off Union Square" is a "delightful" "little bit of Paris", which pros praise for its "consistent" fare ("these people cook with their hearts"), "cozy" setting and "caring service"; it's a particular "find for lunch" or "pre-theater dining."

Antica Trattoria S   21 | 17 | 19 | $32
2400 Polk St. (Union St.), 415-928-5797
■ "Secure your reservation early and bring earplugs", because this "bustling" Van Ness/Polk haunt is "just like a trattoria in Florence" – meaning it serves "excellent pastas" in a "cramped" and "noisy" setting where wits wager that you "can't hear yourself eat."

Anzu L S M   ∇ 22 | 19 | 22 | $43
Hotel Nikko, 222 Mason St. (O'Farrell St.),
415-394-1100
■ Those who have discovered this "lovely" new Japanese-American Downtown in the Hotel Nikko believe the schizophrenic "steak-and-sushi-themed" menu works – thanks to the presence of a master sushi chef who presides over "incredibly fresh" fish and a Swiss executive chef who prepares "delicious" beef with "interesting sauces."

Aperto L S M   20 | 14 | 19 | $27
1434 18th St. (Connecticut St.), 415-252-1625
■ Loyalists on Potrero Hill regard their "cozy" Italian "gathering spot" as a "perfect standby" for "a quick mid-week" lunch or dinner; the menu "offers honest food", but for a more imaginative meal, "stick to the specials."

AQUA 🅛🅜
27 | 26 | 24 | $58 |

252 California St. (bet. Battery & Front Sts.),
415-956-9662

■ Michael Mina's trendy, sleek-as-a-shark Downtowner continues to "set the standard for seafood" with "soaring architectural presentations", "amazing sauces" and "whimsical desserts"; the "understated" dining room, filled with "dazzling flowers", attracts a "glamorous" "power crowd" out "to close that deal"; a small school of critics complains about the "noisy" setting, "snooty service" and the need to "bring your corporate card", but they're outvoted.

Aram's 🅛🅢
20 | 18 | 19 | $34 |

3665 Sacramento St. (bet. Locust & Spruce Sts.),
415-474-8061

■ "An oasis of good food" in Presidio Heights, this "tucked-away", "romantic enclave" pleases neighbors with "great Mediterranean meze" such as "delicious hummus, baba ghanoush and other Middle Eastern fare"; the "intimate dining room" "allows for conversation", but in warm weather, the "adjoining garden patio" is "divine."

Arlequin Food to Go 🅛🅢🅜
▬ | ▬ | ▬ | I |

384B Hayes St. (bet. Franklin & Gough Sts.),
415-626-1211

Sandwiched between its mothership, Absinthe, and its tony wine store sib, Amphora, in Hayes Valley, this tiny take-away cafe offers time-challenged diners a variety of tasty Provençal-style snacks such as upscale sandwiches, artisanal cheeses, housemade pastries and ice creams; a small, stand-up counter is available for those who can't wait until they get home to enjoy their goodies.

A. Sabella's 🅛🅢🅜
16 | 17 | 18 | $35 |

2766 Taylor St. (Jefferson St.), 415-771-6775

■ If a meal at "Fisherman's Wharf is a must for your out-of-town guests", surveyors suggest this seafooder that's been "family owned and operated" for four generations; "great views" and an extensive California-oriented wine list make it a better catch than some of the tourist traps nearby.

AsiaSF 🅢🅜
17 | 19 | 19 | $29 |

201 Ninth St. (Howard St.), 415-255-2742

■ "Who wouldn't have fun with a staff that doubles as a cross-dressing cabaret" act? ask surveyors about this "campy" SoMa supper club serving up Asian tapas and "outrageous" "gender-bending entertainment"; nearly "every table is either a birthday or bachelorette party" and it's also the "perfect place to take your cousin from the Midwest"; even though voyeurs volunteer that the "show is better than the food", "every place is a drag in comparison."

Aux Delices 🄻🅂🄼 18 12 16 $19
2327 Polk St. (bet. Green & Union Sts.), 415-928-4977
■ Fans love that this "quick" neighborhood joint on Polk Street is "easy to get in" to and can't say enough about the "beautifully presented Vietnamese-French specialties" ("I'm still dreaming about their pork in caramel sauce"); wallet-watchers in particular praise the "cheap eats."

Avenue 9 🄻🅂🄼 19 14 18 $26
1243 Ninth Ave. (bet. Irving St. & Lincoln Way), 415-664-6999
◪ A "friendly culinary gem in the Inner Sunset", this New American "bistro" keeps its fervent followers on cloud nine with a "consistently good", "creative menu" prepared in a "lively" open kitchen; however, antis are inclined to nix the "noise" and "cramped" conditions.

Azie 🄻🅂🄼 22 25 19 $51
826 Folsom St. (bet. 4th & 5th Sts.), 415-538-0918
◪ "High-tech meets SoMa" at this trendy newcomer where owner Jody Denton (of LuLu fame) dazzles diners with "brilliant" French-Asian fusion in "inspired" presentations rivaled only by the room's "alluring decor"; the "über hip" hold court at the bar while "curtained booths" and a DJ keep the mood "darkly dreamy"; however, skeptics warn of a "pretentious" and "pricey" scene.

Bacar ⬤🄻🅂🄼 – – – E
448 Brannan St. (bet. 3rd & 4th Sts.), 415-904-4100
EOS chef Arnold Eric Wong and wine director Debbie Zachareas, plus third partner David O'Malley, are expected to open this highly anticipated American brasserie in a three-level converted SoMa warehouse this fall; look for a seafood-centric menu, 60-seat wine salon, 1,000 bottle wine list and live jazz nightly; set in the epicenter of multimedia gulch and serving until 1 AM nightly, it aims to capitalize on the underfed dot-com crowd (several of whom are investors).

Backflip 12 20 12 $27
Phoenix Hotel, 601 Eddy St. (bet. Larkin & Polk Sts.), 415-771-3547
◪ The "cool" crowd braves the dicey Tenderloin to knock back designer drinks at the Phoenix Hotel's "groovy" "ultramarine"-toned nightclub, a notable "party place" for slumming "rock stars"; but the area "swingers" who "go for the pool parties" and "people-watching" tend to torpedo the "underwhelming" Californian 'cocktail cuisine.'

Bagdad Cafe ⬤🄻🅂🄼⇗ 12 10 13 $14
2295 Market St. (16th St.), 415-621-4434
■ "One of the few all-nighters" in the city, this 24-hour diner in the Castro is a "place to watch the boys go by" and refuel with "decent food" "after partying all night"; even advocates admit they turn up mainly "because it's open at 3 AM", so expect a line after the clubs close.

Baker Street Bistro L S   19 | 15 | 19 | $27 |
2953 Baker St. (bet. Greenwich & Lombard Sts.),
415-931-1475

◪ For a "trip to Paris without the flight", Baker Street
Francophiles flock to this "charming bistro" where the
"authentic" touches include "simple", "solid" cooking, a
$14.50 "prix fixe bargain" and "friendly", "enthusiastic"
service ("you'll leave speaking French"); but given the
"tight quarters", it's "not the place for private assignations."

Balboa Cafe L S M   16 | 16 | 17 | $27 |
3199 Fillmore St. (Greenwich St.), 415-921-3944

◪ "Young and single and love to mingle"?; this "old-time
San Francisco institution" in Cow Hollow is "ground zero
for the social register", and fans of the American menu must
"brave the noise and the yuppies" to enjoy the "superior
burgers" and "really good wine list"; dissenters dismiss it
as a "raucous" "pick-up joint" with "boring bar food."

Baldoria S M   18 | 17 | 18 | $32 |
(fka Baraonda)
2162 Larkin St. (Green St.), 415-447-0441

◼ Its name may be new, but this Van Ness/Polk Italian is
still "a cozy place for a date" where the "authentic" "pastas
are winners" and the "attractive staff" "makes you feel
special"; insiders intimate the "gnocchi is not to be missed."

Barcelona L M   16 | 18 | 17 | $31 |
7 Spring St. (California St.), 415-989-1976

◪ This "sexy", colorful Downtowner offers "enjoyable"
eating in "authentic Spanish" style thanks to "classic tapas"
and paella enhanced by a live "flamenco show" on
weekends; though doubters dub the food "disappointing",
the "cool atmosphere" makes it "a find" – literally, given
the "odd location."

Barney's Gourmet   17 | 10 | 12 | $14 |
Hamburger L S M
4138 24th St. (Castro St.), 415-282-7770
3344 Steiner St. (Chestnut St.), 415-563-0307

◼ Loyalists insist this Bay Area chain flips "the best"
"unconventional burgers", featuring "every type imaginable"
including "nonmeat alternatives"; heart-stopping sides
like "giant onion rings" and "addictive curly fries" are just
as popular, and at most locations patio seating "greatly
improves" the "dingy" decor.

Basil L S M   19 | 17 | 17 | $23 |
1175 Folsom St. (bet. 7th & 8th Sts.), 415-552-8999

◪ Thai fanciers favor this "solid", "midpriced" SoMa
Siamese for "elegant", "yummy creations" served in a
"soothing" setting; partisans proclaim it "better than most",
though a few purists protest the "bland" fare ("they try to
cater to Americans").

Beach Chalet Brewery L S M   11 | 19 | 13 | $23 |
1000 Great Hwy. (bet. Fulton St. & Lincoln Way),
415-386-8439
◪ The "homebrews and California sunsets" combine to
impress "landlocked visitors" at this American brewpub
overlooking Ocean Beach; though it's "too bad the food
and service don't match" the "spectacular views", the
"historic building" is a showcase for "beautiful mosaics"
and WPA-era murals depicting old-time SF.

Bella Trattoria S M   21 | 18 | 22 | $29 |
3854 Geary Blvd. (3rd Ave.), 415-221-0305
■ "Old-style pasta – hooray!" cheer amici of this "family-
run" trattoria, known for its "great homemade Italian"
cuisine, "friendly service" and "cozy, inviting atmosphere";
with "such a wonderful spot" in the Inner Richmond, locals
wonder "why head Downtown?"

Belon M   ▽ 24 | 17 | 19 | $44 |
Hotel Metropolis, 25 Mason St. (Turk St.), 415-776-9970
■ Fearless fans venture into the Tenderloin ("bring a
bodyguard") to experience the "supreme" stylings of chef-
owner Paul Arenstam (ex Rubicon) at this new brasserie
in the Hotel Metropolis; the filling fare – including "luscious
oysters" from the raw bar – is "as good as any in France",
though prices are admittedly "high" for the 'hood.

BETELNUT PEJIU WU L S M   22 | 21 | 17 | $31 |
2030 Union St. (Buchanan St.), 415-929-8855
◪ "Still trendy" and "much imitated", George Chen's
"pricey purveyor" of "savory" "tapas-style" Pan-Asian
bites attracts a "young", "hip Union Street crowd" that
doesn't mind the "loooong waits" in the "noisy" bar;
the "exciting vibe" and "innovative" plates ("best green
beans ever!") keep the room "packed", though many
maintain the "staff needs niceness training."

B44 L M   22 | 19 | 20 | $34 |
44 Belden Pl. (bet. Bush & Pine Sts.), 415-986-6287
■ "A great addition to Belden Lane", this "chic" Spaniard
is one of the city's few alternatives for "authentic Catalan"
cuisine; chef-owner Daniel Olivella's "well-executed" menu
features "yummy paellas", and the "bustling" (some say
"deafening") room "brings back memories of Barcelona."

Big Four L S M   22 | 24 | 24 | $45 |
Huntington Hotel, 1075 California St. (Taylor St.),
415-771-1140
■ "Expensive" "men's club" atop Nob Hill that's a bastion
of "civilized dining" where everyone can "feel like a
plutocrat"; chef Gloria Ciccarone-Nehls' "excellent" New
American fare meets its match in the "classy", old-school
service and "Edwardian" interior, which comes complete
with a "vintage bar."

Bill's Place **L S M**   16 | 8 | 14 | $13
2315 Clement St. (bet. 24th & 25th Aves.), 415-221-5262
■ This "cheap", "old-fashioned dive" in the Richmond "fills the craving" for "great greasy burgers and malts", making it an ideal spot "to go with the kids"; in order to "overlook the decor", snag a seat on the "nice patio" on a sunny day.

Biscuits & Blues **S M**   11 | 10 | 12 | $23
401 Mason St. (bet. Geary & Post Sts.), 415-292-2583
■ Even the biggest boosters "come for the blues but nix the food" at this "fun, noisy" Downtown jazz club where the "mediocre" Southern-style "fried" fare is "secondary" to the "great acts that perform."

Bistro Aix **S M**   19 | 15 | 18 | $29
3340 Steiner St. (bet. Chestnut & Lombard Sts.), 415-202-0100
■ "Hip", "charming" bistro off Chestnut Street that's like being in "Aix sans the attitude"; "delicious" and "reasonably priced" Mediterranean fare and a "friendly staff" make this "one of the few places in the Marina where you can relax", as long as you do as the regulars do – eschew the "cramped" dining room and "eat alfresco" in the "wonderful back garden."

Bistro Clovis **L S M**   20 | 16 | 19 | $30
1596 Market St. (Franklin St.), 415-864-0231
■ "A little piece of Paris in San Francisco", this affordable, "oh-so-French" Hayes Valley bistro (think "quaint lace curtains") is a "pre-opera and symphony standby" for "consistently good" onion soup and "delicious tarte Tatin"; oenophiles appreciate the "interesting" wine samplings, in which a tiny trio of different wines from a particular region in France is "nicely presented" on a mini artist's palette.

Bistro Zaré **S**   20 | 17 | 18 | $30
1507 Polk St. (California St.), 415-775-4304
◪ The casual sister to the popular Zaré on Sacramento, this "colorful, unpretentious" Polk Street Mediterranean with a "lovely outdoor patio" garners mixed reports: loyalists like the "big helpings of lusty food", which make it a "great addition to the neighborhood", while the less enthused gripe about only "adequate" fare and "indifferent service."

Bitterroot **L S M**   15 | 13 | 14 | $18
3122 16th St. (bet. Mission & Valencia Sts.), 415-626-5523
◪ "Old West saloon" meets the Mission at this slightly grungy hipster hangout where a "genuinely friendly staff" serves "indulgent portions" of "decent" American "comfort food" at "bargain prices"; although it dishes up three meals a day, fans suggest "get there early" for the "good breakfasts" and Sunday brunch.

Bix ⒧Ⓢ Ⓜ 　　　　　| 22 | 25 | 21 | $42 |
56 Gold St. (bet. Jackson & Pacific Sts.), 415-433-6300
■ "Hidden in an alley" on the edge of the Downtown Financial District, this "retro '30s" supper club ("any moment Bogey might walk in") continues to reign as one of "the most glamorous spots in SF"; the "loud" bar is an "after-work drink mecca" for the "yuppie martini set" who are there "to be seen"; later in the evening, "grown-ups" sup on American "comfort food for the affluent" and soak up the sultry strains of "live jazz."

Bizou ⒧Ⓜ 　　　　　| 23 | 19 | 21 | $38 |
598 Fourth St. (Brannan St.), 415-543-2222
■ Fans blow "a little kiss" to chef-owner Loretta Keller for her "delightful" (albeit "loud") SoMa French bistro featuring "unusual", "sophisticated cooking" ("tempura green beans to die for", "the best beef cheeks") and "amazingly professional service"; once a "culinary gem" for foodies, these days there are "dot-comers everywhere."

Black Cat ●⒧Ⓢ Ⓜ 　　　　| 16 | 18 | 15 | $38 |
501 Broadway (Kearny St.), 415-981-2233
◪ Catty types snipe that Reed Hearon's "trendy", "retro North Beach" haunt is "on its eighth life" 'cause they claim that the cuisine "promises more than it delivers" and is "too expensive for what you get", plus there's plenty of "attitude from the staff"; N.B. however, a post-*Survey* menu revamp and a new focus on French bistro fare may outdate the above food score.

Blowfish, Sushi To Die For ⒧Ⓢ Ⓜ | 21 | 19 | 15 | $31 |
2170 Bryant St. (20th St.), 415-285-3848
■ "Wear black" and "bring your earplugs" to this "raucous" sushi joint in the Mission that reels in a "hipper than thou techno/multimedia crowd" with its "adventurous maki" and "trippy Japanese" cartoons; wallet-watchers warn that while the "fish is so fresh it practically swims to the table", it's a "bit pricey for what you get."

Blue ⒧Ⓢ Ⓜ 　　　　　| 14 | 14 | 16 | $21 |
2337 Market St. (bet. Castro & Noe Sts.), 415-863-2583
◪ "The latest see-and-be-seen" spot in the Castro is this "fun, hip diner" dishing up "down-home comfort food" like fried chicken and other Americana; maybe the "inexpensive" tabs will elevate what some maintain is just a "basic" eating experience.

Blue Plate, The 　　　∇ | 19 | 15 | 16 | $28 |
3218 Mission St. (29th St.), 415-282-6777
◪ Surveyors are split over whether they find this Blue Plate special: devotees dub it a "sleeper in the Mission", serving "creative" Eclectic/International food in an "upbeat, fun atmosphere", but critics counter that it's a "good idea" whose "execution" is "disappointing."

Bocca Rotis 🛇🇸🇲 17 | 15 | 17 | $26
1 West Portal Ave. (Ulloa St.), 415-665-9900
■ West Portal denizens dub this "noisy" but "comfy" French-Italian with a focus on rotisserie dishes a "good old standby"; "stick to" the "to-die-for roast chicken" and "fabulous desserts" and "you can't go wrong."

Bocce Cafe 🛇🇸🇲 13 | 16 | 14 | $21
478 Green St. (Grant Ave.), 415-981-2044
■ This North Beach Italian may not be at the top of its game, but it's a hit with the "just-out-of-college" crowd; "lots of cheap food", a "fun bar" and an "intimate back patio" make it "a great place for a party."

Bontà Ristorante 🇸 20 | 15 | 20 | $30
2223 Union St. (bet. Fillmore & Steiner Sts.), 415-929-0407
■ "Very well-run", "quaint little" Union Street Italian noted for its "fresh homemade pasta"; a staff that "treats guests like family" and "reasonable" tabs also help make it a "fave."

BOULEVARD 🛇🇸🇲 27 | 26 | 25 | $51
1 Mission St. (Steuart St.), 415-543-6084
■ "Paradise found" sums up this "high-energy" Downtown American that's the No. 1 Most Popular restaurant in this *Survey* ("I send everyone here – they always get it right"); "all the raves are well earned" for Nancy Oakes' "outstanding food", Pat Kuleto's "art-nouveau Parisian bistro" setting and a "truly professional staff" that "never fails to impress" the "well-heeled" crowd; insiders suggest: "sit toward the back" or "go early and eat at the counter."

Brandy Ho's 🛇🇸🇲 18 | 11 | 13 | $20
450 Broadway (Kearny St.), 415-362-6268
217 Columbus Ave. (bet. Broadway & Pacific Ave.), 415-788-7527
☑ Devotees dub this duo "better" than the "usual Chinese" "as long as you don't mind the heat"; while detractors declare the fare "greasy" and the service "rushed", wallet-watchers don't waffle about the "reasonable prices."

Brasserie Savoy 🇸🇲 16 | 18 | 16 | $35
Savoy Hotel, 580 Geary St. (Jones St.), 415-441-8080
☑ "Location, location, location" makes this Union Square "traditional" French bistro "convenient" for a "pre-theater" meal; but the majority maintains that the cuisine "quality varies as the chefs come and go", and a slip in the food rating supports that opinion.

Brazen Head ●🇸🇲⌀ 18 | 18 | 19 | $28
3166 Buchanan St. (Greenwich St.), 415-921-7600
■ "If you can find it, you'll love it" rave respondents about this "secret hideaway" near Union Street that serves "hearty" American fare (until 1AM) in an "interior reminiscent of an old wooden sailboat"; just remember there's "no sign" and it "doesn't take reservations or credit cards."

Brother-in-Law's Bar-B-Que 🄻🅂⊘   21   4   11 $14
705 Divisadero St. (Grove St.), 415-931-7427
■ For "awesome", "down-home", "slow-cooked 'cue that can't be beat", fans head for this "great smelling" Western Addition rib joint; sure, it's "grungy" and there's "no concept of service", but that doesn't keep carnivores from "waiting 20 minutes to place an order, another 20 to see it", and taking it out the door.

Brother's Korean Restaurant 🄻🅂🄼   21   6   13 $19
4128 Geary Blvd. (bet. 5th & 6th Aves.), 415-387-7991 ◗
4014 Geary Blvd. (bet. 4th & 5th Aves.), 415-668-2028
■ "As any Korean will tell you", this duo of do-it-yourself wooden-coal barbecue restaurants in the Inner Richmond serves the "real thing" – "delicious grilled meats" and a "panoply" of "complimentary side dishes" of pickles and condiments that are "worth the wait" and the "bare-bones decor"; one caveat: "if you cook it yourself" (you can also have the kitchen prepare it) "wear washable clothing – you'll smell like what you ate."

Bruno's ◗🄼   –   –   –   E
2389 Mission St. (20th St.), 415-648-7701
After a brief hiatus, restaurateur Jon Varnedoe (Foreign Cinema) has restored his beloved Mission nightclub-cum-restaurant to its former glory; chef Ola Fendert's (ex Plouf) menu has more of an Italian focus, but aside from the newly reupholstered red leather booths in the reconfigured dining room and a 500-gallon saltwater fish tank in the bar, the rest of the legendary '60s hot spot's decor remains the same.

Bubble Lounge ◗🄼   12   22   13 $33
714 Montgomery St. (bet. Jackson & Washington Sts.), 415-434-4204
■ "Known for its bubbles" and "bar scene" ("more people in black than a cat-burglar convention") and "not the food" (a limited International menu of caviar and sushi), this "swank" "champagne lounge" is a Downtown "outpost" of the Manhattan original and comes with "a total NY" attitude to match; it draws a clientele of "clique-ish professionals" who come to cruise and drink up the "great atmosphere."

Buca di Beppo 🅂🄼   14   18   16 $23
855 Howard St. (bet. 4th & 5th Sts.), 415-543-7673
See review in South of San Francisco Directory.

Buca Giovanni 🅂   20   18   19 $35
800 Greenwich St. (bet. Columbus Ave. & Mason St.), 415-776-7766
☑ North Beach institution offering "good", "old-fashioned" Italian fare ("try the rabbit") in a "romantic, grotto-like downstairs setting"; a minority maintains that "both the food and decor are getting tired", but they're outvoted.

Butler & the Chef Cafe, The 🅛Ⓜ   –   –   –   I
155A South Park St. (bet. 2nd & 3rd Sts.), 415-896-2075
Charming new cafe on South Park that proves that you can
take it with you when you go, because everything's for sale
here – from authentic cane-back bistro chairs and enamel-
topped tables to vintage posters; the cafe provides pastries
from Boulangerie Bay Bread for breakfast and classic French
baguette sandwiches, salads and table service for lunch.

butterfly ◕   –   –   –   M
1710 Mission St. (bet. Duboce & 14th Sts.), 415-864-5575
Riding on the coattails of the dot-com boom, an Internet
attorney and his wife have transformed this former auto
repair shop into the latest nightspot (replete with a koi pond
and High C-colored seating) in the Mission's burgeoning
Valencia corridor; chef Erik Hopfinger's (ex Backflip) Pacific
Rim cuisine is served in a lively dining room where a DJ spins
tunes till jazz pianists take control of the Steinway grand.

Cafe Bastille 🅛Ⓜ   16   16   15 $24
22 Belden Pl. (bet. Bush & Pine Sts.), 415-986-5673
■ "You can't swing a baguette without hitting a French
person" at this "bustling", "inexpensive" Downtown bistro
avec "great crêpes", Paris "metro decor" and "cute
waiters – even if they do exaggerate their accents"; boastful
regulars add that "there's no better place" to have an alfresco
lunch or listen to "live music" "on a rare warm evening."

Café Claude 🅛ⓈⓂ   16   16   15 $23
7 Claude Ln. (bet. Grant Ave. & Kearny St.), 415-392-3515
■ "If you can't afford airfare to Nice", "practice your
French" at this "quintessential" Downtown bistro with
"authentic cafe decor", a "great croque monsieur" and
other "simple" Gallic favorites; at night, join the
"leather-jacket-wearing Euros" outside in the alley for
some "good" live jazz and a glass of Beaujolais.

Café de la Presse 🅛ⓈⓂ   13   13   13 $21
352 Grant Ave. (Bush St.), 415-249-0900
■ "Pretend you're in Paris" at this "convenient" newsstand/
cafe and bistro near Union Square, which is a resource for a
homesick "international clientele" looking to catch up on
"foreign magazines" over "dark mochas and fluffy quiches",
as well as a "shopper's retreat" for soups, salads and
pastries; others opine it's "unremarkable" in every way.

Café de Paris L'Entrecôte 🅛ⓈⓂ   17   15   17 $33
2032 Union St. (bet. Buchanan & Webster Sts.), 415-931-5006
◪ "When you're in the mood for steak frites" consider this
"reliable", "charming throwback" with open and enclosed
sidewalk seating and copies of Erté paintings on the walls;
those who find it "tired" ("get a new sauce!") and the
signature entrecôte its raison d'être will be pleased to
learn that a new chef has updated some of the Gallic dishes.

Cafe Flore L S M ⌐   13 16 12 $15
2298 Market St. (Noe St.), 415-621-8579
■ Aka "Cafe Hair", and "ground zero for people-watching
in the Castro", this long-standing hip spot's sidewalk tables
continue to be the place for gay men "to check out the
boys" while "looking nonchalant" and "reading foreign
newspapers in the sun" over coffee; the Eclectic victuals
"could be better", but "no one goes for the food" anyway.

Cafe For All Seasons L S M   20 14 19 $24
*150 W. Portal Ave. (bet. 14th Ave. & Vicente St.),
415-665-0900*
◪ An "old favorite" of West Portal locals, this "solid
performer" dishes up "fresh, homey all-American fare",
which makes diners feel "like they're eating at home without
having to cook or clean"; the decor is "bare-bones" and
"the noise level can be pretty bad" ("put some carpet
down"), but there's "good value for the money" here.

Cafe Jacqueline S   25 19 19 $40
*1454 Grant Ave. (bet. Green & Union Sts.),
415-981-5565*
■ "If you and your date have two hours to spend", consider
dining at this "romantic", "charming North Beach spot",
which serves an all-soufflé menu that easily "transcends
its limited format"; while there, "don't forget to peek into
the kitchen and check out the egg crates" and French
owner Jacqueline Marguiles ("she is so cute") as she
whips up each "dreamy, featherlike" dish to order; P.S.
"parking is impossible" so "take a cab."

Cafe Kati S   25 18 22 $41
*1963 Sutter St. (bet. Fillmore & Webster Sts.),
415-775-7313*
■ "All hail vertical food!" salute surveyors dazzled by Kirk
Webber's monthly changing menu of "inventive", "gorgeously
presented" New American cuisine, which tastes "even
better on the way down", especially when paired with
some of the restaurant's hard-to-find California wines;
"great service" and "cozy surroundings" further explain
the "longevity and popularity" of this Japantown jewel.

Cafe Marimba L S M   19 17 15 $24
*2317 Chestnut St. (bet. Divisadero & Scott Sts.),
415-776-1506*
◪ A "twenty- to thirtysomething" "Marina crowd" marimbas
over to this "lively", "upscale" hot spot for its jammed bar
scene ("addictive margaritas"), "out of the ordinary" south-
of-the-border food ("superb moles") and "funky" decor,
which includes walls decked out with "outrageous" Oaxacan
artwork; despite sporadic service gripes (the staff is
"hardly conscious"), this remains a "fun spot for groups."

Cafe Monk ▯▯ 　　　　– – – M
567 Fourth St. (bet. Brannan & Bryant Sts.), 415-777-1331
At this bi-level SoMa Californian newcomer, owned and designed by the ultra-hip Limn design firm, there are artfully hung lighting fixtures, an exhibition kitchen and cinder-block walls hung with photos of assorted 'monks' through the ages, from the Dalai Lama to Thelonious; affordably priced fare is the focus at lunch and dinner, while coffee and pastries pull in the multimedia crowd in the morning.

Cafe Mozart ▯ 　　　　19 19 17 $37
708 Bush St. (Powell St.), 415-391-8480
▨ This "quaint" Nob Hill haven of European fine dining exudes "old-world" "romance" with such trappings as a crackling fireplace and classical music; but what strikes some as "a best-kept secret" for a special-occasion dinner of steak Mozart and ginger crème brûlée is viewed by others as a place that's "getting a little tired."

Cafe Niebaum Coppola ▯▯▯ 　　15 17 15 $26
916 Kearny St. (Columbus Ave.), 415-291-1700
▨ If this tiny Downtown wine bar/eatery/gift shop looks like a stage set for a French bistro, that's probably because it's the brainchild of the director of *The Godfather*; fans like the "simple pizzas and pastas", wines from the namesake's vineyards, bric-a-brac from the "Coppola merchandising empire" and the "potential of having Francis sit next to you"; critics pan "ordinary" food, a "cold" staff and a "commercial" feel ("never trust a restaurant that sells videos").

Cafe Riggio ▯▯ 　　　　17 15 17 $27
4112 Geary Blvd. (5th Ave.), 415-221-2114
▮ Situated in the Inner Richmond, this "unpretentious", "old standby" sports "festive" decor ("upside-down flowerpots act as lamps") and draws long lines for its "reliable", if "not memorable", Italian food; favorites include a calamari salad that "could make a whole meal" and veal piccata.

Cafe Tiramisu ▯▯ 　　　　20 17 18 $30
28 Belden Pl. (bet. Bush & Pine Sts.), 415-421-7044
▮ Set in an alley filled with French cafes, this "informal" Financial District trattoria serves "steady" Italian food (and a mean tiramisu) to harried business people amidst "cool" Pompeii-themed trompe l'oeil paintings; P.S. if the dining room is filled, "ask to sit in the wine cellar" or outside.

Caffe Centro ▯▯ 　　　　18 14 15 $17
102 South Park St. (bet. 2nd & 3rd Sts.), 415-882-1500
▮ Ground zero for the digerati, this South Park java shop attracts "long lines of dot-commers" for "great coffee and pastries" in the morning and "hip sandwiches" and "elegant, filling salads" at lunch; there's limited seating inside and on the sidewalk, so on sunny days most web monkeys "take out and go to the park across the street."

Caffe Delle Stelle L S M　　17 | 14 | 17 | $26
395 Hayes St. (Gough St.), 415-252-1110

☑ This bustling Hayes Valley trattoria, which specializes in "rustic Italian for less" is "always full of pre-opera/symphony/ballet ticketholders" enjoying the staff's *buena serras*, the "complimentary sparkling water" and plenty of al dente pastas, even if some old-timers lament that the place "doesn't have the specialness that it used to" when it was located around the corner.

Caffe Greco ◗ L S M ⌿　　15 | 14 | 14 | $12
423 Columbus Ave. (bet. Green & Vallejo Sts.), 415-397-6261

■ For an authentic North Beach experience, head to this "coffee bar and informal gathering place", which surveyors insist steams up "the best espresso drinks in the city"; long on ambiance and short on food, order a dessert and enjoy the "great people-watching on Columbus Avenue."

Caffe Macaroni M ⌿　　20 | 14 | 18 | $26
59 Columbus Ave. (Jackson St.), 415-956-9737

■ Despite being no larger than "a postage stamp", this North Beach Southern Italian trattoria has a "big personality" thanks to "solid", "homey" pastas whisked to your table by a "friendly" crew of charmers; the "cramped" space is "proof that you can put a good restaurant anywhere."

Caffe Museo L S M　　17 | 17 | 12 | $16
San Francisco Museum of Modern Art, 151 Third St.
(bet. Howard & Mission Sts.), 415-357-4500

■ Culture vultures say the "fresh", "light" Med fare at this SoMa cafe is "better than what one expects from a museum" eatery, making a visit an "awesome finish to a day" of art appreciation; but whether you chow down "outside on a nice day" ("good for people-watching") or inside, "be prepared to compete for a table."

Caffe Proust L S M　　▽ 19 | 18 | 16 | $21
1801 McAllister St. (Baker St.), 415-345-9560

☑ Not a lot of surveyors know this new salmon-colored, antiques-filled Eclectic-Italian in the restaurant-barren Western Addition, but "friends of P" declare it a budget-friendly, "much-needed" addition; whatever your income level, consider ordering the 'Starving Artist' special ($4.95), which is usually a large plate of pasta.

Caffe Sport L ⌿　　16 | 15 | 12 | $28
574 Green St. (bet. Columbus & Grant Aves.), 415-981-1251

☑ North Beach's best-known "tourist trap" is likened to a "Hard Rock [Cafe] of pasta" where "mountains" of "garlicky" Southern Italian staples are dished up amid a "fabulous" "Italo-kitsch interior"; though a few swear the staff's "rude" rep is "undeserved", to others the low service score is no fluke – good sports say "do it once for a laugh", while grinches grouse "go if you like being insulted."

CAMPTON PLACE L S M　　26 ┃ 25 ┃ 25 ┃ $56 ┃
*Campton Pl. Hotel, 340 Stockton St. (bet. Post & Sutter Sts.),
415-955-5555*
■ "Amid the maddening crowd of Union Square", this
Downtown oasis provides "what every hotel restaurant
should" – "subdued elegance", "flawless service" and
"sumptuous food"; chef Laurent Manrique's "interesting"
French Provençal dinner menu complements the long-
renowned "great breakfasts", ensuring its status as "a
special place for special occasions."

Capp's Corner L S M　　14 ┃ 13 ┃ 15 ┃ $21 ┃
1600 Powell St. (Green St.), 415-989-2589
■ "No one leaves hungry" from this "no-frills" "old North
Beach institution" serving "hearty" Italian; though fans
admit the "food is more bountiful than distinguished",
they insist it's a "fun place to stop before *Beach Blanket
Babylon*" and "hang out with the locals"; besides, what
do you expect from a "five-course meal for $20 or less"?

Careme Room L M　　20 ┃ 15 ┃ 18 ┃ $32 ┃
*California Culinary Academy, 625 Polk St. (Turk St.),
415-292-8229*
■ Escoffiers-in-training "take turns" at the stoves whipping
up a "mixed bag" of International cuisine at the California
Culinary Academy's showcase dining room; glassed-in
kitchens allow patrons to observe the preparations, and
the interaction with the chefs is a "nice variation"; P.S.
"bargain" buffets draw crowds on Thursday–Friday nights.

Carnelian Room S M　　19 ┃ 25 ┃ 22 ┃ $47 ┃
*Bank of America Ctr., 555 California St., 52nd fl.
(bet. Kearny & Montgomery Sts.), 415-433-7500*
■ Want to "play tourist"?; the "fabulous city panorama"
from this 52nd-story Downtown aerie is a must for "out-
of-towners", though most agree the "adequate" New
American menu "is not up to" the "spectacular" setting;
those who observe "you can't eat the view" suggest
going for "drinks on a clear night"; N.B. jacket required.

Carta L S M　　18 ┃ 16 ┃ 17 ┃ $33 ┃
1760 Market St. (bet. Gough & Octavia Sts.), 415-863-3516
◪ This "ambitious", "globe-trotting" Upper Market Eclectic
is literally "all over the map", serving "witty combinations
from different regions" of the world that vary "depending
on the month"; the "revolving menu makes it easy to return",
but "uneven execution" seems to come with the territory.

Casa Aguila L S M　　19 ┃ 11 ┃ 16 ┃ $20 ┃
1240 Noriega St. (bet. 19th & 20th Aves.), 415-661-5593
■ It's "totally not Tex-Mex": this "authentic" hole-in-the-
wall in a remote Sunset locale offers "unbelievable amounts"
of "brilliantly spiced" Mexican "home cooking" at "honest
prices"; "friendly service" warms up the "cozy" room.

Cha Am Thai 🅛Ⓜ   19   12   15 $19
701 Folsom St. (3rd St.), 415-546-9711 Ⓢ
307 Kearny St. (Pine St.), 415-956-8241
4621 Lincoln Way (bet. 47th & 48th Aves.), 415-681-9333
■ Pad Thai partialists claim the chow at this chainlet is "a cut above your standard" Siamese, but critics counter the food is "unremarkable" and served in "sterile surroundings"; still, there's consensus on the "reasonable prices."

Cha Cha Cha 🅛ⓈⓂ   19   17   14 $21
1801 Haight St. (Shrader St.), 415-386-5758
Cha Cha Cha @ Original McCarthy's ⓈⓂ
2327 Mission St. (bet. 19th & 20th Sts.), 415-648-0504
■ The "ultragroovy" Haight Street original is "loud enough to give you a lobotomy", and even its tamer Mission Street sib is a "scene" as "college kids" party hearty over "Caribbean-style tapas"; try not to OD on the "incredible sangria" during the "ridiculously long wait" for a table.

CHAPEAU! Ⓢ   25   17   24 $41
1408 Clement St. (15th Ave.), 415-750-9787
■ "Hats off to this French gem" rave backers of "engaging owner" Philippe Gardelle's "first-class bistro", a "feather in the cap" of the Richmond; patrons "can taste the passion" in the "expert preparations" of "authentic" fare, while the "sensational" wine list and "charming" staff more than compensate for "tight", "noisy" quarters.

Charanga   ▽ 21   15   17 $21
2351 Mission St. (bet. 19th & 20th Sts.), 415-282-1813
■ The kitchen's "always experimenting", so "listen to the specials" at this "cozy" Latin American–Caribbean in the Mission, where "creative" chef-owner Gabriela Salas (ex Cha Cha Cha) offers a "vast array" of "tasty" tapas; what the place "lacks in decor it makes up for" with "great prices."

CHARLES NOB HILL Ⓢ   27   25   26 $67
1250 Jones St. (Clay St.), 415-771-5400
■ Chef Ron Siegel is famed for "winning on the *Iron Chef*" Japanese TV show, but these days his audience is Nob Hill "blue bloods" who offer his "sensational" Cal- French fare as "exhibit A for why being civilized matters"; since the "rarified" room and "stellar service" are "luxurious", it's "worth every penny – and plenty of pennies it will be."

Chaya Brasserie 🅛ⓈⓂ   22   23   21 $50
132 The Embarcadero (bet. Howard & Mission Sts.), 415-777-8688
■ "Finally, a new place on the waterfront!"; a "trendy" clientele rejoices over this "polished" and "pricey" SoMa outpost of LA's "hip" French-Japanese fusion house; it boasts an "amazing view" and "delicious" cuisine, but a few contend the menu's combos are "uneven" and "contrived."

Chaz Restaurant **L S**   – – – E

3347 Fillmore St. (bet. Chestnut & Lombard Sts.),
415-928-1211

As we go to press, French-trained but American-born
Charles Solomon is scheduled to return to the local
culinary scene (his highly acclaimed Heights closed in
'97) with this Marina Contemporary American with a
monthly-changing menu; word is that he intends to
offer all the trappings of a fine-dining establishment in
a casual, user-friendly setting.

Cheers **L S M**   17 14 17 $20

127 Clement St. (bet. 2nd & 3rd Aves.),
415-387-6966

■ "Sitting outdoors" to enjoy a breakfast of "great French
toast" is the main attraction at this "casual" Californian in
the Inner Richmond, but its champions cheer the "sunny
atmosphere" that makes it an "undiscovered gem" "for
any meal at any time."

Cheesecake Factory, The **L S M**   – – – M

Macy's Union Sq., 251 Geary St., 8th fl. (bet. Powell &
Stockton Sts.), 415-391-4444

Featuring "huge, almost wasteful portions" of more than
200 menu items (ranging from buffalo wings and Baja
fish tacos to chicken Caesar salad and 34 variations on
cheesecake), this branch of the eclectic American chain
might strike some as an unlikely choice for the top-floor
terrace restaurant in the renovated Macy's at Union
Square, but there you go.

Chez Nous **L S**   – – – M

1911 Fillmore St. (bet. Bush & Pine Sts.),
415-441-8044

Laurence Jossel's (ex sous chef of the popular Kokkari
Estiatorio) "exuberant" Upper Fillmore freshman has fast
become the talk of the town, thanks to his "awesome
little plates" of terrific, stylish Mediterranean tapas and a
"wonderful staff"; since the lilliputian place is "packed",
famished fans withstand the vexing no-rezzie policy and
the wait by indulging in warm olives and Boulangerie
Bay Bread at the narrow bar.

Chloe's Cafe **L S M**   ▽ 22 14 19 $14

1399 Church St. (26th St.), 415-648-4116

■ Noe Valley early birds boast that this "quaint" but
"sophisticated" cafe serves truly "memorable breakfasts"
and brunches, which are highlighted by "the best biscuits,
scones and banana walnut pancakes in town" at very
"inexpensive" prices; while that's quite a contention,
the "long waits on weekends" ("they need to expand")
support the claim.

Chow L S M   18 14 17 $19
215 Church St. (Market St.), 415-552-2469
◪ Tony Gulisano's always "packed" Eclectic eatery in the
Castro is described as a "safety restaurant" "where moms
and nose rings meet" for a "wide range" of "rock bottom–
priced" "home-style bites" ("from Chinese noodles to
Italian" dishes and pizza); puzzled foes say "you get what
you pay for" and question whether the fare is "worth
standing in line" for.

Circadia L S M   12 18 13 $16
2727 Mariposa St. (Bryant St.), 415-552-2649
■ Though corporate bashers gleefully note that this cafe is
owned by "Starbucks in disguise", some Mission slackers
concede that it's "worth breaking your boycott" over as
it's a "good hangout for an Internet coffee klatch", followed
by "dependable" sandwiches, "suds and sounds."

Citizen Cake L S M   – | – | – | M
399 Grove St. (Gough St.), 415-861-2228
Sweet-toothed surveyors couldn't wait for the recent
opening of innovative pastry chef Elizabeth Falkner's new
loft-like Hayes Valley patisserie and California-cuisine
restaurant, which is open for breakfast, lunch and tea and
has her fans once again indulging in divine designer desserts
(try the tarts, drop cookies and cakes) and breads that are
works of art.

Citrus Club L S   ▽ 18 15 14 $17
1790 Haight St. (Shrader St.), 415-387-6366
■ A small, but satisfied contingent of surveyors says this
"cute", red-hued Haight Street "noodle house" serves "huge
portions" of "flavorful, healthy" "fill-up that won't empty
your pockets"; best-sellers include noodles with garlic and
shiitake mushrooms and coconut chicken with spicy lemon.

Clementine S   20 19 19 $37
126 Clement St. (bet. 2nd & 3rd Aves.), 415-387-0408
◪ "Everything about this" "unpretentious", "well-priced"
Inner Richmond venue is "delightfully French", from the
monthly changing menu of "dependably good" authentic
bistro fare (best suited for "a cold night") to the "romantic
surroundings"; Francophiles recommend the "to-die-for"
signature lamb ravioli, "early-bird specials" and "nice"
Sunday brunch; critics call it "solid" but "not memorable."

Clement Street Bar & Grill L S   17 15 18 $24
708 Clement St. (bet. 8th & 9th Aves.), 415-386-2200
■ This "neighborhood stalwart" in the Inner Richmond
serves a nightly changing menu of "simple" but "surprisingly
good" American fare amidst "pub surroundings"; it continues
to attract old-timers by practicing the "dying art of old-
school family dinners complete with meat, potatoes,
vegetable, soup and bread."

Cliff House 🄻🅂🄼
14 | 20 | 16 | $29

1090 Point Lobos Ave. (Great Hwy.), 415-386-3330

◪ Perched over the Pacific, this Ocean Beach landmark is "a must for visiting land-bound relatives who want to see the sea"; though the kitchen is "trying to improve the American food", most city slickers prefer to "have a drink" and fill up on the "to-die-for view."

Cobalt Tavern ●🄻🅂🄼
– | – | – | M

1707 Powell St. (Union St.), 415-982-8123

Although society columnists are still singing the blues over the closing of North Beach's venerable Washington Square Bar & Grill, this promising American brasserie, with live jazz, is rising from its ashes; while retaining the old haunt's cozy tavern atmosphere, new owners have updated the interior, and chef Guy Ferri (a disciple of Jeremiah Tower) is breathing new life into the seafood-centric menu.

Compass Rose 🄻🅂🄼
18 | 25 | 18 | $32

Westin St. Francis, 335 Powell St. (bet. Geary & Post Sts.), 415-397-7000

■ "A gracious place" for a "light lunch" as you "rest your feet after a shopping trip to Union Square", for "afternoon English tea" with your gram or a night of "drinks and dancing" with a date, this "classy" hotel Continental captivates; "though food is secondary" here, the "quiet", "elegant" setting more than compensates.

Connecticut Yankee 🄻🅂🄼
14 | 12 | 14 | $17

100 Connecticut St. (17th St.), 415-552-4440

◪ "If you're missing Boston, this is your spot" claim fans of this "fun", New England–themed, sports memorabilia–filled Potrero Hill American grill with plenty of suds on tap and games on TV.

Coriya Hot Pot City ●🄻🅂🄼
14 | 6 | 10 | $17

852 Clement St. (bet. 9th & 10th Aves.), 415-387-7888

◪ "Bring an empty stomach" and "don't wear anything fancy" when dining at this "hectic", self-serve, "all-you-can eat" Inner Richmond Korean-Taiwanese joint where patrons immerse meat, seafood and veggies into cauldrons of "delicious" bubbling broth; though the "faint of heart" might find the piles of raw meat "gross", fans exclaim "I've never had more fun paying to cook my own food."

Cosmopolitan Cafe ●🄻🄼
– | – | – | M

Rincon Ctr., 121 Spear St. (Mission St.), 415-543-4001

With an eye on the jinxed history of this sequestered spot in Rincon Center, the new owners have moved its entrance to Spear Street and added live music to the mix in an attempt to make for more positive mojo; but probably their most savvy move was hiring chef Steven Levine (ex Sonoma's now-shuttered Freestyle), whose boldly flavored New American cooking should prove congenial to cosmopolitan types.

Crepevine 🅛🅢🅜≠   15 | 11 | 11 | $13
216 Church St. (Market St.), 415-431-4646
624 Irving St. (bet. 7th & 8th Aves.), 415-681-5858
■ SF and East Bay bohemians and college students say these order-at-the-counter crêperies are a "compelling reason to roll out of bed" thanks to "generous portions" of "sweet and savory" crêpes ("from grilled tofu to classic lemon") that are "a lot of bang for not a lot of buck."

Crescent City Cafe 🅛🅢🅜   19 | 9 | 15 | $14
1418 Haight St. (bet. Ashbury St. & Masonic Ave.), 415-863-1374
☑ Bayou boosters have a generally warm response to this Haight Street hole-in-the-wall whose "stick-to-your-ribs" Cajun fare – "great fried-oyster po' boys", gumbo, crab cakes, jambalaya and "the best biscuits and buckwheat pancakes" – makes "great hangover" grub; a "fun", "sweet" staff counters the sparse surroundings.

Crustacean 🅛🅢🅜   22 | 16 | 18 | $39
1475 Polk St. (California St.), 415-776-2722
■ "Put on a bib and dig into" some "outrageous", "habit-forming" "garlic noodles and roasted crabs" (doused in garlic, drunken or tamarind sauce) at this "trendy" Polk Street Vietnamese-seafooder; yes, prices are "expensive", the layout could be better and there's a dress code (no sneakers or jock schlock), but these two dishes make it worth a trip.

Cypress Club 🅢🅜   21 | 26 | 20 | $47
500 Jackson St. (bet. Columbus Ave. & Montgomery St.), 415-296-8555
☑ "Giant lamps shaped like nipples" and curvaceous copper room partitions are some of the many "outrageous decor" elements that "delight visitors" at this "swank" Downtown supper club, which gets a "hip, trendy" crowd at its "gorgeous" bar for martinis and nightly "live jazz"; while the New American edibles are generally "yummy", they're unavoidably overshadowed by the setting.

dalla Torre 🅢   ∇ 18 | 25 | 20 | $41
1349 Montgomery St. (north of Union St.), 415-296-1111
■ Romance-oriented respondents find this "enchanting" bi-level Italian "nestled in Telegraph Hill gardens" "expensive, but worth every penny"; the best seating is upstairs, which affords a "great view of the Bay", or the corner "private booth" downstairs for "maximum privacy."

David's Deli & Restaurant ●🅛🅢🅜   13 | 9 | 11 | $19
474 Geary St. (bet. Mason & Taylor Sts.), 415-276-5950
☑ Some deli-deprived diners may depend on this Downtown stalwart for "comfort food fast", but most matzo-ball mavens moan "oye vey", "it's not New York"; the expensive prices ain't chopped liver" either.

Delancey Street ▯▯ 16 | 17 | 20 | $24
600 The Embarcadero (Brannan St.), 415-512-5179
◪ Surveyors with a "social conscience" believe this
"politically correct" Embarcadero American operated by
"reformed criminals" is "a good place to spend your money";
the food is "decent" and "dependable", "knowing you're
helping the staff" engenders a "feel-good dining experience",
and as a bonus, you can "admire the Bay Bridge views."

DELFINA ▯▯ 25 | 17 | 22 | $35
3621 18th St. (Dolores St.), 415-552-4055
◼ Craig Stoll and Anne Spencer's "recently expanded gem"
has made this "ideal neighborhood trattoria" in the Mission
"even better" (although "reservations are still tough" and
it can be "noisier than a rock concert"); a "hip, mixed crowd"
convenes for "wonderful", "honest Italian country cooking"
and "professional and friendly service"; although a handful
of dissenters complain it "suffers from too much hype",
aficionados assert that "this time the buzz is true."

DINE ▯ ▽ 24 | 22 | 19 | $39
*662 Mission St. (Annie Alley, bet. New Montgomery & 3rd Sts.),
415-538-3463*
◼ "Julia McClaskey does it again" declare devotees who've
discovered this new SoMa New American recently taken
over by the "brilliant" ex chef of the Universal Cafe; diners
dig into "delicious", "unfussy" fare like "tender pot roast",
and there's a "fun bar scene" as well.

Doidge's Cafe ▯▯▯ 20 | 13 | 16 | $19
2217 Union St. (bet. Fillmore & Steiner Sts.), 415-921-2149
◪ "Hearty old-time breakfast" is the main draw at this
"popular" "yuppie brunch hangout" in Cow Hollow; although
pros praise the "great eggs Benedict", the less enthused
opine that this "overpriced" American's saving grace is that
it's "one of the only restaurants to take brunch reservations."

Dot Restaurant ▯▯ – | – | – | M
*Radisson Miyako Hotel, 1611 Post St. (bet. Laguna & Posts Sts.),
415-922-7788*
If you have to ask what the dot stands for, you probably
won't fit in at this youthful hipster hangout, which at press
time is slated to open in Japantown's Radisson Miyako Hotel
(in the space formerly housing Elka's); designed to knock
your knickers off by Joe Boxer creator Nick Graham and
the Fun Display design team, the two-story dining room will
feature chef Noel Pavia's New American fare.

Dottie's True Blue Cafe ▯▯▯ 22 | 14 | 17 | $15
522 Jones St. (bet. Geary & O'Farrell Sts.), 415-885-2767
◼ "Bikers and debutantes" "stand in line" for breakfast at
this "tiny", "funky" Traditional American on the "edge of
the Tenderloin"; "superb frittatas, creative pancakes and
yummy baked goods" keep customers True Blue.

Dragon Well ⬛ⓈⓂ   20 | 17 | 18 | $20
2142 Chestnut St. (bet. Pierce & Steiner Sts.), 415-474-6888
■ This "yuppified" Marina spot lures regulars with "updated", "fresh and creative Chinese" cuisine that's "a lot more affordable and healthy" (the kitchen's "happy to create vegetarian dishes") than some of its brethren; a "simple" but "serene" setting and "warm, friendly" service also make for a "gracious dining" experience.

Dusit Thai ⬛ⓈⓂ   ▽ 20 | 11 | 18 | $18
3221 Mission St. (bet. 29th & Valencia Sts.), 415-826-4639
■ A core group of Bernal Heights devotees claim this tiny Thai with "simple decor but luscious food" is "always good", especially for spicy cooking 'cause "they can make it hot"; it also appeals if you're "on a budget."

E&O Trading Co. ⬛ⓈⓂ   19 | 21 | 17 | $31
314 Sutter St. (bet. Grant Ave. & Stockton St.),
415-693-0303
◪ Cavernous Downtown Asian with a "microbrew pub on the premises" that tempts a "lively young set" and "Union Square shoppers" with a dizzying array of "tasty small plates" and an "Indiana Jones/Disney decor"; while critics contend that it's "noisy" and the "atmo is more interesting than the food", most maintain that it's a "fun" "place to meet after work for drinks and appetizers"; N.B. there's a new branch in San Jose.

E'Angelo Ⓢ⑊   18 | 11 | 19 | $22
2234 Chestnut St. (bet. Pierce & Scott Sts.), 415-567-6164
■ "Out-of-the-way place in the Marina" offering "old-school" style Northern Italian "comfort food" – there's "great pasta" and "where else can you go for veal Parmigiana these days?" – at pleasing prices.

Eastside West ⓈⓂ   17 | 19 | 16 | $34
3154 Fillmore St. (Greenwich St.), 415-885-4000
◪ Not to be confused with a myriad of fusion spots, this upscale Cow Hollow "pickup scene" strives to be the West Coast's answer to an East Coast seafood joint; its fans feel that the "fun raw bar" and "live jazz" make it a "nice addition to the 'hood", but most maintain that the food "needs help."

Ebisu ⬛ⓈⓂ   24 | 13 | 17 | $28
1283 Ninth Ave. (Irving St.), 415-566-1770
◪ "If you can handle the atrocious wait" at this insanely popular Inner Sunset Japanese (it helps to arrive early or do lunch), you'll be rewarded with creative maki and "luscious sushi" that's "so fresh it might swim away before it gets to your mouth"; a few critics carp it's overrated, but they're outvoted by pros who proclaim it's "still a winner."

El Balazo 🅛🅢🅜⊄　　　20　13　15　$9
1654 Haight St. (bet. Belvedere & Clayton Sts.),
415-864-8608
■ "Burritos *sabrosos*" insist amigos of this "brightly painted" Haight Street taqueria where the service is "fast" and the "price is right"; although there's "great music on the loudspeakers", on a nice day, get it to go and walk to nearby Golden Gate Park to eat.

ELISABETH DANIEL, RESTAURANT 🅛🅜　　28　24　25　VE
550 Washington St. (bet. Montgomery & Sansome Sts.),
415-397-6129
■ The former chef-owners of the celebrated Babette's in Sonoma are at the "top of their game" and wowing city slickers at this "great" Downtown newcomer with "fancy shmancy" New French fare ("sweetbread ravioli from heaven") and "amazing" "choreographed service"; "talented chef" Daniel Patterson presents a three-course prix fixe menu at lunch ($35) and six courses at dinner ($68), while his wife, Elisabeth Ramsey, presides over the refined but unpretentious dining room.

Elite Cafe 🅢🅜　　　19　18　17　$32
2049 Fillmore St. (California St.), 415-346-8668
■ Long-standing Upper Fillmore Cajun-Creole "meat market" serving Bayou basics like blackened salmon, gumbo and jambalaya; on Sundays, "yuppies" jam into the "cool wooden booths" to knock back Bloody Mary's and martinis at the "great" "fun" brunch.

Eliza's 🅛🅢🅜　　　22　19　17　$21
2877 California St. (bet. Broderick & Divisadero Sts.),
415-621-4819
1457 18th St. (Connecticut St.), 415-648-9999
■ Looks aren't everything, but the "beautiful art-glass decor and orchids" definitely "enhance the dining experience" at this popular Pacific Heights Chinese and its new sibling on Potrero Hill; while there are whines about the "long lines" and "brisk service", "even food snobs" say it excels at "architectural presentations" of "wonderful" "fresh food" that's "surprisingly inexpensive."

Ella's 🅛🅢🅜　　　21　15　17　$22
500 Presidio Ave. (California St.), 415-441-5669
◪ "Legendary breakfasts" insure that there's "always a line" at this Presidio Heights American, even though it's "newly expanded"; whether the homemade bread, banana pancakes and chicken hash are "worth the ritual of waiting hours" is decidedly a matter of opinion, but if you go for it, be sure to "get there early."

Emma | – | – | – | M |

San Remo Hotel, 2237 Mason St. (bet. Chestnut & Francisco Sts.), 415-673-9090

North Beach Cal-Ital newcomer, named after chef-owner Mark Lusardi's (ex chef-owner of Yabbie's Coastal Kitchen) grandmother, featuring his signature seafood specialties and an emphasis on dishes that rely on local organic produce; co-proprietor and interior designer Anna Veyna has retained the original pressed-tin ceilings and tile floors of the 93-year-old historic San Remo Hotel in which the restaurant resides.

Empress of China 🄻🅂🅜 | 16 | 18 | 16 | $30 |

838 Grant Ave. (bet. Clay & Washington Sts.), 415-434-1345

■ Despite its central Chinatown location and "panoramic view of San Francisco and the Rock [Alcatraz]", most maintain that this "elegant" "old-time Chinese restaurant" serving "disappointing food" is tired and "looks better than it tastes"; critics liken it to "an aging monarch who's become too secure on the throne."

Enrico's Sidewalk Cafe ●🄻🅂🅜 | 17 | 19 | 16 | $30 |

504 Broadway (Kearny St.), 415-982-6223

■ There's "no better SF sidewalk cafe" (a "people-watcher's dream") than this North Beach Italian-Med that's long on atmo and short on service; enjoy lunch alfresco or join the other bohemians in the evening, knocking back an "excellent *mojito*" and listening to live jazz on the "heated patio."

EOS RESTAURANT & WINE BAR 🅂🅜 | 25 | 20 | 21 | $42 |

901 Cole St. (Carl St.), 415-566-3063

■ Oenophiles and foodies "flock from all over" to this cacophonous Cole Valley bistro for chef Arnold Eric Wong's "delicious, inventive" Asian-fusion fare, "exceptional wine list" and "desserts to die for" – don't miss the bananamisu; the "architecturally presented" dishes rise to "distressingly tall heights" (and so have the prices), but most maintain that it's "worth looking for parking"; N.B. walk-ins can opt to eat at the adjoining wine bar.

Eric's 🄻🅂🅜 | 21 | 15 | 16 | $19 |

1500 Church St. (27th St.), 415-282-0919

■ This Noe Valley mainstay, a "pretty storefront" that "looks nothing like a Chinese restaurant", features "kick-ass" cuisine that "draws a festive crowd"; although the "lines are outrageous at times", "unbelievable value" is the payoff.

Esperpento 🄻🅂🅜 | 18 | 14 | 14 | $22 |

3295 22nd St. (Valencia St.), 415-282-8867

■ Flamboyant Mission Iberian with "colorful, lively decor" and a Spanish flamenco dancer that's a "fun place to go with friends"; "reasonable prices" make the "tasty" tapas and "best sangria" even easier to swallow.

FARALLON L S M
24 | 28 | 23 | $53

450 Post St. (bet. Mason & Powell Sts.), 415-956-6969

◪ Dazzled diners Downtown would swim upstream just to eye Pat Kuleto's "over-the-top" "*20,000 Leagues Under the Sea*" decor (swirling with "jelly fish and sea-urchin lamps" and "cast-iron seaweed stair railings") and to eat chef Mark Franz's "inventive" Californian creations; while the unimpressed won't take the bait, calling the coastal cuisine "too splashy for my taste", they're outvoted by surveyors who shout "there's nothing fishy about this place!"

Faz L S M
18 | 17 | 17 | $29

Crocker Galleria, 161 Sutter St. (bet. Kearny & Montgomery Sts.), 415-362-0404

◪ Downtown "corporate lunch place", with other branches in the Bay area, that reels in office workers 'cause its "convenient" and affordable; but whether the Mediterranean fare is "interesting" or "inconsistent" is your call.

FIFTH FLOOR S M
26 | 28 | 27 | VE

Hotel Palomar, 12 Fourth St. (Market St.), 415-348-1555

■ A "palace for the palate" that "seems closer to heaven than just the Fifth Floor" is what surveyors say about this "sensational New French newcomer" in Downtown's Hotel Palomar; chef George Morrone's "sophisticated food" is complemented by a "clubby setting" ("Sinatra could be at the next table"), "polished service" and "phenomenal wine list"; the menu is pricey, but the experience is "exceptional."

Fior d'Italia L S M
16 | 17 | 18 | $34

601 Union St. (Stockton St.), 415-986-1886

◪ Since it claims to be 'the oldest Italian restaurant in America' (circa 1886), it's not surprising that this North Beach institution overlooking Washington Square Park offers "large portions of old-style, non-trendy cooking"; but what some consider "solid" fare served in a "historic" setting, detractors dub a "tired" and "touristy" experience.

Firecracker S
21 | 19 | 19 | $25

1007½ Valencia St. (21st St.), 415-642-3470

■ "Lively", red-hot hipster hangout in the Mission serving up sizzling "innovative Chinese with a twist" in "chic, sexy" surroundings that are as "noisy as its name"; a handful of dissenters feel the fiery fare fizzles in comparison to the "exotic decor", but most maintain that this place is a real "find" that will "blow you away."

Firefly S M
23 | 19 | 20 | $34

4288 24th St. (Douglass St.), 415-821-7652

■ Dinner at this culinary beacon in Noe Valley is like "eating at Mom's house if she was Julia Child" (and required reservations); chef Brad Levy's upscale, Eclectic comfort food ("yummy lentil butter spread instead of butter") shines in a "homey" yet "romantic setting."

Firewood Cafe 🄻🅂🄼
16 | 14 | 13 | $16

4248 18th St. (Diamond St.), 415-252-0999
Sony Metreon Ctr., 101 Fourth St. (Mission St.), 415-369-6199
■ "Great roasted chicken", "tasty thin-crust pizza" and "immense salads" are the draws at these "quick, cheap" and sleek Castro and SoMa spots; although service is limited and the American food doesn't break any culinary grounds, they'll do for a "meal on the run."

First Crush ●🅂🄼
17 | 15 | 17 | $34

101 Cyril Magnin St. (bet. Mason & Powell Sts.), 415-982-7874
■ Some say this "intimate wine bar/restaurant" nestled in a burgundy-colored "basement" Downtown is "the ultimate wine classroom"; its all-American effort extends from the menu to the all-Californian 300-bottle selection; thank goodness for the "knowledgeable staff" without whom you might feel crushed by the "overwhelming" "options."

FLEUR DE LYS 🄼
27 | 27 | 26 | $70

777 Sutter St. (bet. Jones & Taylor Sts.), 415-673-7779
■ Hubert Keller "puts his heart and soul into his food and it shows" swoon fans of this formal Downtown New French where a "sumptuous" canopied setting serves as the backdrop for "creative" cuisine that "continues to be first-rate" (even the "vegetarian tasting menu is awesome"); while some sniff at the "stuffy service", most agree with the romantic who rhapsodized: "this is a restaurant to propose in and I did."

Florio 🅂🄼
20 | 20 | 18 | $35

1915 Fillmore St. (bet. Bush & Pine Sts.), 415-775-4300
■ When Upper Fillmore folk want to "satisfy a bistro yen" they hightail it to this "chic" storefront specializing in Italian-French fare (from "perfect polenta" to pomme frites); the "savvy owners" have created the aura of a "terrific NY–style steak place", even though it also "feels like Paris" due to the "loud, loud, loud acoustics" and hurried Gallic service.

Flying Saucer 🄼
22 | 18 | 17 | $41

1000 Guerrero St. (22nd St.), 415-641-9955
☑ Although this Mission pioneer, which broke culinary bounds in the '90s with its "funky" amusement-park decor and "whimsically presented" eclectic cuisine, changed chefs and ownership last spring, "adventurous" diners still endure "annoying waits" for "three dimensional" French dishes with Middle Eastern and Asian accents; but cutting-edge critics simply sigh: "aren't we over architectural food?"

Fly Trap 🄻🅂🄼
19 | 17 | 18 | $35

606 Folsom St. (2nd St.), 415-243-0580
■ You don't hear much buzz about this SoMa Traditional American steeped in "old SF–style", but traditionalists are content to stick around because it's "one of the few places to serve good liver and onions" and other "internal organs."

Fog City Diner **L S M** | 19 | 20 | 18 | $29 |
1300 Battery St. (The Embarcadero), 415-982-2000
◪ "Crowded", "upscale pseudo-diner" on the Embarcadero that attracts "ad agency and tourist-types" who graze on little dishes that are a mix of "old-fashioned [American] food and creative, fusion fare" ("where else can you get burgers, shakes and ahi tartare"); although cynics warn "all those small plates add up" and gripe about the "hipper-than-thou attitude", advocates insist it's "fun" and a "must stop for anyone visiting SF."

Food Inc. **L M** | 19 | 13 | 12 | $16 |
2800 California St. (Divisadero St.), 415-928-3728
◪ Fans of this "delightful, unassuming" Pacific Heights Cal-Med like its "light breakfasts" and "excellent sandwiches", salads, pizzas and pastas at lunch and dinner, but type A's might consider takeout, as service can be "flaky" and "slow."

Foreign Cinema **S** | 19 | 25 | 17 | $39 |
2534 Mission St. (bet. 21st & 22nd Sts.), 415-648-7600
◪ "Come for the movies, stay for the mashed potatoes" might be the motto of this "hipper-than-hip" Mission newcomer with the "innovative concept" of pairing indie films and "foreign flicks" with "good French food"; serious diners sup inside, while a "super-trendy" "under-30 crowd" shares communal tables in the outdoor courtyard while watching Truffaut; the less cool complain that the reception is chilly and the cell-phone scene "feels like a Motorola commercial."

42° **L S M** | 21 | 21 | 18 | $40 |
235 16th St. (3rd St.), 415-777-5559
◪ Some surveyors need a compass to find this "out-of-the-way", "loud" and "very hip" Mediterranean supper club, located by Potrero Hill near China Basin, but once they do, they deem the "good food", "modern", bi-level setting, "chic", "under-35" crowd and "great jazz" "worth the trip."

Fountain Court **L S M** | 19 | 13 | 15 | $21 |
354 Clement St. (5th Ave.), 415-668-1100
◼ Offering "a nice change" from the endless stream of Mandarin restaurants on Clement Street, this "convenient and dependable" stalwart serves up "good" Shanghai cooking like "juicy pork buns" and vegetable potstickers; N.B. a post-*Survey* redo may outdate the above decor score.

Fournou's Ovens **L S M** | 23 | 23 | 23 | $45 |
Renaissance Stanford Ct. Hotel, 905 California St. (Powell St.), 415-989-1910
◼ Grande dame in the Renaissance Stanford Court Hotel atop of Nob Hill, whose Cal-Med cooking relies on a signature wood-burning oven ("anything roasted is good" and the "lamb is magical"); it's pricey, but the "relaxing", "warm surroundings" make it a "good place to bring the relatives when they visit."

Frascati ⑤Ⓜ　　　　22 | 18 | 21 | $33 |
1901 Hyde St. (Green St.), 415-928-1406

■ "Shhh" beg regulars of this "lovely neighborhood haunt"
in Russian Hill, who prefer to keep this "undiscovered"
(albeit "noisy") Eclectic-Italian with "excellent" food a
"well-kept secret"; no wonder, since it's also "underpriced."

FRINGALE ⓁⓂ　　　　26 | 19 | 22 | $41 |
570 Fourth St. (bet. Brannan & Bryant Sts.), 415-543-0573

■ C'est *"magnifique"* exclaim fans of this "timeless" SoMa
French bistro featuring Gerald Hirigoyen's "consistently
awesome" cuisine; the space-invaded complain "if the
tables were any closer it would be communal dining" and
wish the "tiny restaurant" were "larger so I could get a
reservation", but many maintain that it's the "best meal
for the money in SF."

Fuzio ⑤Ⓜ　　　　13 | 12 | 13 | $17 |
469 Castro St. (bet. 18th & Market Sts.), 415-863-1400
2175 Chestnut St. (Pierce St.), 415-673-8804
1 Embarcadero Ctr. (bet. Clay & Front Sts.), 415-392-7995

◪ This "inexpensive" "fusion pasta" chainlet proffering
oodles of Eclectic-International noodles (from pad Thai to
ravioli) garners mixed reviews: diners on the run insist the
"tasty" fast food is "perfect for a quick lunch" or "after a
movie", but franchise foes dis: "don't fail to miss it."

Ganges　　　　18 | 14 | 16 | $19 |
775 Frederick St. (Arguello Blvd.), 415-661-7290

■ Authentic, family-run Gujarati-style Indian in the Inner
Sunset featuring "fresh", "unique" vegetarian and vegan
fare; "sweet" sari-clad waitresses serve a wide selection
of curries, while customers sit cross-legged on cushions
and enjoy the live Indian music on Friday and Saturday.

GARDEN COURT Ⓛ⑤Ⓜ　　　　19 | 28 | 21 | $41 |
Palace Hotel, 2 New Montgomery St. (Market St.), 415-546-5010

■ The jewel in the crown of Downtown's Palace Hotel, this
airy 1909 dining room showcasing a "huge stained-glass
ceiling" is the "most beautiful room in the Bay Area" and
voted No. 1 for Decor in the *Survey*; critics sigh "if only the
[Californian] food matched" the setting, but that doesn't
stop locals from taking "out-of-town guests here" for high
tea and Sunday brunch.

Garibaldis on Presidio Ⓛ⑤Ⓜ　　　　22 | 20 | 21 | $36 |
*347 Presidio Ave. (bet. Clay & Sacramento Sts.),
415-563-8841*

■ "You can always count on a really nice meal" (try the
"amazing lamb" or "excellent risotto") at this "lively",
"consistently delicious" Cal-Med "neighborhood haunt"
with an offshoot in the East Bay; it's "noisy", but it's been
a "longtime favorite for a good reason."

GARY DANKO ⑤Ⓜ   28 | 27 | 27 | VE
800 North Point St. (Hyde St.), 415-749-2060
■ "Gary's back and better than ever" at this Fisherman's
Wharf French–New American, whipping up "sublime"
creations while his old Ritz-Carlton crony, Nick Peyton,
oversees a staff that "can't do enough to please"; a
"mix-and-match tasting menu" that offers "the best of both
worlds", an "elegant room" and an "impressive wine list"
add up to "the epitome of what fine dining should be" –
no wonder the reservationless lament: "let us in."

Gaylord India Ⓛ⑤Ⓜ   17 | 16 | 16 | $32
Ghirardelli Sq., 900 North Point St. (bet. Larkin & Polk Sts.),
415-771-8822
1 Embarcadero Ctr. (bet. Battery & Sacramento Sts.),
415-397-7775
☑ This Indian duo draws mixed reviews: pros praise the
"good food", "gracious staff" and the Ghirardelli branch's
"fabulous view of the Bay", but detractors dis the "hit-and-
miss" cooking and "high prices."

Gira Polli ⑤Ⓜ   19 | 13 | 16 | $21
659 Union St. (bet. Columbus Ave. & Powell St.), 415-434-4472
■ It's "chicken heaven" at this popular North Beach Italian
rotisserie (with branches around the Bay area) specializing
in "incredibly cheap", "superb, succulent fire-roasted"
birds; since the tiny, plain-Jane dining room is nothing to
crow about, most prefer to "take it home."

Globe ◐Ⓛ⑤Ⓜ   22 | 18 | 18 | $38
290 Pacific Ave. (bet. Battery & Front Sts.), 415-391-4132
☑ While yuppies gather at this Downtown spot for business
lunches, it's best known for its "late-night scene" when a
"trendy" crowd and "chefs kicking back after work" overlook
a "cramped, noisy" room and "long waits" for Joseph
Manzare's "sensational" New American fare; though some
ask "what's all the hype about?", globe-trotters find it "worth
a trip" "if you can bear" the "hipper- than-thou" atmosphere.

Godzila Sushi ⑤Ⓜ   20 | 10 | 14 | $23
1800 Divisadero St. (Bush St.), 415-931-1773
☑ Ironically named, this bite-sized Pacific Heights raw fish
joint scares up a queue for its "fresh", "solid" "sushi at a
great price"; moreover, "what it lacks in atmosphere" ("no-
frills") it more than makes up for with a "delicious" spicy
tuna roll; P.S. since there's often a wait, it's smart to "go early."

Golden Turtle Ⓛ⑤   20 | 16 | 17 | $26
2211 Van Ness Ave. (bet. Broadway & Vallejo St.), 415-441-4419
☑ Labeled "a find" in the ethnically desolate quarter of Van
Ness/Polk, this charming "neighborhood restaurant" on
the first floor of a converted house offers "pretty darn good
Vietnamese" edibles, "friendly service" and traditional decor,
which includes "cool", handmade carved-wood paneling.

Gordon Biersch Brewery 🅛🅢🅜   13 | 15 | 14 | $24 |
2 Harrison St. (The Embarcadero), 415-243-8246
See review in South of San Francisco Directory.

Gordon's House   21 | 20 | 18 | $37 |
of Fine Eats ◗🅛🅢🅜
500 Florida St. (Mariposa St.), 415-861-8900
◪ A "jumping" fun house in "a sleek, futuristic warehouse setting", this bi-level "bright star" in the Mission is where "multimedia pasha's graze" on Gordon Drysdale's down-to-earth Eclectic edibles ("where else can you get donuts for dessert?") after sipping "trendy drinks" at the bar; dissenters don't understand the "disjointed menu" and vote this place "most cacophonous newcomer."

Gourmet Carousel 🅛🅢   18 | 7 | 11 | $18 |
1559 Franklin St. (Pine St.), 415-771-2044
▮ "If you can't get to Chinatown" but want "large portions" of "cheap", "tasty" Chinese in the Pacific Heights area, stop by this "no-frills" ethnic where "nice sweet-and-sour pork", the "best won ton soup" and "wonderful pea shoots" make the world go round for ethnic bargain hunters.

Grand Cafe 🅛🅢🅜   20 | 25 | 20 | $39 |
Hotel Monaco, 501 Geary St. (Taylor St.), 415-292-0101
▮ "Truly grand, as the name implies", this "lively" Downtown brasserie is "one of the most beautiful dining rooms in SF" – 30-foot ceilings, art deco and nouveau touches – and is a fittingly "dramatic" stage for the "great" New French fare; a few spoilers say the "food is not up to the decor", but a plum locale and "gracious service" enhance its rep as a smart choice for lunch after shopping or a pre-theater meal; N.B. however, the departure of chef Denis Soriano may outdate the above food score.

Grandeho's Kamekyo 🅛🅢🅜   22 | 16 | 19 | $26 |
943 Cole St. (bet. Carl St. & Parnassus Ave.), 415-759-8428
2721 Hyde St. (bet. Beach & North Point Sts.), 415-673-6828
▮ This family-run Cole Valley Japanese and its new Hyde Street sibling win kudos for their "unique rolls", "consistently fresh fish prepared with flair" and "very helpful", "multilingual sushi chefs" whose "personalized service" adds to the "homey neighborhood" feel; hint: "eat early to beat the lines."

Great Eastern ◗🅛🅢🅜   21 | 11 | 13 | $25 |
649 Jackson St. (bet. Grant Ave. & Kearny St.), 415-986-2500
▮ "Chose your meal from the live seafood tanks" at this multilevel, Hong Kong–style hole-in-the-wall in Chinatown, whose impressive specialties include steamed abalone with garlic sauce and sautéed geoduck clams with yellow chives; since the size of the catch typically yields large portions, "locals and tourists" tend to come here in "big groups."

Greens ⓁⓈⓂ
22 | 23 | 20 | $33

Ft. Mason Ctr., Bldg. A (Buchanan St. & Marina Blvd.),
415-771-6222

☑ Billed as "SF's temple of haute Vegetarian cuisine", this politically correct (but "expensive") Marina institution boasts Annie Somerville's "zenzational" cooking, a "world-class wine list", "earth-friendly redwood tables" and an "unsurpassed view of the Golden Gate Bridge"; some snipe that it "hasn't kept up with the times", but the majority feels "even a meat lover can't help but like this place."

Hahn's Hibachi
16 | 10 | 14 | $14

1305 Castro St. (24th St.), 415-642-8151 ⓁⓈⓂ
525 Haight St. (Fillmore St.), 415-864-3721 ⓁⓈⓂ
535 Irving St. (7th Ave.), 415-731-3721
1710 Polk St. (bet. Clay & Washington Sts.),
415-776-1095 ⓁⓈⓂ
3318 Steiner St. (bet. Chestnut & Lombard Sts.),
415-931-6284 Ⓜ

■ Called "the perfect in-and-out restaurant when you're short on time" and want to fill up for a song, these "no-frills" Korean BBQ joints dole out "yummy piles of grilled meats", tempting tempura "and good veggie stuff."

Hamano Sushi ⓈⓂ
24 | 13 | 12 | $29

1332 Castro St. (24th St.), 415-826-0825

☑ This frenetic Noe Valley Japanese reels in raw fish aficionados for "Tokyo quality" and "big, thick slabs of fish" (at "US prices"), which rival what's offered at Ebisu and Blowfish; dissenters refuse to put up with the "insane lines" and "surly" waiters who "need to go to charm school", but those who do end the evening satisfied, singing a refrain of "we all scream for green tea ice cream."

Hamburger Mary's ⓁⓈ
15 | 15 | 14 | $17

1582 Folsom St. (12th St.), 415-626-1985

■ "Quintessential hamburger joint" decorated with a "hodgepodge" of "funky" tchotchkes, whose "low-key roadside atmosphere makes you forget that you're in the heart of the city"; though foes feel it's "not what it used to be", plenty of folks still find it a "SoMa favorite" for brunch ("morning-after fare") and simple "late-night" pub grub.

Harbor Village ⓁⓈⓂ
22 | 19 | 16 | $30

4 Embarcadero Ctr. (Drumm St., bet. Clay & Sacramento Sts.),
415-781-8833

☑ "Quality" dim sum and "great views of the Bay" are why this massive Downtown Chinese venue is a popular "place to take out-of-towners", especially on weekends; groups looking "for a special splurge" should consider pre-ordering one of the "sumptuous banquets", which showcase "5,000 years of civilization in ten courses"; critics claim the place "lacks friendly service" and prefer to get their *shu mai* dumplings elsewhere.

Hard Rock Cafe L S M　　11　17　12　$21
1699 Van Ness Ave. (Sacramento St.), 415-885-1699
■ Even though these "shrines to rock 'n' roll" are "the same everywhere", "kids and tourists still make a pilgrimage" to this Van Ness/Polk branch for "deafening" music and "interesting" artifacts (a "wealth of Beatles memorabilia"); cynics roll their eyes and call it a "tired" "sweatshirt shop" where the "only thing worth eating is the overpriced burger."

Harris' S M　　24　22　22　$47
2100 Van Ness Ave. (Pacific Ave.), 415-673-1888
◪ "The vegetarian's anti-Christ", this "traditional" Van Ness/Polk steakhouse is "the place to indulge your craving" for must-try martinis, "superb" dry-aged beef and "the best prime rib"; the "perfect old-school interior" includes mahogany furniture and comfortable leather booths, largely inhabited by bald, cigar-carrying men.

Harry Denton's Starlight Room S M　　14　22　15　$36
Sir Francis Drake Hotel, 450 Powell St. (Sutter St.), 415-395-8595
■ Despite drop-dead views of Downtown and a menu of light American nibbles, reviewers report that playboy Harry Denton's "wanna-be disco" atop the Sir Francis Drake Hotel is a "pre-dinner cocktail and dancing" destination for a "fortysomething clientele trying to relive the good old days."

HAWTHORNE LANE L S M　　26　25　24　$52
22 Hawthorne St. (bet. 2nd & 3rd Sts.), 415-777-9779
■ "Hidden away" in SoMa, Annie and David Gingrass' "chichi" Californian delivers a "deft blend of all the elements for a memorable culinary experience": "imaginative" creations (starting with "wonderful" homemade breads), a "modern", "understated interior" filled with art and ironwork, "excellent", "friendly" service and "marvelous energy", courtesy of a "yuppie expense-account crowd."

Hayes & Vine Wine Bar ◑ S M　　17　20　19　$27
377 Hayes St. (bet. Franklin & Gough Sts.), 415-626-5301
■ Small Hayes Valley wine bar featuring a "comprehensive selection" of vino (800 offerings) by the half-glass, glass, flight or bottle; the menu is "limited", but you can "stave off your hunger" by nibbling on "wonderful snacks like the smoked trout"; the staff is "knowledgeable", but tight-fisted tipplers may find the prices "steep."

Hayes Street Grill L S M　　23　17　21　$37
320 Hayes St. (bet. Franklin & Gough Sts.), 415-863-5545
■ "When you're tired of hip", consider a visit to this "pretension-free" Hayes Valley pre-symphony spot (operated by local restaurant reviewer Patricia Unterman), which serves an over-40 crowd "consistently reliable" renditions of American-seafood classics; however, modernists find the "old SF" decor and menu "a bit boring."

Helmand, The S　　　　　23 | 16 | 20 | $30
430 Broadway (bet. Kearny & Montgomery Sts.), 415-362-0641
■ If you "want to feel like an Afghan prince", have your entourage carry you to this "unique" North Beach standby, "an oasis of calm amid the Broadway tackiness", which offers "excellent" examples of that country's "exotic, distinctive cuisine" ("melt-in-your-mouth lamb", "to-die-for pumpkin ravioli") at "value" prices.

Herbivore L S M　　　　　17 | 14 | 16 | $16
983 Valencia St. (21st), 415-826-5657
◪ Surveyors are divided on this "hardcore" Vegan in the Mission: pleased plant lovers find the "wide array" of cooking (from pad Thai to a veggie sampler) "excellent for the price" and appreciate the blonde-wood paneling and "casual" room; but critics counter that the fare is "bland" and the setting "cold."

Hotei L S M　　　　　14 | 15 | 15 | $17
1290 Ninth Ave. (Irving St.), 415-753-6045
■ "From the people who brought you Ebisu" comes this Inner Sunset "middle-of-the-road noodle house", which serves "simple, homey Japanese fare"; while pros pronounce the udon, soba and ramen offerings "a welcome source of warmth on a cold day" and the interior "soothing" (courtesy of a waterfall), skeptics sniff that the service is "rushed" and the food a "disappointment."

House M　　　　　24 | 17 | 19 | $32
1230 Grant Ave. (bet. Columbus Ave. & Vallejo St.), 415-986-8612 L
1269 Ninth Ave. (bet. Irving St. & Lincoln Way), 415-682-3898 S
■ This Inner Sunset and North Beach pair of "hopping houses" shows off chef Larry Tse's "excellent Asian fusion" cuisine, which "outdoes itself, with its artful main courses" (the "sea bass is still the best on earth") and "yummy desserts"; aesthetes assert the "stark, noisy surroundings diminish the experience", but boosters bark that these "surprisingly affordable" spots "would be on everyone's best list if they charged more."

House of Nanking L S M　　　　　21 | 5 | 9 | $16
919 Kearny St. (bet. Columbus Ave. & Jackson St.), 415-421-1429
◪ How a Chinatown "dive" with infamously "reckless" servers who "cram you in", "tell you what to order" and "throw food at you" became a SF legend worthy of "fashionable people" waiting on long lines is anyone's guess; bargain hunters claim it's because it offers the "best Chinese for the money", but cons counter that the "overrated food for Caucasians" is an "old joke that's better left to the tourists."

House of Prime Rib ⑤Ⓜ | 23 | 18 | 21 | $37 |
1906 Van Ness Ave. (Washington St.), 415-885-4605

■ "Excellent salads" theatrically tossed tableside and "great, heart-stopping servings" of prime rib are the highlights of this Van Ness/Polk beefhouse with an "elegant", "old-folks atmosphere" that hasn't changed in 40 years; up-to-the-minute types find the milieu "tired", but concede they took advantage of the waiter's offer of a free "second helping" of meat.

Hunan Ⓛ Ⓜ | 19 | 9 | 14 | $17 |
1016 Bryant St. (8th St.), 415-861-5808
110 Natoma St. (bet. New Montgomery & 2nd Sts.), 415-546-4999
674 Sacramento St. (bet. Kearny & Montgomery Sts.), 415-788-2234
924 Sansome St. (Broadway), 415-956-7727 ⑤

■ Some like it hot at these perennially packed Chinese "workday lunch" spots, which serve owner Henry Chung's "spicy Hunan regional specialties"; although their "low-rent interiors" "aren't fancy", they enjoy a "cult following" among fiery food fans, who recommend the pan-fried string beans, orange chicken and "A+ smoked ham."

Hunan Home's Restaurant Ⓛ⑤Ⓜ | 20 | 12 | 17 | $19 |
622 Jackson St. (bet. Grant Ave. & Kearny St.), 415-982-2844

■ This spacious Chinatown spot "is not much to look at" (a live fish tank, mirrored walls, tacky chandeliers) "but what it lacks in decor it more than makes up for with excellent" Hunan dishes (especially the prawns with honey walnuts); moreover, unlike some of its competitors, the "friendly staff will cook things the way you want them."

Hungarian Sausage Factory & Bistro ⑤ | ▽ 16 | 15 | 15 | $18 |
419 Cortland Ave. (bet. Bennington & Wool Sts.), 415-648-2847

■ Paging goulash lovers – this "comfortable neighborhood place" in Bernal Heights showcases Hungarian specialties like "good sausages" and stuffed cabbage that add to the culinary melting pot of SF; though some items are "a bit rich" and might not inspire raves from everyone, fans say the "live piano music is a big plus."

Hyde Street Bistro ⑤ | 22 | 17 | 21 | $33 |
1521 Hyde St. (bet. Jackson St. & Pacific Ave.), 415-292-4415

■ Although you can "take the cable car" to this "quaint" Russian Hill bistro, dining here is more "like a visit to a small town in France" (perhaps a Provençal hill town); the "charming" Lyonnaise chef-proprietor "pampers" patrons, who say don't miss his "incredible bouillabaisse."

I Fratelli ⑤Ⓜ | 19 | 17 | 19 | $28 |
1896 Hyde St. (Green St.), 415-474-8240

☑ Surveyors give this Russian Hill "standby" a warm "*bene*" for its "bargain" prices, "fabulous bruschetta", "richly seasoned", "hearty" Italian pastas ("best linguini and clam sauce in town") and "very friendly owner who makes you feel at home."

Il Fornaio ◐ⓁⓈⓂ | 19 | 21 | 19 | $31 |
Levi's Plaza, 1265 Battery St. (bet. Greenwich & Union Sts.), 415-986-0100

☑ Judging from its solid scores, it's obvious that this "popular" Bay Area chain has "found the right formula for a charming Italian restaurant": "super" "chewy" breads, "reliably well-prepared" (if "predictable") pizzas and pastas and "lovely, inviting settings", which include outdoor patios.

Indian Oven ⑤Ⓜ | 23 | 15 | 17 | $24 |
233 Fillmore St. (bet. Haight & Waller Sts.), 415-626-1628

■ Naan-paralleled breads, "delicious vindaloo" and "tasty curries" at "very reasonable" prices are the "reason so many yuppies visit the Lower Haight" to dine at this Indian, which is one of "the best in SF proper"; P.S. a recent expansion of the upstairs back room ("thank God!") may help relieve the "crowded" conditions and "long lines."

Indigo ⑤ | 21 | 20 | 21 | $36 |
687 McAllister St. (bet. Franklin & Gough Sts.), 415-673-9353

■ This "undiscovered gem" serves "imaginative" New American cuisine in a "hip room" with "comfy booths"; while generally regarded as one of "the best pre-theater choices" in the Civic Center area, on weekends it's also a spot for night crawlers, who crowd into the Crimson Lounge, "the racy red bar in the basement"; surprisingly, despite the overall fabulous factor, the staff manages to "treat you like family."

Infusion Bar & Restaurant ⓁⓈⓂ | 17 | 17 | 16 | $29 |
555 Second St. (bet. Brannan & Bryant Sts.), 415-543-2282

☑ As the name implies, the focal point of this "convivial" dot-commer hangout in SoMa is its "rows of fruit-infused vodka" jars and the "stiff drinks" made from them; although some "pass on dinner and go straight to the interesting martini selection", those who eat report that the New American "food is surprisingly good."

Iroha ⓁⓈⓂ | ▽ | 18 | 13 | 14 | $16 |
1728 Buchanan St. (bet. Post & Sutter Sts.), 415-922-0321

■ When surveyors have a yen for "simple and tasty Japanese noodles", they head to this Japantown haunt for some of the "best soba and ramen in SF", which are pleasantly served in an attractive "red-and-black room that makes you feel like a trinket in a bento box"; it also doesn't hurt that the prices (even for sake) are "cheap."

Iron Horse ⅬⅯ
14 | 14 | 15 | $31

19 Maiden Ln. (bet. Geary & Post Sts.), 415-362-8133

◩ Entering this Downtown Italian "San Francisco institution" is like "stepping back in time to the '50s and *Perry Mason*"; though nostalgists are content with the old-school chow, foodies say your best bet is to "stick to the bar" and "pretend you're a gangster" because the "outdated food is only fair"; N.B. as we go to press, a move to another locale Downtown is scheduled.

Irrawaddy Burmese Cuisine Ⓢ
▽ 20 | 12 | 18 | $21

1769 Lombard St. (bet. Laguna & Octavia Sts.), 415-931-2830

◩ Only a handful of surveyors have kicked off their shoes, sat down at the sumptuous sunken tables, taken in the "nice artifacts" and supped on the "wonderful" Burmese specialties (a blend of Indian spices and Chinese techniques) at this "hidden gem" in the Marina; a few caution that the victuals can be "inconsistent", but they're outvoted.

Isobune Sushi ⅬⓈⅯ
18 | 14 | 15 | $23

Japan Ctr., 1737 Post St. (Buchanan St.), 415-563-1030

◩ "Kitschy" Japanese, with branches around the Bay Area, that's a "fun place to grab fresh sushi off of floating boats"; sure, "there's better fish to be had" and some warn "watch out for plates that have been out to sea too long", but since "out-of-towners insist" on trying it, go early so that you "don't have to wait long for your ship to come in."

It's Tops Coffee Shop ⅬⓈⅯ
14 | 15 | 15 | $13

1801 Market St. (McCoppin St.), 415-431-6395

◩ Owned and operated by the same family since 1952, this Upper Market retro diner dishes up nostalgia in the form of "consistently solid" American fare (burgers, shakes, fries) highlighted by "helluva good pancakes" that are served until closing time.

Izzy's Steak & Chop House ⓈⅯ
21 | 16 | 18 | $33

3345 Steiner St. (Lombard St.), 415-563-0487

▉ Although it plays second fiddle to the big-name places, this "endearing, classic neighborhood steakhouse" in the Marina satisfies carnivores with it's "stuck-in-a-time-warp" decor, "friendly service", super sides (try the "incredible creamed spinach" and Izzy potatoes) and "gorgeous steaks" at "reasonable prices."

Jack's ⅬⅯ
18 | 22 | 18 | $42

615 Sacramento St. (Montgomery St.), 415-421-7355

◩ Two years ago this legendary Downtown American-French veteran (SF's oldest restaurant still in its original location) reopened under new ownership with a different look and menu; but while pros praise the "beautiful redo" and say it's "worth a revisit for old-time's sake", the less enthused assert that the edibles are "prosaic" and the place "isn't up to the standards of the original."

Jackson Fillmore Trattoria ⑤Ⓜ   20 | 13 | 16 | $31
2506 Fillmore St. (Jackson St.), 415-346-5288

◪ "If your grandmother was Italian and loved you very much" you might have enjoyed the kind of "hearty, soul-satisfying" Southern Italian cooking prepared at this tiny, always crowded Upper Fillmore trattoria; everything is far from perfect – foes point out that there's "no decor" and the waits for a table are "unbearable" – but all is forgiven after one bite of the "amazing bruschetta."

Jakarta ⑤   ▽ 20 | 18 | 19 | $23
615 Balboa St. (7th Ave.), 415-387-5225

■ For a taste of Indonesia, locals like this ethnic eatery in the Inner Richmond where "interesting" food with "exotic flavors" is served in an elegant setting festooned with shadow puppets and other authentic artifacts; "service is very slow" but "no one complains", probably because it's clear that the staff and owner "really care."

JARDINIÈRE ⑤Ⓜ   26 | 26 | 24 | $56
300 Grove St. (Franklin St.), 415-861-5555

■ "Beautiful people", pre-concert culture vultures and devotees of fine dining make the pilgrimage to this "pricey" Hayes Valley "gastronomical mecca" for "seriously talented" chef Traci Des Jardins' "inventive" Cal–New French cuisine ("amazing scallops") and Pat Kuleto's "gorgeous" interior, which is dominated by a dramatic center bar and a balcony that provides for "great people-watching"; P.S. save room for the "wonderful" cheese course.

Jianna ◐⑤Ⓜ   – | – | – | M
1548 Stockton St. (bet. Green & Union Sts.), 415-398-0442

Marc Valiani (formerly of the LuLu empire) vowed that his new casual North Beach newcomer would be 'ABI' ('anything but Italian') and he's kept his word with this boldly flavored, moderately priced Contemporary American; amber lighting mellows the dining room and bar/lounge area and even the exhibition kitchen hums quietly, maintaining a soothing atmosphere that attracts a mix of old and young; N.B. it's open until midnight, making it one of the best late-night options in the 'hood.

Johnfrank ⑤Ⓜ   20 | 21 | 20 | $42
2100 Market St. (bet. Church & 14th Sts.), 415-503-0333

■ Owners John Hurley and Frank Everett (by way of Garibaldis and Boulevard respectively) break the mold of eateries in the Upper Market with this "chic" New American where a "clamorous", "glamorous" gay crowd ("don't wear anything from last season") poses in between enjoying the "tasty" cuisine and "delightful desserts"; N.B. however, the post-*Survey* departure of chef Richard Crocker and the arrival of chef Lance Velasquez may outdate the above food score.

John's Grill ⬛⬛⬛⬛
63 Ellis St. (bet. Powell & Stockton Sts.),
415-986-0069

| 13 | 16 | 15 | $33 |

⬛ Dating back to 1908, this hard-boiled Downtown institution features a replica of the bird from the *Maltese Falcon*, along with an "old SF menu" (think sand dabs and liver and onions) that Dashiell Hammett might have appreciated; though it remains a "popular lunch spot" for old-timers, most folks find the Traditional American food "mediocre" and suggest "Sam Spade wouldn't come here anymore."

Joubert's ⬛
4115 Judah St. (46th Ave.), 415-753-5448

| 19 | 14 | 22 | $26 |

⬛ South African–Vegetarian cuisine may sound like an unusual combination but most feel this "fascinating" spot way out by the beach in the Sunset pulls it off; try to overlook the "bare-bones decor", which "doesn't hint at the excellent tastes to come" ("they do amazing things with bananas"), the charm of the "fun owner", or the depth of the 50-plus South African wine selection.

Juban ⬛⬛⬛
Japan Ctr., 1581 Webster St. (bet. Geary Blvd. & Post St.),
415-776-5822

| 19 | 19 | 17 | $27 |

See review in South of San Francisco Directory.

Julie's Supper Club ⬛
1123 Folsom St. (bet. 7th & 8th Sts.), 415-861-0707

| 15 | 17 | 15 | $29 |

◪ This "loud and energized" "SoMa pioneer", where the Californian fare "is good, the martinis are better" (especially at happy hour) and "Dean Martin croons in the background", is still the place for "spectacular birthday party celebrations", even if the "bridge-and-tunnel thing is happening."

Julius' Castle ⬛⬛
1541 Montgomery St. (Union St.), 415-392-2222

| 17 | 24 | 20 | $46 |

◪ "On a clear night, you can see forever" (or at least the moon over Treasure Island) from this Telegraph Hill "Valentine's Day staple"; sure, the "unparalleled views of the Bay" go a long way, and the old-world charm of the dining room "is romantic and all", but critics call the Italian "eats disappointing and overpriced."

Kabuto Sushi
5116 Geary Blvd. (15th Ave.), 415-752-5652

| 24 | 10 | 17 | $33 |

⬛ Celebrated sushi maestro Sachio Kojima reels in raw fish aficionados from around the city at this "traditional-style" Japanese joint in the Richmond; the "drab" decor provides "no ambiance", but the offerings are some of "the best in town" and the "salonlike scene at the sushi bar" is full of "regulars who have a rapport with the chef."

Kan Zaman 🅛🅢🅜
17 | 19 | 14 | $19

1793 Haight St. (Shrader St.), 415-751-9656

■ "Decent", "cheap" standards like falafel and baba ghanoush are yours for the taking at this Haight Street Middle Eastern, which surveyors say defines "hippie-souk chic"; enthusiasts advise you "go early or late to avoid the lines", "sit on the floor in a big group", take in the murals depicting a 14th-century Moorish castle and enjoy the weekend belly dancers.

Kate's Kitchen 🅛🅢🅜⊘
20 | 10 | 14 | $15

471 Haight St. (Fillmore St.), 415-626-3984

■ "Bring an empty stomach" to this "funky", no-frills American cafe in the Lower Haight, which some say is "the place for the biggest and best breakfast, if you dare venture to this part of town" and don't mind waiting; expect "goth waitresses" and "reasonable prices" on "fabulous" pancakes, hush puppies and "biscuits and gravy that will stay with you all morning – maybe even all day."

Katia's Russian Tea Room 🅛🅢
20 | 15 | 21 | $25

600 Fifth Ave. (Balboa St.), 415-668-9292

■ "Go for the blinis", stay for the guitarist/accordion player suggest admirers of this light-filled Inner Richmond cafe, which features "traditional", "hearty" Russian food (think beef stroganoff) like "grandma used to make" and "friendly service" led by chef-owner Katia Troosh ("a doll").

Kelly's Mission Rock 🅛🅢
14 | 17 | 13 | $23

817 China Basin St. (Mariposa St.), 415-626-5355

◪ "What a transformation" remark reviewers dazzled by the remodel of this former waterfront dive near the ballpark, which is now an airy, upscale bi-level bistro and a "most welcome" spot to brunch alfresco over chichi American chow while watching the "ships in the Bay"; but bashers say they've "destroyed one of the great hangouts in town."

Khan Toke Thai House 🅢🅜
21 | 23 | 19 | $26

5937 Geary Blvd. (bet. 23rd & 24th Aves.), 415-668-6654

■ "Year after year" this "long-lived" Thai in the Richmond remains a "great place to take out-of-towners" and "first dates" for "sparkling" Bangkok specialties and "fabulous curries", which are served in a sumptuously appointed, artifact-filled setting where patrons must remove their shoes (so "wear clean socks").

King of Thai ◕🅛🅢🅜⊘
19 | 5 | 12 | $12

639 Clement St. (bet. 7th & 8th Aves.), 415-752-5198

◪ It may "look like a dump" ("kill the fluorescent light!") but this Inner Richmond Thai has a loyal following for its "big portions" of "inexpensive" edibles (try the "sumptuous noodles") and long hours "perfect for late-night cravings."

KOKKARI ESTIATORIO ⬛Ⓜ 24 | 27 | 23 | $46
200 Jackson St. (Front St.), 415-981-0983

◼ "Gorgeous", sprawling Downtown taverna where the well-connected Greek community and "beautiful people" lap up "excellent", "rustic" Hellenic fare highlighted by a "killer meze platter", "unbelievable moussaka" and "don't-miss" lamb; reservations are hard to score, but if you can't get a seat "in the front room by the fireplace" or at the "big community table", the "convivial" bar is nice consolation.

Kuleto's ⬛Ⓢ Ⓜ 20 | 20 | 19 | $36
Villa Florence Hotel, 221 Powell St. (bet. Geary & O'Farrell Sts.), 415-397-7720

◪ Adjoining the Villa Florence Hotel, this "always crowded" Downtown trattoria is a "great place to refuel during a Union Square shopping adventure" or after the theater; loyalists return for the "reliable", if "predictable", Italian food, Pat Kuleto's earth-toned, marble-floored setting and the overall "relaxing atmosphere"; P.S. to avoid a wait for a table, "enjoy a meal at the bar."

Kyo-Ya ⬛ 24 | 21 | 22 | $50
Palace Hotel, 2 New Montgomery St. (Market St.), 415-546-5090

◼ Sequestered in the Palace Hotel Downtown, in a "peaceful" dining room with orchids on every table, this notoriously pricey Japanese draws salarymen (and even Yoko Ono once) for impressive sakes, "wonderfully fresh sushi", "refined *kaiseki* dinners" and service that makes you feel "pampered like a passenger in a first-class lounge."

La Cumbre Taqueria ⬛Ⓢ Ⓜ 20 | 9 | 14 | $10
515 Valencia St. (bet. 16th & 17th Sts.), 415-863-8205

◪ This "fun, cheap" taqueria is a "Mission favorite" for "great quesadillas", *carnitas* burritos big enough to feed two and a *pollo asada* that's rumored to be based on "God's recipe"; sorry, at "these prices you don't get decor too."

La Felce ⬛Ⓢ Ⓜ ▽ 22 | 15 | 21 | $30
1570 Stockton St. (Union St.), 415-392-8321

◼ Although it may not be as well-known as it once was (judging from the low voter turnout), this "old-time North Beach Italian" still has a coterie of customers who appreciate the "owners who make everyone feel welcome" and "classic dishes" (particularly the "good veal" renditions), which "haven't changed much" since the day it opened in 1975.

LA FOLIE Ⓜ 28 | 23 | 26 | $68
2316 Polk St. (bet. Green & Union Sts.), 415-776-5577

◼ Chef-owner "Roland Passot continues to make magic" at this "cozy" Van Ness/Polk New French, which "rises above" its Gallic rivals; it's "a real budget buster", but citing the "beautiful presentations" of "memorable" dishes complemented by "impeccable" yet "friendly" service, most agree it's "worth" the beaucoup bucks.

Laghi 🇱🇸🇲   21 | 15 | 20 | $32
2101 Sutter St. (Steiner St.), 415-931-3774

■ Admirers of Gino Laghi's "fantastico" Northern Italian attest the "pastas are still terrific" even though the space is "no longer cozy" since the relocation to roomy Pacific Heights digs; the service remains as "friendly" as ever.

La Méditerranée 🇱🇸🇲   18 | 14 | 17 | $19
2210 Fillmore St. (Sacramento St.), 415-921-2956
288 Noe St. (bet. Market & 16th Sts.), 415-431-7210

☑ This "dependable" duo "fills a niche" with its "flavorful" (if "not spectacular") Middle Eastern–Mediterranean fare, catering to phyllo fans in search of "bargain prices"; but aesthetes assert the "cramped quarters" need "upgrading."

La Palma Mexicatessen 🇱🇸🇲 ▽ 23 | 9 | 11 | $10
2884 24th St. (Florida St.), 415-647-1500

■ "The locals shop" for "fresh" Mexican "groceries" and indulge in the "best *carnitas* in SF" at this hole-in-the-wall Mission market/take-out joint; it's like "a mini-vacation" south of the border – where else can you "watch your tortilla being patted out by hand"?

Lapis Restaurant 🇱🇲   – | – | – | E
Pier 33, The Embarcadero (Bay St.), 415-982-0203

Chef Thomas Ricci's (ex the now-shuttered Elan Vital) menu globe-trots around the Mediterranean Rim, from Southern France down to Egypt, at this waterside gem on The Embarcadero; the massive dining room offers enchanting views of SF Bay, and diners are encouraged to enjoy cocktails and a constitutional out on the pleasant patio.

La Rondalla ◗🇱🇸≠   12 | 15 | 13 | $17
901 Valencia St. (20th St.), 415-647-7474

■ Given its tinseled interior ("Christmas all year round"), mariachis and "margaritas so good you might wake up married", many maintain you "can't beat" this Mission Mexican dive as a "place to party"; though cynics cite "mediocre food", compadres shrug "hey, it's open late."

La Scene Cafe & Bar 🇸🇲   19 | 19 | 21 | $36
Warwick Regis, 490 Geary St. (Taylor St.), 415-292-6430

■ A "hidden gem" tucked away in the Warwick Regis Hotel, this "intimate" Downtown New American earns applause as a "dependable pre-theater" pick based on its "tasty" fare (including a prix fixe "bargain"), "low-key" but "stylish" ambiance and "great service."

La Taqueria 🇱🇸🇲≠   23 | 8 | 13 | $11
2889 Mission St. (25th St.), 415-285-7117

■ For "consistent" quality, it's "worth a trip to the Mission" to sample the "best burritos in the barrio" washed down with "delicious" *aguas frescas* at this "cheap and fabulous" Mexican vet; despite the "cafeteria-style ambiance", purists pronounce it "the real thing."

La Vie ⬛S 22 12 20 $22
5830 Geary Blvd. (bet. 22nd & 23rd Aves.), 415-668-8080
■ "Wonderful roasted crab" and other "authentic" Vietnamese fare prepared with an "artistic touch" ensure this Richmonder is "a hit" in spite of its "spartan" setting; the "gracious service" (host "Han knows every customer") presents patrons with a taste of the good life.

La Villa Poppi ▽ 17 13 19 $34
3234 22nd St. (bet. Mission & Valencia Sts.), 415-642-5044
■ Not many know this lilliputian storefront trattoria in the Mission, but those who have discovered it adore its husband-and-wife team spirit: he prepares the "sophisticated" Tuscan prix fixe menus, she manages the 18-seat dining room; together, they create an "intimate atmosphere" that's "like eating in someone's home."

Le Central Bistro ⬛Ⓜ 20 18 18 $35
453 Bush St. (bet. Grant Ave. & Kearny St.), 415-391-2233
■ Downtown "suits" gather to seal deals over "delish" cassoulet and roast chicken at this "shabby chic" bistro and City Hall hangout ("I actually did see da mayah!"); maybe "it's from a different time and place", but nostalgists insist "it's a classic and never lets you down."

Le Charm French Bistro ⬛Ⓜ 22 17 20 $30
315 Fifth St. (bet. Folsom & Harrison Sts.), 415-546-6128
■ "Wear your beret" at this "unpretentious" "jewel", "an oasis" amid "not-so-charming" "SoMa surroundings", where husband-and-wife owners Alain Delangle and Lina Yew woo diners with "simple but extraordinary French fare"; wallet-watchers tout the prix fixe "bargain", a "gift in this expense-account area."

Le Colonial ⬛SⓂ 20 26 19 $45
20 Cosmo Pl. (bet. Post & Taylor Sts.), 415-931-3600
◪ With its ferns, fans and rattan, this "upscale" Downtown "society hangout" takes diners on a "scenic trip to Saigon" for "sumptuous" French-influenced Vietnamese cuisine; although critics contend it's "a bit too pricey" for the "piddling portions" and service moves at "the pace of the tropics", the "exotic" atmo and "awesome bar" keep the room "awash with dot-commmers."

Left at Albuquerque ⬛SⓂ 13 15 14 $22
2140 Union St. (bet. Fillmore & Webster Sts.), 415-749-6700
See review in South of San Francisco Directory.

Le Soleil ⬛SⓂ 20 13 16 $22
133 Clement St. (bet. 2nd & 3rd Aves.), 415-668-4848
■ This "satisfying" Inner Richmond "jewel" shines with some of "the freshest, tastiest Vietnamese" around; despite its "simple" approach and "sterile setting", advocates agree it's a "great alternative to high-priced Asian fare."

Lhasa Moon L S
17 | 13 | 17 | $20

2420 Lombard St. (bet. Divisadero & Scott Sts.), 415-674-9898

☑ Billed as San Francisco's "unique" source of Tibetan cuisine, this Marina eatery offers a "cultural experience" in which enthusiasts attest the "yummy noodles and *momos* [potstickers]" leave them "satiated and peaceful"; foes find the food "disappointing" ("all tasted alike"), but devotees declare for "Tibetan food – such as it is – it's good."

Liberty Cafe & Bakery L S
22 | 17 | 19 | $27

410 Cortland Ave. (bet. Bennington & Wool Sts.), 415-695-8777

■ Lovers of Liberty claim this tiny New American cafe with a "blue-collar setting" is "not just the best place to eat in Bernal Heights, it's the only place" – thanks to chef Randy Windham's "home cookin' with flair", which features "delicious brunch options" and a chicken pot pie that's "the best in the USA"; at night, the bakery turns into a wine bar that makes seating delays "worth the wait."

Lichee Garden L S M
19 | 10 | 13 | $20

1416 Powell St. (bet. Broadway & Vallejo St.), 415-397-2290

■ Although the decor and service are "nothing fancy", this large Chinatown parlor attracts a "mostly multi-generational [Asian] family clientele" (never a bad sign) for "quality dim sum", "good noodle dishes" and the house specialty – minced squab with pine nuts.

Little City Antipasti S M
16 | 15 | 16 | $29

673 Union St. (Powell St.), 415-434-2900

☑ As the name suggests, "appetizers are the way to go" at this "fun" North Beach Italian whose outdoor seating affords one of SF's best perches for surveying the passing scene; although loyalists like the "nice mix of menu items", antagonists ask: "how does it survive in this food town?"

Little Italy S M
20 | 16 | 20 | $26

4109 24th St. (bet. Castro & Diamond Sts.), 415-821-1515

■ "Fans of garlic should head to this cute Noe Valley" institution where "charming old waiters" serve hearty "down-home Southern Italian food" ("no foo-foo here – just good pasta"); great for families, this local favorite "hasn't changed in 20 years", but that's part of its appeal.

Little Joe's L S M
16 | 10 | 15 | $22

523 Broadway (bet. Columbus Ave. & Kearny St.), 415-433-4343
2642 Ocean Ave. (bet. Junipero Serra Blvd. & 19th Ave.), 415-564-8200

☑ Despite a plain interior – "none of the profits are spent on decor" – this North Beach Italian establishment (with a branch on Ocean Avenue) remains a "tourist mecca", packing 'em in with "big plates of tasty pasta" and "sloppy, satisfying cioppino"; while the discriminating dismiss it as "lots of mediocre food at low prices", good-natured sports just shrug and "watch ESPN on the big screen."

Livefire Grill & Smokehouse **L S M**
15 | 17 | 15 | $33

100 Brannan St. (bet. The Embarcadero & 1st St.),
415-227-0777
See review in North of San Francisco Directory.

Liverpool Lil's **◐ L S M**
16 | 16 | 18 | $24

2942 Lyon St. (bet. Greenwich & Lombard Sts.),
415-921-6664
■ Commuters recommend this self-styled drinking man's saloon where "food is on the back burner" as "the last place before Marin for a drink and a burger"; the Cow Hollow hangout also provides a "home away from home" for an elderly crowd that sighs "where have you gone, Joe DiMaggio?" (the Yankee Clipper used to hang out here).

L'Olivier **L M**
21 | 20 | 21 | $39

465 Davis Ct. (Jackson St.), 415-981-7824
◪ "One of the few quiet, elegant dining places left", loyalists of this Downtown establishment proclaim, praising the "exceptionally charming service", country decor and "classic French food"; but the more revolutionary-minded snipe that this Gallic *grande dame* has "no flair" and has become "deadly dated."

London Wine Bar **L M**
11 | 13 | 16 | $22

415 Sansome St. (bet. Clay & Sacramento Sts.),
415-788-4811
◪ The "well-thought-out selection of wines" by the glass, a "friendly staff" and "the most generous pour in town" make this Downtown watering hole worth a trip; but critics of the self-styled oldest vino bar in America feel "longevity is its only suit" and slam the "limited menu" of Californian fare.

Long Life Noodle Co. **L S M**
13 | 12 | 11 | $16

Sony Metreon Ctr., 101 Fourth St. (bet. Howard & Mission Sts.),
415-369-6188
139 Steuart St. (bet. Howard & Mission Sts.), 415-281-3818
◪ Although some surveyors declare the bowls of "filling" noodles at this SoMa Chinese fast food chainlet "will satisfy every craving", more discriminating diners say the fare "sounds better than it tastes" and the "indifferent service" means "they should rename it Long Lines"; N.B. there's also a Berkeley branch.

L'Osteria Del Forno **L S M ⊘**
23 | 15 | 19 | $22

519 Columbus Ave. (bet. Green & Union Sts.), 415-982-1124
■ Despite a miniscule dining room and perhaps the "smallest kitchen in town", the food at this North Beach "gem" scores big with surveyors; the combo of "incredible" Northern Italian fare (milk-braised pork, pumpkin ravioli, focaccia sandwiches) and "gracious hosts" makes you feel like you're "eating in your best friend's gourmet kitchen" in Italy.

Lovejoy's Tea Room 🇱🇸Ⓜ ▽ 17 | 21 | 16 | $15
1351 Church St. (Clipper St.), 415-648-5895
■ An oasis of "British charm in Noe Valley", this "treasure" promotes relaxation with a cozy afternoon tea that features "real Devonshire cream" over "yummy scones"; although the interior's a bit "shabby", it's a "fun place to hold a bridal shower" or to shop ("if you're sitting on it or eating off it, you can buy it").

LuLu 🇱🇸Ⓜ 22 | 20 | 17 | $37
816 Folsom St. (bet. 4th & 5th Sts.), 415-495-5775
☑ This "boisterous", cavernous SoMa warehouse-turned-bistro remains a great choice if you "go with a group and order tons of lusty Mediterranean dishes" served family-style ("don't miss the fire-roasted mussels"); but for naysayers, the "earsplitting noise" and "horribly rude waiters" "overshadow the food."

Luna Park 🇱🇸Ⓜ – | – | – | M
694 Valencia St. (18th St.), 415-553-8584
Inspired by turn-of-the-century amusement parks of the same name, the youthful owners of this hip Mission newcomer are aiming for an equally entertaining experience; the French-Italian menu includes a few American and Asian dishes and ranges from goat cheese fondue to all the fixin's for making sweet s'mores.

Macaroni Sciue Sciue 🇱Ⓜ ▽ 22 | 16 | 21 | $26
124 Columbus Ave. (bet. Jackson & Kearny Sts.), 415-217-8400
■ Located a stone's throw away from its more well-known sibling, Cafe Macaroni, this casual North Beach venue lives up to its name (*sciue sciue* roughly means 'quick' in Italian) with prompt service from an "enjoyably" "sassy" staff that's as "fresh" as the food; signature items include seafood Amalfi over black pasta and tiramisu.

MacArthur Park 🇱🇸Ⓜ 17 | 17 | 17 | $30
607 Front St. (bet. Jackson St. & Pacific Ave.), 415-398-5700
☑ "When the diet is over" Downtowners head to this "reliable if not innovative" American "standby" for "large, messy portions of good BBQ ribs" and "stacks of onion rings"; although the concept still draws large happy-hour crowds, "big groups" and families (kids love the crayons), foodies find "the formula tired."

Magnolia Pub & Brewery 🇱🇸Ⓜ 15 | 14 | 16 | $17
1398 Haight St. (Masonic Ave.), 415-864-7468
■ "A good place to grab a pint and burger" or brunch in the Haight, this neighborhood microbrewery (which pays homage to its former tenant, the infamous hippie hangout Magnolia Thunderpussy's) serves "an amazing array of beers" and a "slim selection" of "basic American pub fare"; house specialties include "great root beer", mussels steamed in ale and apple crisp.

Maharani L S M 19 | 16 | 16 | $28

1122 Post St. (bet. Polk St. & Van Ness Ave.), 415-775-1988

■ If your date can appreciate "amazing *chana masala*" (garbanzo beans in a curry-and-tamarind sauce) and other "unusual, delicious Indian dishes", then head to this "romantic", pink-colored Tenderloin hideaway; its private booths (request them ahead of time) and "spicy" fare are a surefire way to heat up the evening.

Maki L S ▽ 25 | 17 | 21 | $36

Japan Ctr., 1825 Post St. (Webster St.), 415-921-5215

■ Asiaphiles say you'll "never have Japanese food in surroundings that are more intimate" than this "authentic" spot nestled in Japantown, which gets high marks for its "delightful" cuisine; favorites include "delicious" *chawan mushi* (a savory steamed custard) and the signature *wappa meshi* (seafood, vegetables, chicken or beef served in a wooden basket with steamed rice).

Mama's on Washington Square L S ⊄ 23 | 15 | 16 | $19

1701 Stockton St. (Filbert St.), 415-362-6421

■ Locals and tourists insist that this North Beach American is a breakfast institution that's "worth the huge lines" for its "best baked goods", "banana-bread French toast" and savory dishes using the "freshest ingredients", like heirloom tomatoes from the owner's garden; if you hate crowds, "wake up early" or go "during the week."

Mandalay L S M 19 | 11 | 15 | $18

4348 California St. (6th Ave.), 415-386-3895

■ Loyal patrons of this "quiet" Inner Richmond Burmese call it a "tried-and-true" choice for ginger salad, "good mango chicken" and "sublime coconut chicken noodle soup"; aesthetes note that the interior is in "desperate need of renovation" and therefore suggest "takeout."

Mandarin, The L S M 21 | 23 | 20 | $39

Ghirardelli Sq., 900 North Point St. (bet. Larkin & Polk Sts.), 415-673-8812

◪ "Fancy Chinese", plus a "great view of the Bay" equals "high prices" and high expectations from those who dine at this recently renovated Wharf restaurant; while most praise the "excellent squab" and "elegant", "romantic" atmosphere with "well-spaced tables", those de-Mandarin more claim it's "good but not particularly memorable."

Mangiafuoco S M 20 | 18 | 18 | $30

1001 Guerrero St. (22nd St.), 415-206-9881

■ "Decadent homemade pastas" and "scrumptious seafood" are part of why this "cozy Mission Italian" is a "dependable, neighborhood" choice for young diners, who also appreciate its "intimate" seating and "quiet", "romantic" atmosphere that's ideal for dates.

Manora's Thai Cuisine L S M 22 | 14 | 17 | $21
1600 Folsom St. (12th St.), 415-861-6224
■ Surveyors "keep going back" to this SoMa Thai, which is "still one of the best" in town because it does "not feel cramped, even when full" and serves "great lemongrass soup" and other "delicious" dishes at "value" prices.

Mario's Bohemian Cigar Store Cafe L S M 19 | 17 | 16 | $17
566 Columbus Ave. (Union St.), 415-362-0536
2209 Polk St. (bet. Green & Vallejo Sts.), 415-776-8226
■ Grab a hot meatball or eggplant foccacia sandwich and "watch the world go by" at this "funky" North Beach Italian coffee shop (with an outpost on Polk); while more "go for the ambiance", "best cappuccinos" and food than the cigars, the original branch does have a smokin' "good selection" of stogies to boot.

Marnee Thai L S M 22 | 13 | 16 | $20
2225 Irving St. (bet. 23rd & 24th Aves.), 415-665-9500
◪ This "very crowded" neighborhood Sunset Thai "lacks ambiance", but wins high marks for its "spicy angel wings"; however, what really sets it apart from its brethren is the opinionated, self-proclaimed clairvoyant owner: loyalists say "do exactly what she says and your meal will be delicious" (and "she might read your palm, if you're lucky"), but dissenters find her "bossy" and "annoying."

MASA'S 28 | 25 | 27 | VE
Hotel Vintage Court, 648 Bush St. (bet. Powell & Stockton Sts.), 415-989-7154
◪ Judging from ratings, the "departure of [former chef] Julian Serrano has not hurt" this Downtown Classic French destination where chef Chad Callahan continues the tradition of "astonishingly creative", "outstanding" cuisine (in four- and five-course menus) and the staff "makes you feel like royalty"; for those who are less impressed with the "dark", "gloomy" and "formal" setting, a scheduled renovation should help lighten things up.

Massawa L S ▽ 22 | 11 | 17 | $17
1538 Haight St. (Ashbury St.), 415-621-4129
■ Platters of food scooped up with *injera* (a sour, spongy bread) are the hands-on way to dine at this Haight Street Eritrean, a "hole-in-the-wall" with "nicely spiced, flavorful" choices such as the vegetarian-combination plate.

Ma Tante Sumi S M 22 | 19 | 22 | $35
4243 18th St. (bet. Castro & Diamond Sts.), 415-626-7864
■ "Cozy and romantic" French-Asian featuring "carefully prepared", "wonderful" cuisine such as a "fantastic duck confit" and a wasabi-and-lime-cured salmon nigiri that you will "dream about"; exasperated boosters find it "maddening that this first-rate restaurant isn't better known."

Matsuya Ⓜ   ▽ 21 | 15 | 19 | $22
3856 24th St. (Vicksburg St.), 415-282-7989
■ Although it's often eclipsed by the glitz and hype of other Japanese restaurants, regular visitors to this small sushi bar in Noe Valley still consider it the "nicest", largely due to its charismatic owner Fusae Ponne, who has operated it since 1951, back when it was located in Japantown.

Matterhorn Swiss Restaurant Ⓢ   18 | 18 | 19 | $33
2323 Van Ness Ave. (bet. Green & Vallejo Sts.), 415-885-6116
◪ "Instead of a trip to Zermatt", fans longing for a taste of the Alps hike to this Van Ness/Polk venue for its "authentic Swiss-style setting" and fondue-focused menu; double-dippers declare it's "great for a romantic rendezvous for two", as long as you're prepared to "eat your weight in cheese."

Max's Diner Ⓛ Ⓢ Ⓜ   16 | 14 | 16 | $20
311 Third St. (Folsom St.), 415-546-0168
◪ "Convenient to the Moscone Convention center", this '50s-style retro diner serves "NBA-player-sized portions" of Jewish-style comfort food from an "extensive menu"; while it's a "good place to sit in a booth and get a Reuben and chocolate malt" with the kids, detractors say the "massive servings do not compensate" for the "average" edibles.

Max's on the Square Ⓛ Ⓢ Ⓜ   15 | 14 | 16 | $23
Maxwell Hotel, 398 Geary St. (Mason St.), 415-646-8600
■ Similar in concept to its sibs, this Downtown branch of the popular deli chain is most popular for breakfast and for informal pre-theater meals; expect the same max-out portions of favorites such as eggs Benedict, French toast, 'grandma's' chicken and old-fashioned cheesecake.

Max's Opera Café Ⓛ Ⓢ Ⓜ   16 | 15 | 16 | $22
Opera Plaza, 601 Van Ness Ave. (Golden Gate Ave.), 415-771-7300
◪ "Talented waiters and waitresses" serenade guests with nightly arias (after 7PM) at this "festive" Civic Center deli that pays homage to the nearby opera house; despite being a bustling place for a pre- or post-concert meal, detractors find the predictably "large portions" of food "mediocre", but concede that the desserts can be "great."

Maya Ⓛ Ⓢ Ⓜ   21 | 22 | 19 | $39
303 Second St. (bet. Folsom & Harrison Sts.), 415-543-2928
◪ Set in a "pretty", earth-toned room with traditional decor (Mayan masks) as well as more predictably "posh" elements, this SoMa Mexican "doesn't serve burritos", but does offer "lovely presentations" of "stupendous haute" dishes whose flavors "aren't buried in heavy cheese and sour cream"; budget-watchers resent the "high prices", but that sure doesn't stop the dot-commers.

Maye's Oyster House L S M   15 | 12 | 15 | $27 |
1233 Polk St. (bet. Bush & Sutter Sts.), 415-474-7674
◪ In a town focused on the latest new thing, this no-frills, "old-fashioned" Italian-seafooder on Van Ness/Polk has a steady stream of regulars who savor its "traditional and consistent" "fresh fish dishes" like sand dabs and historical "SF atmosphere" (it's the second oldest restaurant in town); modernists may find it a "disappointment."

Mayflower L S M   20 | 12 | 13 | $23 |
6255 Geary Blvd. (27th Ave.), 415-387-8338
◼ This Richmond Chinese is known for its "excellent dim sum" and "superb" Cantonese seafood specialties; now under new ownership, management has snared a former chef from the popular Hong Kong Flower Lounge.

Maykedah L S M   ▽ 24 | 17 | 21 | $28 |
470 Green St. (bet. Grant Ave. & Kearny St.), 415-362-8286
◼ One of the few Persian restaurants – and arguably "the best" – in the Bay Area, this "elegant" (and undiscovered) North Beach spot is a "perfect" place to explore this variety of Middle Eastern cuisine, aided by an "extremely friendly and helpful" staff.

McCormick & Kuleto's L S M   18 | 22 | 18 | $35 |
Ghirardelli Sq., 900 North Point St. (bet. Larkin & Polk Sts.), 415-929-1730
◪ Locals head to this gargantuan Ghirardelli Square haunt at Fisherman's Wharf to treat their out-of-town guests to "seafood and sea view"; although cynics find the fare "mundane" and the service "slow", pros posit that the "spectacular atmosphere may help you forget" the flaws.

mc² L M   21 | 23 | 20 | $46 |
470 Pacific Ave. (Montgomery St.), 415-956-0666
◪ A "stark interior"– either "sleek" or "sterile", depending on your taste – provides a minimalist backdrop for chef Yoshi Kohma's "innovative", "architecturally inspired" Californian-French cuisine; although detractors complain of "total culinary con-fusion" and expensive portions that you "need a magnifying glass to see", admirers respect the "great wine list" and suggest this "with-it" Downtowner is "much improved since opening."

Mecca S M   20 | 22 | 18 | $40 |
2029 Market St. (bet. Dolores & 14th Sts.), 415-621-7000
◪ There's "always an eclectic show" of trendy types at this "very happening spot" on Upper Market surveyors say; while the "Castro-meets-Downtown crowd" at the bar is "too hip" and "too loud" for some, late-night diners who "just want a good, relaxed dinner" amidst the candelabras and velvet drapes report the New American menu has gotten much better since chef Mike Fennelly took over the kitchen.

Meetinghouse, The ⑤Ⓜ   25 | 21 | 23 | $41
1701 Octavia St. (Bush St.), 415-922-6733
■ Located in residential Pacific Heights, this "perfect, pretty little secret" specializes in "mom's cooking, if your mom's Martha Stewart"; enthusiasts find the simple New American dinners here a "pleasure from start to finish" (there's an "awesome bread basket of buttery biscuits" and "the dessert chef rocks!") and, despite occasional seating delays, deem the service pleasantly "down-to-earth."

Mel's Drive-In ●Ⓛ⒮Ⓜ⇄   13 | 14 | 14 | $15
2165 Lombard St. (Steiner St.), 415-921-2867
3355 Geary Blvd. (bet. Parker & Stanyan Sts.), 415-387-2255
Richelieu Hotel, 1050 Van Ness Ave. (Geary St.), 415-292-6357
■ "*Happy Days* are here again" at this trio of "classic '50s diners" with their retro "juke boxes" (but, alas, "no drive-in window"); when it comes to the food, grease is the word – but that doesn't stop "foreign tourists" and "teens" from wolfing down burgers and fries, or after-hours eaters knocking off a "milkshake and pancakes" either.

Memphis Minnie's   – | – | – | I
BBQ Joint ⓁⓈ⇄
576 Haight St. (bet. Fillmore & Steiner Sts.), 415-864-7675
Peripatetic pitmaster Bob Kantor has led a nomadic existence hawking his finger lickin' BBQ in various short-leased locales in the city for the past five years, but he and his signature slow-smoked Southern-style ribs seem to have settled down at this homey Lower Haight Street spot, replete with a plethora of porcine paraphernalia and lots of napkins.

Mescolanza ⑤Ⓜ   20 | 15 | 19 | $25
2221 Clement St. (bet. 23rd & 24th Aves.), 415-668-2221
■ This "standout Northern Italian spot", located "in the midst of restaurant row in the Richmond", is your classic "cozy" trattoria; "good pasta dishes" and what some call "the best pizza in town" help regulars overlook the "tight quarters."

Metropol ⓁⓂ   19 | 14 | 16 | $21
168 Sutter (bet. Kearny & Montgomery Sts.), 415-732-7777
■ Offering either "sit-down or take-away" fare, this Downtown underground eatery is "a cut above" the other fast-food options in the area, thanks to the Mediterranean flair of its "reliably fresh food" (with especially "creative salads") and decor that "makes the place warm."

Michelangelo Cafe ⑤Ⓜ⇄   18 | 15 | 16 | $22
579 Columbus Ave. (Union St.), 415-986-4058
■ Decorated with Sistine Chapel-esque artwork, this "cramped" Italian is a "North Beach standard" for many out-of-towners who insist the "hearty pasta" and "free Gummi Bears and cookies" are worth "lining up for"; while a few dis the "boring food", people-watchers advise: "get the corner table to see the Washington Square happenings."

Mifune 🄻🅂🄼
19 | 11 | 14 | $15

Japan Ctr., 1737 Post St. (bet. Buchanan & Webster Sts.), 415-922-0337

■ "Nobody does noodles better" than this Japantown soup shop, whose steaming bowls of arguably the "best soba and udon in town" provide "comfort at a fast pace and a great price"; although slightly "run-down" looking, it's "great for cold, rainy days" or a "good quickie before a movie" at the nearby Kabuki theater.

Millennium 🅂🄼
23 | 21 | 22 | $33

Abigail Hotel, 246 McAllister St. (bet. Hyde & Larkin Sts.), 415-487-9800

■ "Meat lovers won't miss a thing" at this "elegant" Civic Center showcase for chef and cookbook author Eric Tucker's "imaginative Vegetarian menu" (which includes options for dairy-skipping vegans too); though occasionally "the food tries too hard", most feel the "truly artful" cuisine served by an "attentive staff" makes the experience "a real adventure."

Miss Millie's 🅂
20 | 19 | 18 | $21

4123 24th St. (bet. Castro & Diamond Sts.), 415-285-5598

■ They trek from all over SF to Noe Valley, where this "fabulous weekend brunch spot" dishes up New American "homey food" with "a sophisticated twist" (i.e. lemon ricotta pancakes with blueberry syrup) in a "cute and quaint" retro setting; while no reservations are accepted, fans insist it's "worth the wait."

Moishe's Pippic 🄻🄼≠
15 | 7 | 13 | $14

425A Hayes St. (bet. Gough & Octavia Sts.), 415-431-2440

■ While a few praise the pastrami, most surveyors say "feh" to this Hayes Valley Jewish delicatessen, labeling the stuffed-sandwich menu as "far from what it aspires to be"; at best, some allow "it's not my deli, but it's good for SF."

Mom is Cooking 🄻🅂🄼
20 | 7 | 13 | $17

1166 Geneva Ave. (bet. Edinburgh & Naples Sts.), 415-586-7000

■ This Excelsior hole-in-the-wall draws raves for its "authentic, un-Americanized Mexican food" (especially the "fluffy tamales") and drink ("margarita central") from regulars who disregard the mañana-syndrome service and "low-rent setting"; however, the cuisine "can be inconsistent", so make sure you go "when mom [aka Abigail Murillo] is actually cooking."

MoMo's 🄻🅂🄼
18 | 20 | 17 | $36

760 Second St. (The Embarcadero), 415-227-8660

◪ "Location, location, location" is what matters at this eatery just opposite Pacific Bell Park, a primo "after-work pickup spot for the cell-phone crowd"; although some like the Traditional American cuisine, most surveyors go for the "party atmosphere" on the "sunny deck" and prefer to leave the "overpriced ordinary fare" to Giants fans on game days.

Montage L S M
16 | 18 | 15 | $38

Sony Metreon Ctr., 101 Fourth St. (Mission St.), 415-369-6111

▣ Despite the "hugely comfortable" setting and the "fresh, clean California flavors" of chef Jennifer Cox's "beautifully presented" cuisine, this young destination restaurant in the Sony Metreon does draw some criticism: the disenchanted note the "confused service" and "ridiculous prices" and are unable to escape the sense of "eating in a mall."

Moose's L S M
21 | 20 | 20 | $39

1652 Stockton St. (bet. Filbert & Union Sts.), 415-989-7800

■ "Host Ed Moose is the master of schmooze" at his eponymous Cal-Med brasserie, which has supplanted the now-shuttered Washington Square Bar & Grill as the "power spot of North Beach" (albeit one that forbids cell phones); although the "swinging" scene gets "noisy", most regulars chow down on the Moose Burgers or Caesar salads while they "people-watch and listen to jazz" at the lively bar.

Morton's of Chicago S M
23 | 20 | 21 | $54

400 Post St. (bet. Mason & Powell Sts.), 415-986-5830

■ At this Downtown outpost of the national string of steakhouses, "big prices and big portions" rule; while a few lament the "chain restaurant mentality" ("it left its heart in Chicago") and "can do without the pre-dinner meat presentation", to most it remains unbeatable for "an honest hunk of beef" and "Godiva chocolate cake"; insiders advise "ask for the prime rib" (not listed on the menu).

Mo's Burgers L S M
21 | 10 | 14 | $14

Yerba Buena Gardens, 772 Folsom St. (bet. 3rd & 4th Sts.), 415-957-3779

Mo's Grill L S M

1322 Grant Ave. (bet. Green & Vallejo Sts.), 415-788-3779

■ Carnivores happily report "you can [still] get them rare" at these SoMa and North Beach diners – each one an "uncut diamond of a burger joint" that mixes up "thick, milk shakes" to accompany the flame-broiled beef; N.B. the SoMa branch also boasts a "great view" of Downtown.

Murasaki ● M
▽ 24 | 8 | 16 | $34

211 Clement St. (bet. 3rd & 4th Aves.), 415-668-7317

■ To the few who frequent this unobtrusive "jewel in Inner Richmond", owner Toshihiro Sasaki "is the best and most friendly sushi maker in town"; don't expect any "fancy chef gimmicks" here – just the "freshest fish."

Narai L S
▽ 20 | 13 | 18 | $21

2229 Clement St. (bet. 23rd & 24th Aves.), 415-751-6363

■ "Huge portions" of "sophisticated Thai" food attract a "mostly neighborhood" crowd to this hideaway in the Richmond ("don't tell anybody – keep it secret!"); despite "unattractive decor", it makes a "nice stop to or from the California Palace of The Legion of Honor."

Neecha Thai Cuisine L S M   21 | 14 | 19 | $20
2100 Sutter St. (Steiner St.), 415-922-9419

■ "The chef knows what to do with spices" declare devotees of this "solid, dependable" Pacific Heights Thai joint, celebrated for its 47 "unique veggie options" (e.g. "gluten satay"), along with more conventional "warming curries" and equally "warm service."

Ne O S   24 | 22 | 22 | $40
1007 Guerrero St. (bet. 22nd & 23rd Sts.), 415-643-3119

■ "If ultra-trendy – including the patrons – is what you are looking for", this Mission newcomer is the place; reactions to the pristine scene – from the backless chairs to the servers' white uniforms – range from straight "out of Woody Allen's *Sleeper*" to "a metaphor for the purity of the culinary artistry" being displayed; however, a shift from chef Lance Velasquez's New American menu to Jason Tuley's Asian-French fare may outdate the above food rating.

New Korea House L S M   20 | 12 | 14 | $25
1620 Post St. (Laguna St.), 415-931-7834

■ Attention action-oriented diners: this Japantown Korean allows you to grill your own meat, shrimp, squid or octopus tableside, though lazy eaters can "choose to have the kitchen cook it"; the "staff speaks very little English", but most patrons don't seem to mind.

New Pisa L S M   16 | 15 | 17 | $22
550 Green St. (bet. Columbus & Grant Aves.), 415-989-2289

■ Low-priced portions of "basic Italian food served family style", "cool baseball memorabilia" and a "good old-timer's bar scene" makes this hole-in-the-wall a "North Beach staple" – even if its similarity to another well-known bargain spot in the neighborhood earn it the nickname "copy Capp's."

Nippon Sushi L S M ⊄   ▽ 19 | 8 | 13 | $15
314 Church St. (15th St.), no phone

■ No one denies it's "an absolute dive", but maki mavens point out this "dirt cheap" Upper Market/Church Street Japanese joint gives you "twice as much as any other place in town", so it's "worth waiting in the line out the door."

Nob Hill Cafe L S M   19 | 14 | 19 | $27
1152 Taylor St. (bet. Clay & Sacramento Sts.), 415-776-6500

■ Tiny and "tavern-like" trattoria servicing Nob Hill with "fabulous pizza and pasta" at "the most reasonable price"; while a "cute neighborhood spot", the no-reservations policy means you better come prepared to "wait out on the sidewalk" for a table, especially at dinner.

Nonna Rose Seafood Cafe 🄻🅂🄼 _ | _ | _ | E
7 Fisherman's Wharf (bet. Jefferson & Taylor Sts.),
415-359-1200
Although this SF seafood cafe is a newcomer, it has a
century-old connection to the area: the original Nonna Rose,
grandmother of restaurateurs Joe and Nunzio Alioto, was
one of the first women to operate a fish stall on the Wharf
and the founder of the venerable Alioto's upstairs; her
namesake restaurant, specializing in wood-grilled fish,
affords a charming view of the fishing boats.

North Beach Pizza 🄻🅂🄼   18 | 9 | 13 | $16
1499 Grant Ave. (Union St.), 415-433-2444
715 Harrison St. (3rd St.), 415-371-0930 ◗
4787 Mission St. (bet. Persia & Russia Aves.), 415-586-1400
800 Stanyan St. (Haight St.), 415-751-2300 ◗
North Beach Pizza Express 🄻🅂🄼
3054 Taraval St. (41st Ave.), 415-242-9100
☑ Applauded for serving "the best dinner to have delivered
to your office if you're still at work at 8 PM" (or even later),
this SF chainlet is known for its "lip-smacking good pizza"
with "heart-stopping slugs of cheese"; the unconverted
sniff the "greasy" pie is "overrated" and wistfully ask
"when will we get real pizza on the West Coast?"

North Beach Restaurant ◗🄻🅂🄼   19 | 18 | 19 | $35
1512 Stockton St. (bet. Green & Union Sts.), 415-392-1700
☑ This "family-oriented place" continues to dish up "old-
style North Beach Italian" cuisine (think veal scallopine
and warm zabaglione) as it has done for 20 years – and
"that's good" according to some reviewers, who like to "eat
with regulars"; dissenters say the only thing impressive
about "old reliable" is its massive "Italian wine list."

North India 🄻🅂🄼   19 | 14 | 16 | $29
3131 Webster St. (bet. Greenwich & Lombard Sts.),
415-931-1556
☑ Surveyors with a taste for tandoori split pretty evenly over
this Marina institution: while pros praise the "sophisticated
flavors" and "expert preparation" of Indian food, gourmets
gripe that the place "has fallen in quality" to the point that
it has gotten "expensive for what it is."

Northstar 🄻🅂🄼   21 | 18 | 20 | $29
288 Connecticut St. (18th St.), 415-551-9840
■ "Sunny and scrumptious", this Potrero Hill spot – a
"younger brother" of the popular Firefly – beams brightly
as an "upscale take on the friendly neighborhood bistro";
a "caring staff" serves "hearty portions of simple, old-
fashioned" American fare and Asian specialties ("fab
tempura appetizer"); don't forget to take home some
goodies from the adjacent Little Dipper, which supplies
the restaurant's desserts.

Occidental Grill L M   19 | 18 | 19 | $32
453 Pine St. (bet. Kearny & Montgomery Sts.), 415-834-0484
■ Although better known as a "great after-work cocktail stop" (especially for twentysomethings) than a restaurant, many find the duck ravioli and other New American dishes just fine at this "quintessentially clubby" Downtown hangout.

One Market L M   22 | 21 | 20 | $44
1 Market St. (Steuart St.), 415-777-5577
◪ Cool and cavernous, Bradley Ogden's Embarcadero establishment remains a "hot lunch spot for Financial District movers and shakers" who do deals over New American fare while being coddled by "impeccable service"; cynics say since chef George Morrone moved on, this is "one market that's not as high flying as it used to be", but most maintain those lucky enough to snare the chef's table with its tasting menu are in for "a unique experience."

O'Reilly's Irish   15 | 19 | 17 | $21
Pub & Restaurant L S M
622 Green St. (bet. Columbus Ave. & Powell St.), 415-989-6222
■ "Have a pint, a shepherd's pie and feel like a Dubliner" at this "classic Gaelic" pub on the shores of North Beach; although it's known for the "great Guinness" that flows during the "fervent bar scene", many return the next morning seeking "hangover relief with an Irish breakfast."

Original Joe's ◐ L S M   18 | 13 | 17 | $24
144 Taylor St. (bet. Eddy & Turk Sts.), 415-775-4877
■ "Travel back in time" to this family-run Italian-American "throwback to the '40s", where the 88-year-old founder still tends bar seven days a week; brave hearts say "forget the neighborhood" ("ground zero of the Tenderloin") and "sit at the counter" to watch the "best side show in town", which consists of the cooks and the seedy local clientele.

Oritalia S M   23 | 23 | 20 | $43
Juliana Hotel, 586 Bush St. (Stockton St.), 415-782-8122
◪ While this pioneer of "creative Cal-Asian hybrid cuisine" has changed chefs again and relocated to bigger Downtown digs, fusion fans find dining here "delightful in all regards": "stunning decor", "informative staff" and "schizophrenic [food] combinations that somehow aren't that crazy"; but skeptics gripe that since the move, the fare's been "going downhill" while the "pricing is getting stratospheric."

Osaka Grill L S M   ▽ 21 | 20 | 21 | $30
1217 Sutter St. (bet. Polk St. & Van Ness Ave.), 415-440-8838
◪ If you dig the drama of tableside preparation, then head to this Van Ness/Polk Japanese grill that features "friendly service" and "delicious teppanyaki"; however, foes find the food and ambiance "lackluster" and sniff they'd "rather go to a Benihana's"; N.B. still, if you want to be a wasabi master, the chef leads a weekly hands-on cooking class.

Osome ⓛⓈⓜ   20 | 13 | 17 | $28
3145 Fillmore St. (bet. Filbert & Greenwich Sts.), 415-931-8898
■ When hosting a small group, it's fun to "reserve a tatami room, kick off your shoes and sip some saki" at this Cow Hollow haunt with "basic but fine" Japanese cuisine; fans warn the "wait can be long but it's worth it" – especially "if you get to know the sushi chef."

Osteria ⓛⓈ   21 | 17 | 21 | $31
3277 Sacramento St. (Presidio Ave.), 415-771-5030
■ This "perfecto" Presidio Heights Italian place pleases its "mostly over-50 clientele" with "reliable pastas" and what some call the "best calamari steak" around; despite the sometimes "abrupt service", dining at this local favorite "almost makes you wish you lived in the neighborhood."

Ovation Ⓢⓜ   22 | 26 | 21 | $52
Inn at the Opera, 333 Fulton St. (bet. Franklin & Gough Sts.), 415-553-8100
☑ Its devoted admirers applaud this Hayes Valley performer as the "best place for a romantic pre-opera dinner" – even if the New French-Continental food isn't quite "up to the prices" or the luxurious decor; still, the "polished and intimate" scene is too "staid" for tougher critics, who snipe "it's like dining in a mortuary."

Pacific ⓛⓈⓜ   24 | 22 | 23 | $48
Pan Pacific Hotel, 500 Post St. (Mason St.), 415-929-2087
■ Tucked away in the Pan Pacific Hotel Downtown, this "quiet beauty" is "a Union Square sanctuary"; despite a recent chef change, fans insist there's "always something superfresh and spectacular" about its Californian cuisine and can't understand why, with its "handsome room" and "attentive service", "this place is still a secret."

Pacific Cafe Ⓢⓜ   21 | 15 | 19 | $27
7000 Geary Blvd. (34th Ave.), 415-387-7091
☑ The lines seem never-ending at this Richmond seafoodery, but the "free-flowing wine" served during the delay –along with the "fresh fish, prepared simply but impeccably" – has helped this place find "a loyal clientele"; those unmollified by the complimentary vino, however, gripe it's "overly crowded and noisy" and there's "a long wait for nothing special."

Palio d'Asti ⓛⓜ   21 | 20 | 21 | $38
640 Sacramento St. (bet. Kearny & Montgomery Sts.), 415-395-9800
■ Snazzy Downtown "power lunch spot" that's a "business staple" for many surveyors who appreciate the "friendliest hostess in SF" and the "amazing service" as much as the Italian fare ("if you know of better pasta, let me know"); night crawlers point out that "it's even better at dinner" "when you can dine leisurely" and sip at the Enoteca (wine bar), which showcases selections from Piedmont and Tuscany.

Palomino ● L S M
18 | 21 | 18 | $34

345 Spear St. (bet. Folsom St. & The Embarcadero), 415-512-7400

■ A "beautiful view of the Bay Bridge" and a varied menu of Cal-Med fare draw crowds to this hopping Embarcadero branch of a national chain; while sophisticates sniff it's for tourists and twentysomething "bridge-and-tunnel folk – not SF-ers" – the more easygoing like to "sit on the deck before the ballgame", feasting on the "terrific" gorgonzola potatoes.

Pancho Villa Taqueria ● L S M
21 | 11 | 14 | $10

3071 16th St. (bet. Mission & Valencia Sts.), 415-864-8840

■ "This is the Mission, these are the burritos, end of story" summarize aficionados of this "clean, bright restaurant" that offers great "value prices" and, many say, the "best Mexican food in the city"; unfortunately, "its popularity means unbearably long lines", but a doorman keeps the "street parade" in order, and they serve until midnight.

Pane e Vino L S M
24 | 19 | 20 | $34

3011 Steiner St. (Union St.), 415-346-2111

■ Dining at this Cow Hollow trattoria is like "being in Northern Italy" – "crowded", "loud" and "hectic" – but the food is "*squisito*" and "every dish is a winner"; try to book a table, though be warned: "reservations are a mirage."

Paragon L S M
– | – | – | M

701 Second St. (Townsend St.), 415-537-9020

Although oxtail and duck confit sure don't sound like ballpark fare, that's what this SoMa American newcomer, located in striking distance from Pacific Bell Park, has on its opening lineup; soaring ceilings and sliding-glass doors are balanced by a high-tech interior that most likely mirrors the workplaces of the Internet types that pack the joint.

Park Chow L S M
20 | 16 | 18 | $20

1240 Ninth Ave. (Irving St.), 415-665-9912

■ Chef-owner "Tony Gulisano does it again", duplicating the reasonably priced, "Eclectic homestyle cooking" (American/Asian/Italian, to name just a few influences) of his original Chow; however, the atmosphere at this Inner Sunset outpost, with its "funky hippie setting" and working fireplace, is a little more "homey" than its Castro cousin's.

Park Grill L S M
24 | 22 | 24 | $37

Park Hyatt Hotel, 333 Battery St. (Clay St.), 415-296-2933

■ The "who's who of the Financial District meet to eat" and strike deals at this Downtown "oasis" in the Park Hyatt; since there's "impeccable service" and excellent New American cuisine at breakfast, lunch and dinner, this "sophisticated spot" is "what a good hotel dining room should be" – so "if you have no club, make this your club."

Parma M
18 | 14 | 18 | $27 |

3314 Steiner St. (bet. Chestnut & Lombard Sts.), 415-567-0500
■ Family-run, "crowded" trattoria in the Marina that's an "old favorite" for those who love the "rich Northern Italian food" and the "down-to-earth feel" of the place; extra kudos to the "friendly" waiters who make you "feel like you're a regular even if you aren't."

Pasta Pomodoro L S M
15 | 12 | 15 | $16 |

2027 Chestnut St. (Fillmore St.), 415-474-3400
816 Irving St. (9th Ave.), 415-566-0900
2304 Market St. (Castro St.), 415-558-8123
1865 Post St. (Fillmore St.), 415-674-1826
655 Union St. (Columbus Ave.), 415-399-0300
1875 Union St. (Laguna St.), 415-771-7900
■ "Huge portions" of "cheap Italian chow" and fast service "account for the Starbucks-like expansion" of these conveniently located pasta purveyors – "one chain [you] don't cringe at"; while reviewers confess the food's "no winner in the gourmet department", at least "you get what you pay for" – and you don't have "to do the dishes."

Pastis L M
23 | 19 | 22 | $39 |

1015 Battery St. (Green St.), 415-391-2555
■ This "stylish" Downtown bistro has "more elbow room, less noise" and is a hell of a lot "easier to get into than its sister restaurant Fringale", while offering similarly "imaginative" New French cuisine created by the same chef (Basque-born Gerald Hirigoyen) and served by "charming, heavily accented waiters"; P.S. patio dining is "wonderful."

Pauline's Pizza
22 | 13 | 16 | $21 |

260 Valencia St. (bet. Duboce & 14th Sts.), 415-552-2050
■ "Inventive combos" of "delicious organic" ingredients (pesto pie, anyone?) are what set this "upscale" pizzeria in the seedy Mission apart from the rest; although admirers concede the "pricey" pies and salads can make "the bill creep up", they insist "it's worth every penny."

paul K S
– | – | – | M |

199 Gough St. (Oak St.), 415-552-7132
Everything seems A-ok at Paul Kavouksorian's stylish Hayes Valley rookie; Rick Eldon's (ex Bitteroot and Valentine's Cafe) menu mines Cal-Mediterranean territory, so expect anything from sumac-encrusted duck breast to a dessert of cardamom fritters with sour-cherry compote.

Pazzia Caffe & Pizzeria L M
▽ 22 | 13 | 19 | $24 |

337 Third St. (bet. Folsom & Harrison Sts.), 415-512-1693
■ Just a stone's throw from SFMOMA and the Moscone Convention Center, this small SoMa trattoria draws folks who "love those thin-crust pizzas" and other Italian dishes; surveyors also single out the friendly, personalized service ("the owner always asks if you liked it").

Perlot 🕒Ⓜ   – | – | – | VE
(fka Cafe Majestic)
Hotel Majestic, 1550 Sutter St. (Gough St.), 415-441-1100
Beautiful hotel restaurant near Japantown, perennially
praised as one of the most romantic dining rooms in the
city, that recently underwent a name change and major
metamorphosis; the refurbished Edwardian interior has
been restored to its former elegance and a new chef has
also upped the dining ante, offering guests a choice between
a three- or six-course prix-fixe American menu.

Perry's ◑ⓁⓈⓂ   13 | 13 | 15 | $24
1944 Union St. (bet. Buchanan & Laguna Sts.), 415-922-9022
Perry's Downtown ◑ⓁⓈⓂ
*Galleria Park Hotel, 185 Sutter St. (bet. Kearny &
Montgomery Sts.), 415-989-6895*
☑ An "older crowd" loves to socialize at this pair of "warm
and welcoming watering holes" (the 30-year-old original in
Cow Hollow, the other Downtown), but the beery atmosphere
and "uninspired" Traditional American menu isn't for the
young and hip; if you want to eat, order the "manly bar
food" (the burger is a good bet).

Piaf's Ⓢ   18 | 20 | 19 | $37
1686 Market St. (Gough St.), 415-864-3700
■ Fans of the French chanteuse don't regret coming to
this "charming" Hayes Valley bistro where the walls are
covered with photos of the Little Sparrow and performers
pay her musical tribute nightly; the Gallic fare may not
sing, but it's "surprisingly good."

Picaro ⓈⓂ   ▽ 18 | 16 | 16 | $20
3120 16th St. (bet. Guerrero & Valencia Sts.), 415-431-4089
■ "Fun" and "hip" Mission Spanish that's a "great place to
go with a group" of bohemians and "share" "really good"
tapas; although the decor isn't "exciting", "quick service"
allows for a tasty meal "before a movie at the Roxie."

Pier 40 Roastery & Cafe ⓁⓈⓂ ▽ 15 | 15 | 12 | $17
Pier 40, The Embarcadero (Townsend St.), 415-495-3815
☑ What this "casual, pier-side" South Beach Californian
has got going for it is "good views" of the Bay (especially
if you can snag one of the "outdoor tables") and its
proximity to the ball park; however, the breakfast and lunch
fare proffered is only "ok" and service can be "slow."

Pier 23 Cafe ⓁⓈⓂ   13 | 16 | 13 | $23
Pier 23, The Embarcadero (Greenwich St.), 415-362-5125
■ "Funky" Traditional American on the Embarcadero
packed with "Financial District yuppies playing hooky"
out on the "back patio"; the young crowd is there for the
drinks, the music and the "waterfront" view, not the
"so-so" seafood specialties.

Pintxos 🖪🅂
17 | 18 | 18 | $33 |

557 Valencia St. (bet. 16th & 17th Sts.), 415-565-0207

◪ "Spanish newcomer" on "Valencia's Restaurant Row" in the Mission serving Basque-inspired tapas that garners mixed reviews; amigos admire the "different" and "delicious" fare and the "vibrant" setting, but enimigos cite "slow service" and "disappointing" cooking, so whether it's "up-and-coming" or "hit-or-miss" will have to be your call.

Pizzetta 211 🖪🅂⌿
– | – | – | I |

211 23rd Ave. (California St.), 415-379-9880

Cozy Richmond cafe offering gourmet sandwiches, calzones, farm salads bursting with organic produce and house-baked desserts; still, the real showstoppers here are the individual rustic pizzas that emerge from the double-decker oven.

P.J. Mulhern's 🖪🅂🅼
– | – | – | M |

570 Green St. (Columbus Ave.), 415-217-7000

This North Beach rookie generates star power from its co-owners, former Golden State Warriors coach P.J. Carlesimo and former Moose's manager Bob Mulhern; the kitchen goes through hoops to ensure that the Contemporary American cuisine scores points, and the dining room heats up when fellow NBA sports personalities dribble into town.

PJ's Oyster Bed 🅂🅼
21 | 15 | 16 | $29 |

737 Irving St. (bet. 8th & 9th Aves.), 415-566-7775

◪ Cajun-Creole eats like gumbo and "a wide selection of fresh oysters", combined with a "fun, raucous" atmosphere, "make this Inner Sunset spot hop"; some devotees are delighted that a renovation's made the place "brighter and bigger", but others opine that "it's gone downhill by trying to go upscale."

Planet Hollywood 🖪🅂🅼
8 | 13 | 10 | $23 |

2 Stockton St. (Market St.), 415-421-7827

▪ Despite the plethora of movie memorabilia on display at this Downtown branch of the celluloid-centered chain, the consensus is that "unless you're a tourist or a kid" there's "nothing on the [American] menu that redeems" this "shrine to Hollywood" save the "good drinks."

Plouf 🖪🅼
22 | 17 | 18 | $32 |

40 Belden Pl. (bet. Bush & Pine Sts.), 415-986-6491

▪ "Devotees of mussels will sop up every drop of the yummy broth" at this "delightful" Downtown bistro tucked away in the "*très* French" alley of Belden Place; outdoor seating (when weather permits) and authentic Gallic waiters who flirt as much as the sailors they are garbed to resemble help replicate the "real flavor of the streets of Paris."

PlumpJack Cafe ⬛Ⓜ   25   21   23 $45
3127 Fillmore St. (bet. Filbert & Greenwich Sts.), 415-563-4755

■ "Come for the wine list, stay for the food" urge enthusiasts of this "elegant" "Cow Hollow destination" showcasing "sensational" Mediterranean cuisine, along with its now-famous "well-priced" vinos and "knowledgeable staff"; "the only downside is it's small", which makes for cramped seating and "hard-to-get reservations."

Pluto's ⬛ⓈⓂ   18   11   12 $14
627 Irving St. (8th Ave.), 415-753-8867
3258 Scott St. (Chestnut St.), 415-775-8867

☑ It's "Thanksgiving every day" at this "cafeteria-style" chainlet serving "home-style" American "comfort food" (like "fresh-cut turkey", "huge salads" and gigantic sandwiches) at "student prices"; while detractors declare the service is "often chaotic" and the fare is "not celestial", more maintain that for a "cheap", "quick" "well-balanced meal", it's "very serviceable."

Ponzu ◗ⓈⓂ   –   –   –   M
Serrano Hotel, 401 Taylor St. (bet. Geary & O'Farrell Sts.), 415-775-7979

Vibrant Downtown hot spot, named after the kicky Japanese dipping sauce, that offers an arresting array of visual stimuli, from a curvaceous bar to illuminated aquariums to John Beardsley's (of Betelnut Pejiu Wu) signature pan-Asian small plates and platters; its proximity to the theater district also makes it an ideal spot for a pre- or post-performance dinner.

Pork Store Cafe ⬛ⓈⓂ   18   10   15 $13
1451 Haight St. (bet. Ashbury & Masonic Aves.), 415-864-6981

■ "Go when you're starving and pig out" encourage fans of this "greasy neighborhood joint" (billed as the oldest restaurant on Haight Street) known for its "hearty breakfasts" ("delicious biscuits" and pancakes) and piping "hot coffee served while you wait on line"; for those who don't mind the "noisy", "funky atmosphere", it's like being in "hog heaven."

POSTRIO ⬛ⓈⓂ   26   26   24 $53
Prescott Hotel, 545 Post St. (bet. Mason & Taylor Sts.), 415-776-7825

■ Wolfgang Puck's Downtown Californian is still the "gold standard" of SF dining, dishing up just the right mix of "beautiful people", "professional service" and "consistently great food"; who doesn't "feel like a movie star descending the staircase" into the "dramatic dining room" and supping on Steve and Mitchell Rosenthal's "remarkable" Asian-accented Mediterranean fare and "amazing desserts"?; although "the bar is a total meat market", it's still one of the best spots for "fun, late-night dining."

Potrero Brewing Company L S M 15 | 17 | 15 | $23 |
537 Florida St. (bet. 18th & Mariposa Sts.),
415-552-1967
☑ "If you like beer, you'll love this place" say surveyors of this "fun", "out-of-the-way" Mission pub, which is praised for its pool tables, "good microbrews" and "pleasurable outdoor seating"; most maintain the food is "unremarkable" and the service is "scattered", but those in search of the "young" and "noisy" head here.

Powell's Place L S M ▽ 19 | 6 | 13 | $14 |
511 Hayes St. (bet. Laguna & Octavia Sts.),
415-863-1404
■ "Soulful" Soul Fooder owned and operated by gospel singer Emmet Powell that's been serving locals (and of late, Hayes Valley hipsters) "the crispiest, flakiest fried chicken" and a helping of Southern comforts like cornbread and collard greens for over 25 years; although the "'70s interior" is serviced by an exceptionally "friendly staff", the aesthetically inclined advise "take out."

Prego Ristorante ◗ L S M 18 | 17 | 18 | $31 |
2000 Union St. (Buchanan St.), 415-563-3305
■ This "reliable" Cow Hollow Italian "has been around for years" and still manages to win over fans with "good" standards; "friendly service" and "easy reservations" are other pluses.

Presidio Cafe L S M ▽ 15 | 18 | 14 | $22 |
300 Finley Rd. (Arguello Blvd.), 415-561-4661
☑ Tiger Woods wannabes can "pretend they're country clubbers" at this casual Californian cafe, the Presidio's first full-service restaurant since the golf course opened to the public; putters can choose from "outdoor seating" affording expansive views of verdant fairways, or the "airy" Mission-style "dining room", while refueling on salads and hamburgers.

Primo Patio Cafe L M ⇗ ▽ 21 | 9 | 11 | $16 |
214 Townsend St. (bet. 3rd & 4th Sts.), 415-957-1129
■ The sunny "patio" is primo at this funky Caribbean SoMa "lunchtime spot" serving up the likes of jerk chicken; although the tiny interior is not much more than a walkway and service can be "very slow", easygoing enthusiasts insist it's "one of the fun spots in the area."

Puccini & Pinetti L S M 15 | 15 | 15 | $28 |
Monticello Inn, 129 Ellis St. (bet. Mason & Powell Sts.),
415-392-5500
☑ Downtown trattoria serving up "basic Italian food" at "reasonable prices" in "a fun, party atmosphere"; it's "convenient" to the theater district, but non–ticket holders find the "unfocused menu" "disappointing."

Radicchio Trattoria S　　▽ 17 | 15 | 18 | $29
1809 Union St. (bet. Laguna & Octavia Sts.), 415-346-7373
◪ "Warm neighborhood" trattoria in "trendy" Cow Hollow,
where "friendly waiters" serve "solid" "traditional Northern
Italian cuisine"; but some say there's "not much innovation"
here, which may explain why it's "fairly undiscovered."

R & G Lounge L S M　　21 | 9 | 13 | $23
631 Kearny St. (bet. Clay & Sacramento Sts.), 415-982-7877
■ Connoisseurs of Cantonese cuisine confirm "if you want
authentic, here it is" at this bi-level Chinatown joint; it's
"popular with local businessmen" who "ignore the decor"
(the upstairs is "more spacious") and "spotty" service in
order to order the "exquisite crab dishes" and "whatever
seafood is in the fish tank."

Rasselas Ethiopian S M　　▽ 16 | 14 | 14 | $23
2801 California St. (Divisadero St.), 415-567-5010
1534 Fillmore St. (bet. Geary Blvd. & O'Farrell St.),
415-346-8696 ●
◪ Although this Pacific Heights hangout entertains guests
with "excellent" live music nightly, the vote is split on the
eating experience: fans like its "fascinating" Ethiopian
cuisine, which brings "a whole new meaning to finger
food", but conformists craving the familiar find the menu
"limited" and confess they "go for the jazz", not the only-
"ok" edibles; N.B. there's a new branch on Fillmore Street.

Red Herring L S M　　21 | 20 | 20 | $41
Hotel Griffon, 155 Steuart St. (bet. Howard & Mission Sts.),
415-495-6500
◪ "Wonderful", "inventive seafood dishes" (who would
have thought of serving "super lobster cones"?) are your
clues that this "good newcomer", rising from the ashes of
the old Roti along The Embarcadero, is not your average fish
tale, although finatics hope that there will be a "smooth
transition" now that opening chef James Ormsby has sailed
off elsewhere; P.S. the "plush" dining room is "best if you
can get a Bay window table."

Rick's S M　　▽ 16 | 15 | 18 | $27
1940 Taraval St. (30th Ave.), 415-731-8900
■ "Dependable" "neighborhood place" in the Sunset
serving groaning portions of chef Rick Oku's American-
Eclectic cooking that goes Island-oriented on the first
Monday of the month when he whips up a luau dinner replete
with poke; on weekends, there's also live Hawaiian music.

Ricochet Restaurant & Bar S　　▽ 18 | 15 | 14 | $33
215 West Portal Ave. (bet. 14th Ave. & Vicente St.), 415-566-5700
◪ This Twin Peaks haunt, with an "inviting bar" and
"artistically presented" New American fare, brought a
breath of fresh air when it opened, but now ex boosters
backfire that the food is "iffy" and the experience is only "ok."

Ristorante Bacco ⑤Ⓜ   22 | 18 | 21 | $32
737 Diamond St. (bet. Elizabeth & 24th Sts.),
415-282-4969

■ "Now the crowds have moved on to the next trendy place", but this "convivial" Noe Valley trattoria still provides "excellent Italian fare", an "imaginative wine list", "attentive service" and "lovely decor"; regulars blow kisses to the kitchen for its "decadent risotto" and wonder why others "aren't lined up outside the door."

Ristorante Ecco ⓁⓂ   22 | 22 | 20 | $37
101 South Park St. (bet. 2nd & 3rd Sts.), 415-495-3291
■ Acolytes appreciate this "mercifully quiet", "authentic" and "excellent" Italian overlooking "charming" South Park; although it's a popular "lunch spot in Silicon Gulch" and makes for a "romantic" evening out, web monkeys warn it's "elegant" and "kind of upscale for the dot-com crowd" ("don't go in jeans").

Ristorante Ideale ⑤   20 | 17 | 20 | $31
1309 Grant Ave. (bet. Green & Vallejo Sts.),
415-391-4129
■ "Yes, there *is* good food in North Beach" insiders insist about this "hidden gem" tucked among the "tourist traps" in the nabe; if you're looking for "sophisticated Italian fare" served by "charming waiters" and a "fun" time, this ristorante may be ideal.

Ristorante Milano ⑤   21 | 15 | 21 | $32
1448 Pacific Ave. (bet. Hyde & Larkin Sts.), 415-673-2961
■ "Old favorite" on Russian Hill, where "good, solid" Northern Italian fare (like homemade pasta dishes), "warm, inviting service" and "attentive co-owners" add up to "the perfect neighborhood place."

Ristorante Umbria ⓁⓂ   20 | 16 | 19 | $28
198 Second St. (Howard St.), 415-546-6985
■ While this unassuming SoMa spot "close to the Moscone Convention Center" serves "pleasant" Italian food "without a lot of fuss", fans detect a "passion and soul" in the "staff and the owner" that make a difference; the wine list also features complementary wines from the region of Umbria.

RITZ-CARLTON DINING ROOM Ⓜ   28 | 28 | 28 | $68
Ritz-Carlton Hotel, 600 Stockton St. (bet. California & Pine Sts.),
415-773-6198
■ Expect the "transcendental" at this "blow-the-bank" Nob Hill "grande dame" featuring Sylvain Portay's "outstanding" New French cuisine; since the staff is among the "finest in the USA" (rated No.1 for Service in the *Survey*) and the "elegant" ambiance is that of a "great European hotel", "it doesn't get any better than this"; N.B. jacket required.

Ritz-Carlton Terrace 🇱🇸🇲 | 24 | 24 | 25 | $48 |

Ritz-Carlton Hotel, 600 Stockton St. (bet. California & Pine Sts.), 415-773-6198

■ It's "not as fancy as the Dining Room", but this "luxurious" Nob Hill Mediterranean, replete with "gracious service", still "exemplifies why the Ritz is the Ritz"; although it serves three meals a day, including a seafood celebration buffet on Fridays, most come for lunch alfresco or to get "pampered" at the "upscale brunch buffet" on the veranda – an experience that "you and your wallet will long remember."

Rocco's Seafood Grill 🇸🇲 | 19 | 18 | 18 | $32 |

2080 Van Ness Ave. (Pacific Ave.), 415-567-7606

■ Modest Van Ness/Polk Continental-seafooder serving "generous portions" of "consistently good" SF– style specialties (think sand dabs, cioppino, crab Louie) at prices that won't put a "huge dent in one's wallet"; landlubbers won't be lost at sea since there are also items like prime rib.

Roosevelt Tamale Parlor 🇱🇸 | 18 | 10 | 12 | $15 |

2817 24th St. (bet. Bryant & York Sts.), 415-550-9213

■ Operating since 1922, this "institution in the Mission" is a destination for the adventurous, who hit the non-trendy part of 24th St. for "excellent" handmade tamales; just be warned that the "no-frills" setting is "gritty" and service can be "slow."

Rooster, The 🇸🇲 | 20 | 20 | 19 | $32 |

1101 Valencia St. (22nd St.), 415-824-1222

■ "Cozy, neighborhood" Mission spot that showcases "hearty" Eclectic country cooking from around the world in a "funky, homey" setting; it's "an oasis in a desert of trendy places" and "good for a date."

Rosamunde Sausage Grill 🇱🇸🇲 | ▽ 23 | 10 | 16 | $9 |

545 Haight St. (bet. Fillmore & Steiner Sts.), 415-437-6851

■ Snausage fans say "they do one thing and they do it perfectly" at this counter-service only emporium of "good, cheap sausages" on Lower Haight; here's how it works: take your pick from 15 "delicious varieties" and then head next door to the Toronado and "wash it down" with a beer for a match made in heaven.

ROSE PISTOLA 🇱🇸🇲 | 22 | 20 | 18 | $40 |

532 Columbus Ave. (bet. Green & Union Sts.), 415-399-0499

◪ "The energy is palpable" at Reed Hearon's "hip-and-happening" North Beach North Italian–seafooder, which continues to be packed nightly with out-of-towners and locals who consider themselves lucky to get in; while less-trendy types are tired of the din ("I've been in quieter steel plants") and "hype", advocates insist that "it's got everything going for it" ("delicious food" and a "vibrant" atmo), so "sit up front for less noise and more people-watching."

Rose's Cafe 🇱🇸🇲   17 | 15 | 15 | $24
2298 Union St. (Steiner St.), 415-775-2200

▣ "This pleasant, European-style cafe" attracts the "yuppies of Cow Hollow" who wait patiently to snare a "nice sidewalk seat in the sun" so they can order "some of the same good [Northern Italian] dishes served at Reed Hearon's other places" (like oven-roasted mussels) "at half the price"; but cynics sniff you'll get the same "inconsistent" food and "snotty attitude" associated with his other eateries as well.

Rotunda 🇱🇸🇲   20 | 24 | 20 | $33
Neiman Marcus, 150 Stockton St. (Geary St.),
415-362-4777

■ "For those who shop till they drop", this oh-so-very Downtown retreat, "nestled on top of Neiman Marcus and overlooking Union Square", attracts the ladies who lunch under the dramatic glass dome and nibble on upscale, "expensive" Americana like the "great lobster club"; N.B. it's scheduled to start serving dinner as we go to press.

Rouge 🇸🇲   – | – | – | M
1500 Broadway (Polk St.), 415-346-7684

Whether the name is derived from the racy lipstick left on his face by giddy admirers or the red-hot spot that Harry Denton's forthcoming Van Ness/Polk nightclub will probably become remains to be seen, but at press time, the bon vivant was banking on a fall opening for his latest party venue, said to be a mix of equal parts cocktail food and live entertainment.

Royal Thai 🇱🇸🇲   22 | 16 | 19 | $23
951 Clement St. (11th Ave.), 415-386-1795

See review in North of San Francisco Directory.

Roy's 🇱🇸🇲   – | – | – | E
101 Second St. (Mission St.), 415-777-0277

Internationally acclaimed Hawaiian chef-restaurateur Roy Yamaguchi's first outpost in SF opened in late summer, and fans of his signature Euro-Asian cuisine were waiting with bated breath to say 'aloha'; the SoMa locale offers an expansive, airy dining room, an exhibition kitchen and a cutting-edge wine list.

Rubicon 🇱🇲   24 | 21 | 22 | $49
558 Sacramento St. (bet. Montgomery & Sansome Sts.),
415-434-4100

▣ "Classy" Downtowner that's a top "choice for impressing clients", thanks to chef Scott Newman's "superb" Cal-French fare and master sommelier Larry Stone's "incredible" "world-class wine list"; although detractors dis "the corporate power vibe", oenophiles insist the "food-and-wine pairings are mind-blowing" and "suggest you settle in, pay the money and enjoy."

Sam's Grill & Seafood Restaurant L M
| 20 | 17 | 18 | $34 |

374 Bush St. (bet. Kearny & Montgomery Sts.), 415-421-0594
■ To "step back in time", head for this Downtown American-seafooder where "crusty waiters" serve "real crusty sourdough" and "old-style" fish-house fare to "stockbrokers" and an "older crowd" that still relish the "creamed spinach", curtained booths and "heavy male atmosphere."

Sanppo ◑ L S M
∇ | 16 | 10 | 14 | $22 |

1702 Post St. (Buchanan St.), 415-346-3486
☑ This street-level Japantown Japanese is almost hidden by the sign for its upstairs neighbor, Denny's, but it manages to stay afloat serving "low-cost" sushi and "hearty donburri"; its proximity to the Kabuki also makes it "convenient for pre- or post-movie dining."

Sanraku Four Seasons L S M
| 24 | 14 | 17 | $27 |

704 Sutter St. (Taylor St.), 415-771-0803
Sony Metreon Ctr., 101 Fourth St. (Mission St.), 415-369-6166
■ Japanese duo Downtown and in the Sony Metreon Center that's noted for serving "always reliable", "unbelievably fresh sushi"; although the "simple decor isn't worth noting", fans insist the "focus is on the food", where it should be.

Savor L S M
| 17 | 14 | 16 | $19 |

3913 24th St. (Sanchez St.), 415-282-0344
☑ Some surveyors savor the "satisfying, creative crêpes" served at breakfast, lunch and dinner at this "affordable" and "popular" Noe Valley French-Med, but foodies "can't understand why it's crowded" 'cause meals are "mediocre."

Scala's Bistro ◑ L S M
| 23 | 22 | 21 | $38 |

Sir Francis Drake Hotel, 432 Powell St. (bet. Post & Sutter Sts.), 415-395-8555
■ Scala's still "soars" despite the departure of original chef Donna Scala from this "always humming" Downtown bistro boasting "excellent" French-Italian fare, a "gracious staff" and "warm ambiance"; although the noise sensitive say it's "too loud", most maintain that it's the "quintessential restaurant" après "Union Square shopping" or "pre-theater" – "if you can get in."

Schroeder's L M
| 15 | 15 | 16 | $27 |

240 Front St. (bet. California & Sacramento Sts.), 415-421-4778
■ If this Downtowner has nothing else, it's certainly got "tradition", having served sauerbraten, Wiener schnitzel and other "hearty" German-Continental fare to a mostly male clientele for more than a hundred years; although nostalgists find it "fun for lunch", most say the "tired food" is "a long way from Deutschland."

Scoma's ⒧Ⓢ Ⓜ   19 | 17 | 17 | $35
Pier 47 (bet. Jefferson & Jones Sts.), 415-771-4383
◼ Legendary, weather-beaten waterfront haunt known for "generous portions" of "good" if not "memorable" "seafood standards" and "even better views"; it may be "touristy" and "commercial", but many maintain that it's the "best" of that ilk on Fisherman's Wharf.

Scott's ⒧ Ⓜ   18 | 17 | 17 | $34
3 Embarcadero Ctr., promenade level (Drumm St.), 415-981-0622
◼ "Franchisey", "no-nonsense" seafooder/steakhouse (with branches throughout the Bay Area) catering to a business-lunch crowd that finds the "nice Embarcadero setting" and "quiet" atmosphere perfect "for work meetings"; but whether the food is "reliable" or only "average" (there's "no imagination in the cooking") will have to be your call.

Sears Fine Food ⒧Ⓢ Ⓜ≢   17 | 10 | 15 | $16
439 Powell St. (bet. Post & Sutter Sts.), 415-986-1160
◼ "If you want good pancakes sprinkled with tons of nostalgia, eat here" advise advocates of this "popular" Traditional American and "perennial favorite on Powell"; but while they single out the "delicious Swedish pancakes", critics counter that "Aunt Jemima would run screaming from this overpriced joint."

Shalimar ⒧Ⓢ Ⓜ≢   23 | 5 | 8 | $14
532 Jones St. (Geary St.), 415-928-0333
◼ Indian-Pakistani dive delivering "cheap and tasty" food that's the "real thing"; mostly packed with natives and locals from the 'hood, brave hearts insist the "spicy-beyond-control" curries and naan are "worth the chaos and the scary location" in the Tenderloin.

Shanghai 1930 ⒧ Ⓜ   20 | 22 | 18 | $41
133 Steuart St. (bet. Howard & Mission Sts.), 415-896-5600
◼ George Chen's "swanky" SoMa supper club exudes a "glamorous atmosphere" that "takes you to another era" (you "expect Rita Hayworth to walk in"), as well as boasting a "great jazz-bar scene"; most maintain that the "haute Chinese cuisine" is "good", but a minority moans "small portions" and "insane prices" make them feel "Shanghaied."

Silks ⒧Ⓢ Ⓜ   24 | 25 | 25 | $55
Mandarin Oriental Hotel, 222 Sansome St. (California St.), 415-986-2020
◼ A "classy" "sleeper" in the Mandarin Oriental, this Downtown hotel restaurant offers "excellent", "innovative" Cal-Asian cuisine; since the setting is also "deluxe" and "service is as smooth as its name", admirers ask "why is this such a secret?"; however, the departure of chef Dante Boccuzzi may outdate the above food rating.

SLANTED DOOR, THE 🅛🅢   26 | 18 | 19 | $34
584 Valencia St. (17th St.), 415-861-8032
■ Charles Phan's "outstanding", "inventive Vietnamese" creations served in "cool digs" have "yuppies slumming in the Mission", hitting "automatic redial to get a reservation" at this "trendy" place that's "hell to get into"; patrons overlook the "deafening din" for the "brilliant flavors" of the small dishes and "the perfect wines to complement" them.

Slow Club 🅛🅢🅜   21 | 19 | 17 | $29
2501 Mariposa St. (Hampshire St.), 415-241-9390
■ "Slow is a misnomer" for this "stylish", "urban" Mission "hangout" that's "always happening"; it attracts a "hip" crowd that knocks back cosmos and enjoys the "consistently good" New American fare; just be warned that a "no-reservations" policy may mean a long wait.

Sno-Drift ●🅛🅢🅜   – | – | – | M
1830 Third St. (16th St.), 415-431-4766
Boys just want to have fun seems to be the motto at this new tongue-in-cheek, ski-lodge–themed restaurant (look for kitschy sno-cone drinks at the bar) near Potrero Hill; it's the first ownership venture for Craige Walters and Charles Doell, the talent behind the whimsical design team Fun Display (responsible for Backflip and The Zodiac Club, among others); the kitchen turns out affordable New French–American fare at lunch and small plates in the evening.

South Park Cafe 🅛🅜   21 | 18 | 19 | $33
108 South Park (bet. 2nd & 3rd Sts.), 415-495-7275
■ "Are we in France?" ask fans of this "quaint bistro", an "easy to like" "grand little place" on South Park, with a "wonderful Left Bank atmosphere" and sidewalk seating; although "lunch is swarming with SoMa Interneters", "dinner is lovely" for "steak frites and inexpensive Bordeaux."

Splendido 🅛🅢🅜   20 | 21 | 19 | $37
4 Embarcadero Ctr. (Drumm St.), 415-986-3222
◪ "With a great view of the Bay Bridge", "elegant decor" from designer Pat Kuleto and a "fun after-work bar scene", this "gorgeous spot in a high-rise mall" transcends its "slick, corporate" Embarcadero locale; but whether the "rustic Italian fare" is "reliable" or "hit-or-miss" is your call.

Stars ●🅛🅢🅜   21 | 22 | 20 | $46
555 Golden Gate Ave. (Van Ness Ave.), 415-861-7827
◪ Although it's "not the legend it used to be" when Jeremiah Tower ruled the roost at this Civic Center icon in its "heyday", the majority maintains that the "new Stars is shining and twinkling", with a "more inviting" remodeled dining room and less "attitude"; however, the post-*Survey* transfer of chef Chris Fernandez (a Paul Bertolli protégé) to Stars' Seattle branch has left Amaryll Schwertner in charge of the Cal/French/Italian menu and may outdate the above food score.

Stelline ⬛🆂Ⓜ 14 | 12 | 16 | $23
429 Gough St. (bet. Hayes & Ivy Sts.), 415-626-4292
☑ For those looking for a "quick inexpensive meal before
the opera", this "casual" Hayes Valley Italian with a "mom-
and-pop feel" will do "in a pinch"; but the food is only
"ok" and "Caffe Delle Stelle [it's neighboring sib] it's not."

Stinking Rose ⬛🆂Ⓜ 14 | 14 | 15 | $26
*325 Columbus Ave. (bet. Broadway & Vallejo St.),
415-781-7673*
☑ Many "tourists love" this "crowded" North Beach Italian
with "garlic everything", including "garlic ice cream";
however, locals lament that the food is "poor" and "anyone
with taste buds should stay away"; P.S. the amorous assert
"never go here on a date."

Straits Cafe ⬛🆂Ⓜ 22 | 18 | 18 | $29
3300 Geary Blvd. (Parker Ave.), 415-668-1783
☑ A meal at chef-owner Chris Yeo's Inner Richmond "secret"
spot is like a "mini-trip to Singapore", with "innovative
and tasty" Southeast Asian fare, "colorful, zany" tropical
decor and "fun cocktails" with a "plastic monkey hanging
off your glass"; NB. there's also a branch in Palo Alto.

Suppenküche 🆂Ⓜ 21 | 17 | 18 | $25
601 Hayes St. (Laguna St.), 415-252-9289
■ This hip "country German" hangout, with "beer hall
ambiance" and a "huge imported selection" of brews on
tap, is a "little piece of the old country" in Hayes Valley;
despite Deutschland's reputation for heavy fare, the meals
are "lite and bright" and served at communal tables.

Sushi Groove 🆂Ⓜ 22 | 20 | 15 | $30
1916 Hyde St. (Union St.), 415-440-1905
1516 Folsom St. (11th St.), 415-503-1950 ⬛
■ "Candlelit walls", a live DJ in the waiting area and sake
cocktails help sushi fans get into the groove at this tragically
"hip", "fun" Russian Hill Japanese; black-clad "yuppies"
hang out in the "coolest wine bar in town" until they get
their shot of "excellent, innovative sushi" that's as fresh
as the "icy cold staff"; there's a new branch in SoMa.

Swan Oyster Depot ⬛Ⓜ⌀ 25 | 13 | 22 | $25
*1517 Polk St. (bet. California & Sacramento Sts.),
415-673-1101*
■ "Almost nothing beats oysters and a cup of chowder" at
this landmark on Van Ness/Polk that's in a "class by itself";
despite the "funky decor", "tourists and locals alike continue
to line up for the privilege of sitting at the counter" at lunch
for "simple" but "excellent quality seafood" "served by
friendly brothers who love what they do."

Tadich Grill 🇱 Ⓜ   20 | 18 | 18 | $33
240 California St. (bet. Battery & Front Sts.), 415-391-1849
🗹 When "you miss the old boys' club", join "Downtown suits" and "out-of-towners" at this "Financial District stalwart" (reportedly the oldest restaurant in California, circa 1849) for its "authentic, old-school" SF fare; although foes feel that the food is "tired", the waiters are "crusty" and the "memorabilia makes it feel like a tourist trap", most suggest "sit at the counter and step back into time."

Taiwan 🇱 Ⓢ Ⓜ   19 | 7 | 12 | $16
445 Clement St. (6th Ave.), 415-387-1789
289 Columbus Ave. (Broadway), 415-989-6789
■ "Eat like a Mandarin for less than 10 bucks" boast boosters of these Chinese sibs in the Inner Richmond and North Beach, where you can get "consistently good dumplings" and "great soups for a song"; at these prices, no one seems to mind the "grungy decor" or "abysmal service."

Taqueria Cancun 🇱 Ⓢ Ⓜ ⇗   21 | 8 | 13 | $9
1003 Market St. (6th St.), 415-864-6773
2288 Mission St. (19th St.), 415-252-9560 ●
3211 Mission St. (Valencia St.), 415-550-1414 ●
■ Chainlet of "authentic taquerias" sprinkled throughout the seediest parts of town that's renowned for its "monstrous burritos" made with hefty fillings and "fresh, whole strips of avocado"; of course, there's no decor and service can be "sullen", but oh those "dirt cheap prices."

Tavolino 🇱 Ⓢ Ⓜ   17 | 18 | 16 | $33
401 Columbus Ave. (Vallejo St.), 415-392-1472
🗹 "Sitting on the sidewalk on a sunny day" "people-watching" from this "stylish" North Beach corner and sampling flavorful *cicchetti* ("tapas, Italian-style") is the "next best thing to being in Venice" claim fans; but critics counter that the cooking has "gone downhill", and a slip in the food rating supports that point of view.

Ten-Ichi 🇱 Ⓢ Ⓜ   20 | 16 | 18 | $28
2235 Fillmore St. (bet. Clay & Sacramento Sts.), 415-346-3477
■ "Lovely Japanese spot on Upper Fillmore" that's "appreciated" by regulars who return for the "broad menu of choices", including an "excellent", "non-hyped sushi bar"; "sweet service" and a "quiet atmosphere" add to its appeal.

Terra Brazilis Ⓢ   21 | 19 | 20 | $33
602 Hayes St. (Laguna St.), 415-241-1900
■ This "happening" spot in the "up-and-coming area" of Hayes Valley offers an "amazing introduction to Brazil's cuisine" and an "innovative wine list"; despite cramped quarters ("tables on top of each other"), which makes the place "unbelievably noisy", the adventurous find it "a nice change of pace" and a "wonderful pre-opera spot."

Thai House ⑤Ⓜ
21 | 13 | 19 | $19

2200 Market St. (bet. 15th & Sanchez Sts.), 415-864-5006 Ⓛ
151 Noe St. (Henry St.), 415-863-0374
■ These twin, "easy-on-the-budget" eateries in the Castro
are "always good", especially "for those who are looking
for more than just pad Thai and curry"; "friendly service"
and "good prices" are other pluses.

Thanh Long ⑤
24 | 14 | 16 | $37

4101 Judah St. (46th Ave.), 415-665-1146
■ There's "no need for a menu" at this Vietnamese Sunset
joint – simply strap on a bib and order the "incredibly
messy" but "indescribably delicious roasted crab" and
"garlic noodles from heaven"; N.B. the wait can be as
long as its name implies.

Thanya & Salee Ⓛ⑤Ⓜ
▽ 19 | 15 | 15 | $21

1469 18th St. (Connecticut St.), 415-647-6469
■ "Consistently good" neighborhood Thai on Potrero Hill
serving "great, quick curries" that's a good alternative
"when everyone is waiting in line at Eliza's"; although
the dining room is "not a destination", the adjoining Lilo
Lounge lures in a lively local crowd with it's "great drinks
and tropical decor."

Thep Phanom Thai Cuisine ⑤Ⓜ
25 | 16 | 19 | $24

400 Waller St. (Fillmore St.), 415-431-2526
■ "Authentic" Lower Haight Thai "standout" that's a "real
Phenom-ena" according to surveyors who rate it "best
in the city"; sure, it's got "attentive service" and a "cozy
neighborhood feel", but it's the "creativity, spice and
freshness" of the food that set it apart; budget-watchers
concede "it's good" (and "worth the parking nightmare"),
"but don't let people tell you this is cheap."

Thirsty Bear Brewing Co. Ⓛ⑤Ⓜ
17 | 14 | 14 | $26

661 Howard St. (bet. Hawthorne & 3rd Sts.), 415-974-0905
◪ "Good microbrews" and "unusual tapas" are the bill of
fare at this "incredibly noisy" SoMa brewpub that attracts
"frat boys and big-haired girls" who can "barely" find a
spot at the "standing-room only" bar for "after-work
socializing"; critics find the "high-tech warehouse
setting" "sterile" and say the apps are "hit-and-miss."

Three Ring ⑤Ⓜ
20 | 18 | 18 | $32

995 Valencia St. (21st St.), 415-821-3210
■ This addition to the "crowded Valencia restaurant
corridor" in the Mission – actually a "reincarnation of [the
shuttered] Val 21" – features Keith Handelsman's (ex French
Laundry) "tasty" Eclectic-French fare at "affordable
prices"; the subtle, vintage circus decor encompasses
colorful murals and "complimentary cotton candy."

Ti Couz L S M | 21 | 15 | 15 | $20 |

3108 16th St. (bet. Guerrero & Valencia Sts.),
415-252-7373

■ "Deservedly popular", "bustling crêperie" (the "original that others around the city are still trying to copy") that's "a touch of Brittany in the Mission"; enthusiasts endure the "long wait" for "unusual, thick, square, rustic crêpes" stuffed with "a yummy assortment" of fillings, from mushrooms to Nutella, as well as fresh seafood at "*incroyable*" prices; despite its success, it retains an "informal", "artsy" air.

Timo's S M | 18 | 12 | 16 | $26 |

842 Valencia St. (bet. 19th & 20th Sts.), 415-647-0558

◪ For a fun-filled evening of "excellent sangria" and "an astounding variety of tapas", loyalists still like this Mission favorite; however, foes feel the Spanish tidbits are only "ok" and gripe about the "cramped seating" and "poor service."

Tin-Pan Asian Bistro L S M | 20 | 19 | 18 | $25 |

2251 Market St. (bet. Noe & Sanchez Sts.),
415-565-0733

■ "Upscale" "Castro scene" with a "delightful", "expansive menu" specializing in "tasty" pan-Asian noodles; it also makes a "good first date" place suggest cynics, 'cuz there's "great people-watching if it fails"; but what some call a "lively, energized" atmosphere, others simply dub "noisy."

Tita's L S M ⇴ | ▽ 16 | 13 | 18 | $19 |

3870 17th St. (bet. Noe & Sanchez Sts.), 415-626-2477

■ "If you hanker for a Hawaiian-style plate lunch, this is the place" claim Big Island boosters of this "very friendly" Castro spot dishing up "excellent teriyaki anything"; the "down-home ambiance" and an "aloha spirit" are also guaranteed to "put a smile on your face."

Tokyo Go Go S | 22 | 22 | 18 | $30 |

3174 16th St. (bet. Guerrero & Valencia Sts.), 415-864-2288

■ "Trendy", "fun and funky with fine fish" is what surveyors say about this Japanese hangout in the Mission (brought to you by the folks who gave the Marina the equally hip Ace Wasabi); a "young and beautiful crowd" "breaks in groovy outfits" while knocking back cucumber-garnished saketinis and "killer sushi" in a *Jetsons* atmosphere."

Tommaso's S | 23 | 16 | 19 | $24 |

1042 Kearny St. (bet. Broadway & Pacific Ave.),
415-398-9696

■ "Great, old-time Italian" in North Beach, specializing in "wood-fired pizzas" baked in the same "historic oven" that's been there since the '30s, where "*The Sopranos* would feel right at home"; devotees declare that "the Crotti family still does the best" pies and lasagna in the city.

Tommy's Joynt ◑ L S M ⇄   13 | 14 | 12 | $16 |
1101 Geary Blvd. (Van Ness Ave.), 415-775-4216
◪ "Old, sleazy hangout" on Van Ness/Polk that's the "last of the hofbraus", with "real turkey carved to order" and other "filling" fare; although some say "give it a pass unless you're in the nabe and hungry", its "late-night" hours and "cheap prices" pull in night owls and wallet-watchers.

Tommy Toy's   25 | 24 | 24 | $52 |
Cuisine Chinoise L S M
655 Montgomery St. (Washington St.), 415-397-4888
◪ Surveyors who "want to be spoiled" head to this "upscale" Downtowner featuring "luscious, French-influenced Chinese" cuisine, "impeccable service" and an "elegant" (though "dark") setting; while foes feel it's "over the top" and "overpriced", most expense-accounters insist it's "excellent" for "entertaining your customers."

Tonga Room S M   11 | 25 | 16 | $33 |
Fairmont Hotel, 950 Mason St. (California St.), 415-772-5278
■ "Despite being cheesy and touristy", this "kitchy" Nob Hill Asian with a "faux-tropical setting", featuring "simulated storms" and "wonderful alcoholic concoctions", is "sure to put a smile on even the most cynical person's face"; but just "go for the band" and dancing and "make sure you eat at home."

Ton Kiang L S M   25 | 13 | 17 | $23 |
5821 Geary Blvd. (bet. 22nd & 23rd Aves.), 415-387-8273
■ Voted No. 1 for the "best dim sum" in the *Survey* is this Richmond Chinese, chalking up kudos for its "never-ending supply" of "yummy" dumplings; "you'll get the most for the least", so "it's worth the wait [on weekends] for those little plates"; fans of "fine Hakka cuisine" also make the trek here (they certainly "don't go for the atmosphere").

Top of the Mark S   18 | 26 | 20 | $42 |
Mark Hopkins Hotel, 1 Nob Hill (California & Mason Sts.), 415-616-6916
■ "Incredible views" (just "hope it's not foggy"), a "wonderful", "classy" atmosphere with a "great band" nightly, drinks and dancing (complimentary lessons on Tuesday evenings) draw devotees to this swanky stop atop Nob Hill; while some say skip the "overpriced" Californian food, which can miss the mark, the exception is the bountiful Sunday brunch that's "good, especially with visitors."

Tortola L   16 | 11 | 14 | $18 |
Crocker Galleria, 50 Post St., 3rd. fl. (bet. Kearny & Montgomery Sts.), 415-986-8678 M ⇄
3640 Sacramento St. (bet. Locust & Spruce Sts.), 415-929-8181 S
Stonestown Galleria, 3251 20th Ave. (Winston St.), 415-566-4336 S M ⇄

Tortola (Cont.)
*UCSF Medical Ctr., 500 Parnassus Ave., Millberry Union
Bldg. (2nd Ave.), 415-731-8670* Ⓜ⇔
◪ Those looking for "healthy food in a hurry" head for this
Cal-Mexican chain featuring "fresh enchiladas", tamales,
tostados and the like; but enamigos object to the "expensive",
"small", "bland" portions and insist there's better "south-of-
the-border fare" in SF.

Town's End | 20 | 16 | 18 | $25 |
Restaurant & Bakery Ⓛ Ⓢ
2 Townsend St. (The Embarcadero), 415-512-0749
■ Folks flock to this New American restaurant/bakery for
its "wonderful brunches", "incredible bread basket" and
"great Embarcadero view"; while it's "ideal for breakfast"
(no wonder there's "a wait on weekends"), lunch and dinner
are also offered; regulars just "hope it doesn't get too
popular" with the crowds at the nearby "new ball park."

Trattoria Contadina Ⓢ Ⓜ | 21 | 17 | 21 | $30 |
1800 Mason St. (Union St.), 415-982-5728
■ Unpretentious, family-run trattoria serving "simple but
delicious" "Italian standards" that are overseen by a
"gracious owner who makes you feel like you're visiting
relatives"; it's a "favorite" because it's "what a North Beach
restaurant should be" and without the "hustle and chaos"
that are so prevalent at other eateries in that area.

Truly Mediterranean ●Ⓛ Ⓢ Ⓜ | 22 | 6 | 12 | $10 |
1724 Haight St. (Cole St.), 415-751-7482
3109 16th St. (Valencia St.), 415-252-7482 ⇔
■ These "spartan" purveyors of "delicious", "cheap"
Middle Eastern fare in the Haight-Ashbury and Mission
are a "gift from heaven when you're starving" ("fantastic
falafel and schwarmas to swoon over"); although there's
no ambiance to speak of at either, both offer entertainment
in the form of "great people-watching."

Tu Lan Ⓛ Ⓜ⇔ | 22 | 3 | 9 | $12 |
8 Sixth St. (Market St.), 415-626-0927
◪ Surveyors willing "to take a walk on the wild side" on
this seedy stretch of SoMa (reportedly, Julia Child once
did) are rewarded with "huge portions" of "delicious
Vietnamese" food that are as "tasty as the interior is trashy";
no, it's definitely "not for neatniks", but the "cheap prices"
pull in plenty of penny-pinchers.

Twenty Four Ⓛ Ⓢ Ⓜ | – | – | – | E |
24 Willie Mays Plaza (King & 3rd Sts.), 415-644-0240
Paying homage to Willie Mays' jersey number, this new,
no-nonsense American grill is close enough to Pacific Bell
Park to catch a fly ball, but diners are more likely to get a
buzz at the art deco bar or fill up on American classics
like steak or banana splits.

2223 Restaurant S M   21 | 18 | 19 | $36
2223 Market St. (bet. Noe & Sanchez Sts.), 415-431-0692
■ "Cruisy", "hipster" "hot spot" in the Castro with "lots of boy-watching" that also offers a "fine meal", thanks to chef/co-owner Melinda Randolph's flavorful riffs on "feel-good [American] comfort food"; sure, it's "crowded" and "noisy", but for most that's what makes for a "fun" "scene."

Universal Cafe L S   23 | 17 | 19 | $33
2814 19th St. (bet. Bryant & Harrison Sts.), 415-821-4608
■ Chic "little" cafe "in the middle of nowhere" in the Mission serving "universally good" New American fare to those who find it; despite "cramped" quarters and a sometimes "snippy" staff, the "high-tech decor" and "great outdoor seating" go over big with the "dot-com" crowd; N.B. despite the departure of chef Julia McClaskey, reports say the cafe seems to be "navigating the transition nicely."

Valentine's Cafe S   21 | 15 | 20 | $24
1793 Church St. (30th St.), 415-285-2257
■ Tucked away in Upper Noe Valley, this modest dinner-and-weekend brunch spot wins hearts with its "friendly service" and "surprisingly good" Vegetarian and vegan menu; after sampling the cuisine's "bold cross-cultural" flavors (with a strong Indian strain), all but die-hard carnivores find themselves falling "in love with Valentine's."

Venticello S M   22 | 22 | 21 | $38
1257 Taylor St. (Washington St.), 415-922-2545
■ The combination of "superb fare" and "an exquisitely warm setting" makes this Nob Hill Northern Italian "great for a romantic evening" (and "the Italian waiters aren't bad either"); however, when you go, "plan to meet your dining neighbors", as the quarters are "very tight."

Venture Frogs Restaurant ❂ L S M   – | – | – | M
1000 Van Ness Ave. (O'Farrell St.), 415-409-2550
Owned by two youthful Internet zillionaires turned technology incubators, this Civic Center start-up logs in with a Pan-Asian menu that reads like a tear sheet from *The Industry Standard* – 'AOL miso-glazed cod', 'eBay eggplant' and 'Netscape pan-fried noodles'; the high-tech design, including a fiber-optic illuminated bar embedded with computer chips, reflects from whence they come.

Via Vai Trattoria L S M   19 | 16 | 18 | $29
1715 Union St. (bet. Gough & Octavia Sts.), 415-441-2111
■ Man cannot live on bread and wine alone, so the owners of Pane e Vino opened this Italian Cow Hollow "charmer" that specializes in thin-crust pizza from a wood-burning oven; reviewers deem the rest of the menu "good, not great", saving their praise for sitting out back "on the patio drinking excellent red wine – all's well with the world."

Vicolo L S M   21 | 11 | 13 | $18
201 Ivy St. (bet. Franklin & Gough Sts.),
415-863-2382

■ Named after the tiny alley (*vicolo*) in which it's tucked
away, this modest Hayes Valley Italian serves deep-dish
"cornmeal pizza to die for" with "cool, yuppie toppings"
and "delicious" gourmet greens ("you can't beat the beet
salad"); although there's not much ambiance to speak of,
performing-arts patrons know it's a great "quickie before
the opera" or "a good fallback" for those nights when you
can't score "reservations near Civic Center."

Vivande Porta Via L S M   22 | 16 | 18 | $33
2125 Fillmore St. (bet. California & Sacramento Sts.),
415-346-4430

◪ Chef-owner Carlo Middione's Upper Fillmore trattoria,
serving down-home Italian food either to eat in or to go,
draws a mixed response: while advocates love to watch
chefs prepare the "wonderful homemade pastas" and
other "reliable" fare, critics carp it's "overpriced for the
deli setting" and feel "uncomfortable eating at tables by
take-out counters."

Wa-Ha-Ka   14 | 11 | 12 | $14
Oaxaca Mexican L S M
1489 Folsom St. (11th St.), 415-861-1410
1980 Union St. (Buchanan St.), 415-775-4145 ⊅

■ "Cheap food", "cheap beers" and cheap atmosphere
are the draws at this pair of fast-food outlets in SoMa and
Cow Hollow; although they praise the "fresh ingredients"
in the "funky" fare (prawn burritos, crab-cake enchiladas),
most Tex-Mex mavens see the joints mainly as "great
places to start out the night" before hitting the clubs.

Walzwerk   ▽ 24 | 15 | 24 | $25
381 S. Van Ness Ave. (bet. 14th & 15th Sts.),
415-551-7181

■ "East German cooking gets a deft liposuction" at this
newcomer in a sketchy part of the Mission, where the
"two absolutely adorable" owners lure schnitzel-seeking
surveyors and ex-patriate Berliners with "comfort food in
an über-hip setting"; like good socialists, everyone breaks
brown bread at the long, communal tables.

Waterfront   21 | 23 | 19 | $44
Restaurant & Cafe L S M
Pier 7, The Embarcadero (Broadway), 415-391-2696

■ Embarcadero institution with a split personality: the
formal upstairs restaurant, offering a Cal-French menu, has a
"magnificent Bay view" – and, naturally, "you pay for it";
the casual cafe downstairs, with its dockside patio, serves
Cal-Med cuisine at reasonable prices; so no wonder
surveyors say this 35-year-old veteran is still a "fave for
showing off the city to guests."

Watergate 🆂 Ⓜ   23 | 20 | 22 | $40
1152 Valencia St. (bet. 22nd & 23rd Sts.), 415-648-6000
■ They do fusion right at this "sophisticated spot" in the Mission, where the New French–Asian food "is prepared with great finesse" and "intense attention to detail"; throw in the friendly service – the "owners really care" – and you have reviewers wondering why the place isn't more crowded ("maybe it's the name"); N.B. ask about the extensive list of exotic teas.

We Be Sushi Ⓛ Ⓜ   16 | 8 | 14 | $17
3226 Geary Blvd. (bet. Parker & Spruce Sts.), 415-221-9960
94 Judah St. (Sixth Ave.), 415-681-4010 🆂 🍴
538 Valencia St. (bet. 16th & 17th Sts.), 415-565-0749 🆂
1071 Valencia St. (22nd St.), 415-826-0607 🆂 🍴
☑ If you're cash-strapped and craving sushi, this "bare-bones" Japanese chain "is the place to go"; but while "it be a great bargain" to its fans, foes sniff the "industrial-type franchise" is "cheap and nothing more."

Woodward's Garden 🆂   25 | 16 | 21 | $40
1700 Mission St. (Duboce St.), 415-621-7122
■ "An oasis under the overpass", this miniscule Mission eatery draws big praise for its "flawless, fresh" New American cuisine; though a handful carp about the "weird location" and "too cramped" quarters, most say the "masterfully prepared, full-flavored food" is "so good you forget where you are"; N.B. the restaurant plans to expand next door, which should double capacity to a roaring 51 seats.

Xyz Ⓛ 🆂 Ⓜ   19 | 22 | 18 | $45
W Hotel, 181 Third St. (Howard St.), 415-817-7836
☑ Brought to you by the owners of the Universal Cafe, this hip SoMa "hot spot" in the equally "cool" new W Hotel (WXYZ, get it?) is dripping in "ultra-contemporary" decor, "beautiful people" and attitude – perfect "when you need a shot of chic"; unfortunately, "the show interferes with the service" snipe the critics, who wonder "Y eat here?" – the Californian-French "food doesn't match the hype or the price."

Yabbies Coastal Kitchen 🆂 Ⓜ   23 | 18 | 21 | $37
2237 Polk St. (bet. Green & Vallejo Sts.), 415-474-4088
■ "Go for the oysters" urge fans of this lively Van Ness/ Polk fish house – and stay to sample the rest of the menu, which features "out-of-the-world seafood" (especially the tuna poke appetizer) that's "always superbly fresh"; "attentive service" adds to the "attractive" ambiance; N.B. Max Martinez, who cut his teeth at Aqua, has assumed the top toque from original chef Mark Lusardi.

Yank Sing L S M 24 | 16 | 18 | $27
427 Battery St. (bet. Clay & Washington Sts.), 415-781-1111
Rincon Ctr., 101 Spear St. (bet. Howard & Mission Sts.),
415-957-9300
49 Stevenson St. (bet. 1st & 2nd Sts.), 415-541-4949
■ "Scarf up the delectables as the carts roll by" at this trio of SoMa parlors that "churn out" a never-ending parade of "delicious" "piping hot" Chinese choices (the "individual portions of Peking Duck [alone] are worth the visit"); while this "Rolls Royce of dim sum" does have the "price tag to match", that doesn't deter "the suits who line up around the corner" for the lunch-and-brunch-only service – so make reservations or "get there early."

Ya-Ya Cuisine L M 21 | 16 | 20 | $27
663 Clay St. (bet. Kearny & Montgomery Sts.),
415-434-3567
■ Unique "hole-in-the-wall" Downtowner that will convince even those "who think they don't like Middle Eastern food to think again" – the fatoosh salad and other "exquisite" fare from the Fertile Crescent will put you in "paradise"; yet despite a "warm staff" and the loyal following developed by Yahya Salih's previous venture in the Sunset, the dining room is often "tragically empty."

Yoshida-Ya L S M 20 | 17 | 17 | $30
2909 Webster St. (Union St.), 415-346-3431
☑ Longtime Cow Hollow Japanese offering "good hibachi cooking", as well as sushi and an "authentic upstairs" (where you can sit on the floor at the traditional low tables); some suspect it "fell off its pedestal a long time ago", but families still enjoy coming here "with the kids" – it's a nice "alternative if you don't want to wait hours at Ace Wasabi."

Yuet Lee ● L S M ⊄ 21 | 4 | 12 | $20
1300 Stockton St. (Broadway), 415-982-6020
■ "Ignore the decor" – it's heavy on fluorescent green – at this "low-budget" hole and you'll be rewarded with simple, "well-sauced" seafood (the salt-and-pepper squid alone is an "SF treasure") and other Chinese staples; with a kitchen that's open until 3 AM, this is "one of the best places to eat in Chinatown" – for night owls, anyway.

Yukol Place Thai Cuisine S M ▽ 21 | 12 | 21 | $19
2380 Lombard St. (bet. Pierce & Scott Sts.),
415-922-1599
■ Especially "nice service" elevates this neighborhood Marina spot to a status of "our favorite Thai" for many reviewers; while a few critics dismiss the fare as "just average", there are those who "will drive an hour just to get their chicken satay."

Zao Noodle Bar ⓛⓢⓜ   15 14 15 $17
2406 California St. (Fillmore St.), 415-345-8088
2031 Chestnut St. (Fillmore St.), 415-928-3088
3583 16th St. (bet. Market & Noe Sts.), 415-864-2888
◪ This burgeoning chainlet of "young and fun" pan-Asian noodle shops serves "oodles of noodles for the money"; but while nearly everyone agrees that it's a "great concept", specific reactions are as mixed as the dishes' origins: cheerleaders find it a "good place for a quick bite" of "hearty and healthy fare", but real ramen mavens insist the "uninspired" and "bland" dishes "fall short of their potential."

Zaré on Sacramento ⓛⓜ   22 20 21 $36
568 Sacramento St. (bet. Montgomery & Sansome Sts.), 415-291-9145
■ "Small and cozy", this Downtown hideaway is "a romantic spot in the [otherwise buttoned-up] Financial District"; the "warmth" largely stems from "oh-so-charming" executive chef-owner Hoss Zaré, "a master of hospitality" (ladies receive a rose as they leave), whose "gutsy" Med cooking is delivered with "impeccable service."

Zarzuela   23 17 19 $30
2000 Hyde St. (Union St.), 415-346-0800
■ Although the competition has increased, this six-year-old spot remains the "city's most authentic place for Spanish food" insist Castilian connoisseurs, who cite its "perfect paella", "good sangria" and "an outstanding tapas menu" that allows guests to experience "many tastes without [eating] too much"; the "friendly" staff "does everything right", except take reservations and procure a parking place – the only drawback to the Russian Hill neighborhood.

Zax   24 20 23 $41
2330 Taylor St. (Columbus Ave.), 415-563-6266
■ It's a "limited menu, but everything works" at this husband-and-wife-run bistro in North Beach, a "tucked-away haven" that "deserves to be better known" for its "finely crafted combinations of Mediterranean" fare (don't miss the "killer goat cheese soufflé"); add in a quiet atmosphere and a "knowledgeable staff" and you have a "sophisticated" dining scene for "grown-ups."

Zazie ⓛⓢⓜ   19 17 18 $23
941 Cole St. (bet. Carl St. & Parnassus Ave.), 415-564-5332
■ This *charmant* cafe in Upper Haight-Ashbury attracts a "cosmopolitan clientele" that appreciates the "high-quality cuisine for less than you'd expect" and overlooks the "painfully slow", "pretentious service"; on sunny mornings, the place to be is on the "lovely garden patio", sipping jumbo lattes and enjoying the "very good breakfast with a French accent" (although "weekend brunch can be impossible to get into").

Zinzino 🅂🅜   19 | 18 | 18 | $30 |
2355 Chestnut St. (bet. Divisadero & Scott Sts.),
415-346-6623
■ While many admirers of this "funky little spot" in the
Marina come in search of the "micron-thin", wood-
oven-baked pizza, the "high-energy" place also pumps out a
"nice variety" of Cal-Italian dishes such as "succulent
spaghetti and meatballs baked in parchment paper"; you
can either dine in an interior crammed with memorabilia
(from Vespas to Venetian masks) or in the covered, heated
garden out back.

Zodiac Club, The 🅂🅜   18 | 21 | 18 | $33 |
718 14th St. (Market St.), 415-626-7827
■ Although this rising star in Upper Market/Church Street
serves a Cal-Med menu that changes with the monthly
constellations, hipsters admit they head to this horoscope-
themed hangout more for the "very, very dark" "*Jetsons*-
esque" atmosphere and exotic cocktails (each sign has a
different libation); P.S. with a kitchen open until 12 AM on
weekends, it's "perfect for a late-night dinner" (although
the "prices and service are from another planet").

ZUNI CAFE ◑🅛🅢   24 | 20 | 19 | $38 |
1658 Market St. (bet. Franklin & Gough Sts.),
415-552-2522
■ More than 20 years after it opened, this "legendary"
Italian-Mediterranean mainstay on the edge of Hayes Valley
"maintains the hip vibe" that still attracts the city's rich
and famous ("you just feel cool eating here"); loyalists
swoon "ah, the Caesar salad, the oven-roasted chicken,
the burgers" – Zuni standards that "set the standard" for
all others; despite a few of the inevitable "overrated"
comments, it remains the "quintessential SF" scene.

East of San Francisco

Ajanta 🅛🅢🅜   22 | 16 | 19 | $24
1888 Solano Ave. (bet. Alameda & Colusa Aves.), Berkeley, 510-526-4373
■ Naan-partisans swear this "family-run" Berkeley Indian "never disappoints" with its monthly "changing menu" of "wonderful" "nonstandard" regional specialties; "courteous service" and "beautiful" reproductions of Ajanta cave murals add to the "cheerful" experience; "locals hope others don't catch on."

Autumn Moon Cafe 🅛🅢🅜   18 | 15 | 17 | $24
3909 Grand Ave. (Sunny Slope Ave.), Oakland, 510-595-3200
◪ "Like eating at home, but without the fuss or the dishes" sums up the appeal of this "comfortable" Oakland American that draws "long lines on weekends" for its "reasonably priced" and "consistently good homestyle" brunches brought to table by "friendly" folks; however, "the moon doesn't shine brightly" for a handful of heretics who complain of "mediocre food" and "scattered service."

Barney's Gourmet Hamburger 🅛🅢🅜⌀   17 | 10 | 12 | $14
1591 Solano Ave. (Tacoma Ave.), Berkeley, 510-526-8185
1600 Shattuck Ave. (Cedar St.), Berkeley, 510-849-2827
5819 College Ave. (Chabot Rd.), Oakland, 510-601-0444
4162 Piedmont Ave. (Linda Ave.), Oakland, 510-655-7180
See review in San Francisco Directory.

Battambang 🅛🅜   ▽ 21 | 11 | 17 | $17
850 Broadway (9th St.), Oakland, 510-839-8815
■ This modest Oakland "favorite" doling out "delicate but full-flavored" Cambodian cuisine "has got to be the number one bargain" in town, according to admirers who enthuse equally about the "great appetizers" ("the pineapple-coconut soup is quite a find"), "delicious entrees" and "must" desserts; at these prices, there are "no complaints."

Bay Wolf 🅛🅢🅜   25 | 21 | 23 | $40
3853 Piedmont Ave. (Rio Vista Ave.), Oakland, 510-655-6004
■ "Wonderful Piedmont Avenue staple" (housed in a converted Victorian) that's "still great after all these years" with its "well-done marriage" of "warmly welcoming" service and Michael Wild's "beautifully presented" Cal-Med menu focusing on "fresh" ingredients, which prompts fans to refer to it as the "Chez Panisse Cafe of Oakland"; despite howls about "small portions" and "high prices", almost "everyone would want this in their neighborhood."

Bette's Oceanview Diner 🄻🅂🄼   21 15 16 $17
1807 Fourth St. (Hearst Ave.), Berkeley, 510-644-3230
■ "There's no ocean view", but there is a Bette and boy is she "fabulous" at whipping up "mega portions" of "yummy soufflé pancakes" and other "terrific" breakfast treats at this "funky, fun" "institution" on Berkeley's Fourth Street; "lines are long on weekends", but you can always "skip the wait" and sample the "take-out options next door"; P.S. there's "no dinner" at this diner.

Bighorn Grill 🄻🅂🄼   ▽ 15 17 16 $33
2410 San Ramon Valley Blvd. (Crow Canyon Rd.), San Ramon, 925-838-5678
☑ "Bring an appetite" because "hearty portions" of meat are the hallmark of this Pat Kuleto–designed steakhouse in San Ramon; cinema-goers say it's a "great stop after the movies", but many more carnivores counter it "should be horned out of town" based on beefs about "inconsistent food and service."

Bistro Viola 🅂🄼   18 16 17 $33
1428 San Pablo Ave. (Page St.), Berkeley, 510-528-5030
☑ With its "challenging menu" of Cal-French specialties and "lovely little touches", this "great newcomer" to the somewhat "sketchy" San Pablo dining scene of Berkeley is a "valiant effort" to bring "a bit of the big city across the bridge"; however, doubters feel it's "trying too hard to be haute" and is "too expensive for the location"; N.B. Danny Cohen has taken over the stoves from opening chef Mark Zeitouni.

Blackhawk Grille 🄻🅂🄼   20 21 19 $38
Blackhawk Plaza, 3540 Blackhawk Plaza Circle (Camino Tassajara), Danville, 925-736-4295
☑ If "grand" water views float your boat, this "beautiful", "trendy" Danville Cal-Med attracting a "very upper-crust clientele" is the place to be; a revolving door of chefs means that the "innovative" fare can be "unpredictable", but most find the "patio by the lagoon" a "lovely setting for lunch" before or after touring the nearby Behring Auto Museum; N.B. the 7,000-bottle wine collection may be worth more than the vintage cars.

Blue Nile 🄻🅂   18 14 14 $16
2525 Telegraph Ave. (Dwight Way), Berkeley, 510-540-6777
■ Surveyors in search of a "different dining experience" head to this "hole-in-the-wall" Berkeley Ethiopian where guests scoop up "flavorful" family-style "finger food" with pieces of "good" spongy bread; it's "dark and a little shabby" and the "service is slow", but wallet-watchers say it's "so cheap, who cares?"

Brazio 🅛🅢🅜   ▽ 18 | 20 | 16 | $41
*Blackhawk Plaza, 3421 Blackhawk Plaza Circle
(Camino Tassajara), Danville, 925-736-3000*
■ Peripatetic chef-owner Fred Halpert (whose burgeoning restaurant empire includes two wine country restaurants, Brava Terrace and Live Fire, plus a second location of the latter in SF) has brought his predilection for playing with fire to this Danville Tuscan steakhouse with two lovely terraces overlooking a man-made waterfall; despite early buzz for the stylish newcomer, voters are curiously mum on its progress, beyond reports of "no one on the floor is trained."

Breads of India 🅛🅢🅜⊉   22 | 9 | 15 | $18
*2448 Sacramento St. (Dwight Way), Berkeley,
510-848-7684*
☑ Customers confess they "die from hunger smelling and watching the yummy breads go by" while they endure the inevitable "long wait" (no reservations) at this "tiny" Berkeley storefront serving "intense, well-layered curries" and other "scrumptious" Indian specialties from a "daily-changing menu"; critics can't get past the "bare-bones decor", "communal seating" and "hurried" service, but they're in the minority.

Bridges Restaurant 🅢🅜   23 | 24 | 21 | $44
44 Church St. (Hartz Ave.), Danville, 925-820-7200
☑ "Upscale" patrons "sit on the charming patio" and enjoy the "soothing atmosphere" and "imaginative", "well-prepared" food served at this "beautiful", "romantic", "expensive" Danville Cal-Asian immortalized in *Mrs. Doubtfire*; only a few have their doubts, feeling it's "all style but little substance" and resting on its big-screen "laurels."

Britt-Marie's 🅛🅢⊉   18 | 16 | 18 | $23
*1369 Solano Ave. (bet. Carmel & Ramma Aves.), Albany,
510-527-1314*
■ "Cozy European" cafe and wine bar in Albany that "feels like home" to admirers who appreciate the "funky" "old-world atmosphere", "friendly" service and "ample helpings" of "remarkably good" globe-trotting comfort food at "reasonable prices"; "if only they'd take reservations."

Bucci's 🅛🅜   19 | 18 | 17 | $28
*6121 Hollis St. (bet. 59th & 61st Sts.), Emeryville,
510-547-4725*
■ This "high-energy" "'in' spot and power scene in the up-and-coming Emeryville district" draws the "heavy hitters" from nearby dot-com businesses with its "very good pizzas", "wonderful" Mediterranean standards and "friendly staff"; although it's been around long before the high-tech industry moved in, the "warehouse setting" seems like the "perfect fit for the district."

Cactus Taqueria 🄻🅂🄼   19   11   13 $11
1881 Solano Ave. (The Alameda), Berkeley, 510-528-1881
5525 College Ave. (Shafter Ave.), Oakland, 510-547-1305
■ "Fresh and healthy" "no-frills" taquerias in Berkeley and
Oakland that are "notches above" the "heavy Mexican"
competition, earning olés for the "tastiest tamales", "best
burritos ever" and "crispy tacos [that] can't be beat"; a
few enemigos find it "a little pricey" for fast food, but
most maintain it's ideal for a "meal on the go" or "to go."

Cafe de la Paz 🄻🅂🄼   19   15   16 $21
1600 Shattuck Ave. (Cedar St.), Berkeley, 510-843-0662
■ There's a "great variety" of "unusual and interesting"
Spanish/Latin American tapas – ranging from Venezuelan
corn cakes to "Guatemalan tamales like *mamita's*" – at this
"warm, welcoming" café that got its start at Le Peña
Cultural Center and moved up the food chain to Berkeley's
Gourmet Ghetto; "service can be slow" (let's just call it
Latin time), so be sure to order a pitcher of the "excellent
sangria" or a bottle of Chilean wine to ease the wait.

Cafe 817 🄻🄼   ▽ 21   16   14 $14
817 Washington St. (bet. 8th & 9th Sts.), Oakland, 510-271-7965
■ A taste of Tuscany in Downtown Oakland may sound
like an oxymoron, but "charming" chef-owner "Sandro
Rossi's love for his native cuisine permeates" this "truly
classy" Northern Italian serving "wonderful" breakfasts
and lunches including "excellent sandwiches" and "terrific
coffee to boot" (no pun intended) in a "very European"
atmosphere; the only downside – it's not open for dinner.

Cafe Fanny 🄻🅂🄼   22   13   14 $16
1603 San Pablo Ave. (Cedar St.), Berkeley, 510-524-5447
■ "Part of the Berkeley triumvirate", flanked by Acme
Bread and Kermit Lynch Wine Merchant, Alice Waters'
"tiny" New French is the "perfect stand-up or take-out
breakfast and lunch" place, proffering "crêpes to die for",
"yummy granola", the "best latte anywhere" and other
"pricey" items prepared with the same organic ingredients
as the mother ship, Chez Panisse; "seating is limited to a
few tables in the parking lot", giving a whole new meaning
to the term tailgate party.

Cafe Rouge 🄻🅂🄼   19   18   18 $32
*1782 Fourth St. (bet. Hearst Ave. & Virginia St.), Berkeley,
510-525-1440*
☑ With an in-house meat market and charcuterie, this "way
cool" French bistro on "vibrant" Fourth Street is a "meat
lover's paradise" ("how un-Berkeley!") where Francophiles,
shoppers and "hip folks" come to "sit at the big zinc bar" and
"pretend to be in France" over "great steak frites" and
freshly shucked oysters; but there are cynics who say it's
"too expensive" for "good but not exciting" food and
"hit-or-miss service."

California Cafe 🄻🅂🄼   20 | 18 | 20 | $31
1540 N. California Blvd. (bet. Bonanza St. & Civic Dr.),
Walnut Creek, 925-938-9977

■ "Newly remodeled" "chain of reliably good restaurants"
serving "high-quality California cuisine" in strategic
locations near some of the Bay Area's toniest malls, making
it "always a solid choice" for "doing lunch while shopping";
surveyors see it mostly as a "backup, not a destination point."

Cambodiana 🄻🅂   ▽ 19 | 13 | 19 | $22
2156 University Ave. (bet. Oxford St. & Shattuck Ave.),
Berkeley, 510-843-4630

■ "A real find!" rave reviewers of this "charming",
"unassuming" "little place" in Berkeley with a "lovely
staff" serving "wonderful, unique" Cambodian specialties
including "superb" marinated and grilled lamb chops;
it's especially "handy" after a performance at the nearby
Zellerbach or Berkeley Rep.

Casa Orinda 🅂🄼   19 | 18 | 18 | $31
20 Bryant Way (Moraga Way), Orinda, 925-254-2981

■ "Lots of regulars" return again and again to this "original
gathering place" in Orinda for the "outstanding fried
chicken", "fun Western decor" (you "must see the gun
collection") and "very friendly" service; the kitchen also
whips up "ample" portions of other American "comfort
food" like steak.

César 🅂🄼   20 | 20 | 18 | $27
1515 Shattuck Ave. (bet. Cedar & Vine Sts.), Berkeley,
510-883-0222

■ A "limited menu" of "excellent tapas" ("addictive fried
potatoes", "splendid salt cod") is paired with an "amazing"
250-plus wine and spirits list at this "hip", "lively" Spaniard
run by alums of neighbor Chez Panisse, securing it as
"Berkeley's best and only bar for grown-ups" and one of
the few places to dine that's "open late."

Cha Am Thai 🄻🄼   19 | 12 | 15 | $19
1543 Shattuck Ave. (Cedar St.), Berkeley, 510-848-9664
See review in San Francisco Directory.

CHEESEBOARD 🄻⊄   27 | 11 | 19 | $11
1504 Shattuck Ave. (Vine St.), Berkeley, 510-549-3055

■ Okay, we admit it, this "wonderful" Berkeley "cheese
mecca"/bakery is "not a restaurant per se", but food lovers
unite over this "worker-owned" "collective" offering
"heavenly" "specialty pizzas that change daily" and an
"amazing array of cheeses" and breads ("the best baguette
in the world"); so "grab a slab of cheese and a crusty
roll" (or homemade English muffin) and discover one of
the East Bay's culinary secrets and the *Survey*'s No.1
Bang for the Buck.

CHEZ PANISSE Ⓜ   28 | 25 | 26 | $65 |
1517 Shattuck Ave. (bet. Cedar & Vine Sts.), Berkeley,
510-548-5525
■ Disciples of "the Church of Alice" Waters beat a path to
this "high altar of food" in Berkeley to "pay homage" to the
"reigning matriarch of California cuisine", savor the "simple"
yet "sublime" seasonal organic fare and be coddled by
"superb service"; some wonder "what's all the fuss?", but
they're drowned out by a choir of believers who vow "heaven
must be something like this"; P.S. the only potential downside
(aside from snagging reservations) is playing "prix fixe
roulette" – what they serve is what you get.

CHEZ PANISSE CAFE Ⓛ Ⓜ   27 | 23 | 24 | $41 |
1517 Shattuck Ave. (bet. Cedar & Vine Sts.), Berkeley,
510-548-5049
■ "There is nothing second class" about Alice Waters'
"relaxed and casual" upstairs cafe; followers feel it's "just
as good" but "a lot cheaper" than its downstairs "sister"
and appreciate the fact that it is "less intense", "easier to
get into" and offers "more choices" of "seasonally fresh"
Cal-Med cuisine (including a particularly noteworthy pizza);
N.B. the cafe now accepts reservations up to one month
in advance for lunch and dinner.

Christopher's Ⓛ Ⓢ Ⓜ   19 | 18 | 18 | $29 |
1501A Solano Ave. (Curtis St.), Albany,
510-525-1668
☑ After a long hiatus, fusion pioneer Christopher Cheung
is back behind the stoves at this "elegant" but "mercifully
unpretentious" "neighborhood restaurant" in Albany,
churning out "creative Californian cuisine" (laced with lots
of "sublime" Southwestern and Asian spices) in a bi-level
dining room with "high ceilings" and a "spacious" feel;
although skeptics say the "inventive menu" is "hit or miss",
most maintain "it works."

Citron Ⓢ Ⓜ   24 | 20 | 22 | $43 |
5484 College Ave. (bet. Lawton & Taft Aves.), Oakland,
510-653-5484
■ Change is a constant at this "hip" Oakland Regional French
featuring a new "small but tantalizing" menu every two to
four weeks; despite the ephemeral nature of the lineup, chef
Chris Rossi manages to execute "consistent" – "sometimes
brilliant" – creations "that make your taste buds sing";
"attentive service", a "wonderful" patio and "one of the
best wine lists in the Bay area" round out the experience.

Crepevine Ⓛ Ⓢ Ⓜ ⊄   15 | 11 | 11 | $13 |
5600 College Ave. (Ocean View Dr.), Oakland,
510-658-2026
See review in San Francisco Directory.

Doña Tomás　　▽　22　18　19　$28
*5004 Telegraph Ave. (bet. 49th & 51st Sts.), Oakland,
510-450-0522*

■ This "little treasure" in North Oakland "makes you realize that Mexican can be one of the great world cuisines" according to surveyors who've sampled the "fabulous, juicy *carnitas*", "magical margaritas" and other "addictive" items on the "daring menu"; the "staff is a little shell shocked", but most amigos nominate it for "rookie of the year."

FatApple's 🅛🅢🅜　　18　13　16　$17
*7525 Fairmount Ave. (Colusa Ave.), El Cerrito, 510-528-3433
1346 Martin Luther King Jr. Way (Rose St.), Berkeley,
510-526-2260*

■ These "reasonably priced", all-American "neighborhood gathering places" plastered with Jack London photos and serving (what else?) "mile-high" apple pie, "outstanding burgers" and "large portions" of other "mom-style" "comfort food" also attract long lines of families and coeds for their "great breakfasts" and homemade baked goods.

Faz 🅛🅢🅜　　18　17　17　$29
*600 Hartz Ave. (School St.), Danville, 925-838-1320
5121 Hopyard Rd. (bet. Gibraltar & Owens Drs.), Pleasanton,
510-460-0444*
See review in San Francisco Directory.

Garibaldis on College 🅛🅢🅜　　22　20　21　$36
*5356 College Ave. (bet. Clifton & Hudson Sts.), Oakland,
510-595-4000*
See review in San Francisco Directory.

Ginger Island 🅛🅢🅜　　17　17　16　$27
*1820 Fourth St. (bet. Cedar St. & Hearst Ave.), Berkeley,
510-644-0444*

◪ Everyone finds the menu "interesting" at this ginger-accented New American on Berkeley's Fourth Street, but diners are divided on everything else: "very good creative cuisine" and "friendly staff" vs. "inconsistent food" and "spotty service"; best bet: "stick with the baby-back ribs" and "homemade ginger ale" "for lunch while shopping."

Gira Polli 🅢　　19　13　16　$21
1616 N. Main St. (Civic Way), Walnut Creek, 925-945-1616
See review in San Francisco Directory.

Hotel Mac 🅛🅢🅜　　18　20　20　$34
50 Washington Ave. (Park Pl.), Point Richmond, 510-233-0576

■ "Funky little hotel" dining room, set in a "rather historic spot in Point Richmond", serving "always delicious", "reasonably priced" Continental "basics" such as rack of lamb and "creamed spinach that has spoiled every future creamed spinach elsewhere"; but it's the "inviting interiors", "friendly" service and "spectacular monthly wine dinners" that "make it memorable."

Il Fornaio 🇱🇸🇲　　19　21　19　$31
1430 Mt. Diablo Blvd. (bet. Broadway & Main St.), Walnut Creek,
925-296-0100
See review in San Francisco Directory.

Il Porcellino 🇱🇸🇲　　▽　16　15　17　$28
6111 La Salle Ave. (bet. Moraga Ave. & Mountain Blvd.),
Oakland, 510-339-2149
◪ A statue similar to the famous good luck pig of Florence
(from which Il Porcellino gets its name) greets guests at
the entranceway of this Northern Italian in Oakland's tony
Montclair district; locals label the food "hit or miss, mostly
hit", but the service is "friendly" and it's "nice for the nabe."

Isobune Sushi 🇱🇸🇲　　18　14　15　$23
5897 College Ave. (south of Chabot Rd.), Oakland, 510-601-1424
See review in San Francisco Directory.

Italian Colors 🇱🇸🇲　　18　18　18　$29
2220 Mountain Blvd. (bet. Park Blvd. & Snake Rd.),
Oakland, 510-482-8094
Jack London Sq., 101 Broadway (Embarcadero W.),
Oakland, 510-267-0412
■ "Relaxed neighborhood dining" duo that's a "favorite
weekly eatery" for Oaklanders who welcome the "large
portions" of "consistently good" Cal-Italian fare, "soothing
atmosphere" and "nice service"; N.B. the Jack London
Square location is new.

Jade Villa 🇱🇸🇲　　17　10　12　$19
800 Broadway (bet. 8th & 9th Sts.), Oakland, 510-839-1688
◪ "Forget dinner and do dim sum" urge enthusiasts of this
Oakland Chinese where it's "mobbed and noisy", and the food
is served with a side order of "attitude", but the reward
is a "dizzying" number of "tasty" (if "a bit greasy") tidbits
"priced right"; some say it's "disappointing", but that doesn't
deter devotees who consider it the "best in the East Bay."

Jimmy Bean's 🇱🇸🇲　　17　10　13　$17
1290 Sixth St. (Gilman St.), Berkeley, 510-528-3435
■ This "casual" "industrial-zone hangout" in an otherwise
"depressing part" of Berkeley (run by the owners of the
fancier Lalime's) is "not much to look at", but the "wonderful
salads, pizzas, quesadillas" and other "moderately priced"
Californian standards are "popular" for breakfast and
lunch; "too bad they closed for dinner."

Jojo　　–　–　–　M
3859 Piedmont Ave. (Rio Vista), Oakland, 510-985-3003
Homey, bite-sized bistro in Oakland that has all the right
ingredients to become a neighborhood staple: a small but
carefully constructed country French menu that changes
according to the market, and enticing desserts prepared
by co-owner and ex Chez Panisse pastry chef Mary Jo
Thoresen in the dining room's open kitchen.

Jordan's L S M ▽ 19 | 22 | 20 | $45

*Claremont Resort, 41 Tunnel Rd. (Claremont Ave.),
Berkeley, 510-549-8510*

■ Situated in Berkeley's chic Claremont Resort, this hotel
Californian with "a spectacular view", "professional service"
and "some inspirational dishes" is "improved" thanks to a
remodel and new chef; it's many East Bayers "secret place."

Juan's Place L S M 19 | 12 | 15 | $16

941 Carleton St. (9th St.), Berkeley, 510-845-6904

■ "It feels like you've been transported to Mexico when you
step in the door" of this "festive", "old-school" "dive" (we're
talking "lot's o' lard"); in reality, it's a Berkeley "institution"
bustling with "Cal students, families and all sorts of people
from all over the East Bay" who come for the "huge portions"
at "cheap prices"; better still, it's so "unpretentious you
can go in grubby clothes and no one cares."

Kirala L S M 26 | 15 | 17 | $29

2100 Ward St. (Shattuck Ave.), Berkeley, 510-549-3486

■ "Unbeatably the best Japanese food in the East Bay" –
"fantastic robata" and "superfresh sushi" – can be found
at this "king of the grill" in Berkeley; the inevitable result is
"devastatingly long lines" (despite a recent expansion),
although the majority maintains it's "worth the wait"; some
have just "one word" on the subject: "reservations" – "they
should take them"; P.S. there's now a "cool bar" pouring
more than 20 premium sakes from Japan.

Koryo Wooden ▽ 23 | 10 | 12 | $21
Charcoal BBQ ❂ L S M

4390 Telegraph Ave. (Shattuck Ave.), Oakland, 510-652-6007

■ "Forget Brother's in San Francisco – this is by far the
best Korean BBQ place outside of Korea and LA" insist Seoul
food lovers who've discovered this "bustling" cook-it-
yourself joint in Oakland that also happens to serve a
mean bibimbop (vegetable dish); just remember to "wear
clothes you can wash the smokiness out of" and "bring a
skilled barbecuer to avoid looking foolish."

Lalime's S M 25 | 20 | 23 | $39

*1329 Gilman St. (bet. Neilson St. & Peralta Ave.), Berkeley,
510-527-9838*

■ Dubbed the "insider's Chez Panisse" by admirers, this
"romantic" North Berkeley Med-Eclectic set in a converted
white stucco house has a "cult following" for its "ever-
changing menu" of "creative", "intelligently prepared" fare;
penny-pinchers report the "amazing" "prix fixe is pricier
than before", "but the food and wine are always tops."

La Mediterranée L S M 18 | 14 | 17 | $19

2936 College Ave. (Ashby Ave.), Berkeley, 510-540-7773
See review in San Francisco Directory.

La Note 🛱🆂🅼
20 | 20 | 16 | $21

*2377 Shattuck Ave. (bet. Channing Way & Durant Ave.),
Berkeley, 510-843-1535*

■ "*Très charmant*", "casual" French bistro in Downtown Berkeley that woos aficionados with its "delicious evocations of France", including "authentically Provençal breakfast and lunch items" (don't miss the jumbo-sized salad Niçoise) and "hurried" Gallic service; "expect a nice wait for weekend brunch" and, if it's warm enough, request a table on the "lovely garden" patio; N.B. dinner is served on Friday and Saturday only.

Lark Creek 🛱🆂🅼
22 | 21 | 21 | $38

1360 Locust St. (Mt. Diablo Blvd.), Walnut Creek, 925-256-1234

☑ "California-fresh" twists on "very good basic American fare" ("famous garlic-mashed potatoes", "where else can you get meat loaf like this?") are the signature of this "popular" East Bay outpost of Bradley Ogden's Lark Creek Inn; but there are dissenters who declare that it "doesn't hold a candle to the original in Marin"; N.B. there's also a branch in the South Bay.

Le Cheval 🛱🆂🅼
22 | 15 | 16 | $22

1007 Clay St. (10th St.), Oakland, 510-763-8495

■ You'll find a "dizzying" array of "not too expensive" choices (and have a "50/50 chance of getting help" to sort it all out) at this Vietnamese "gold mine" in Oakland; despite the "noise", "chaos" and "waits" in the "massive" dining room, the "diverse crowd" says the "magnificent flavors and aromas that make your mouth sing" are "worth it."

Long Life Noodle Co. 🛱🆂🅼
13 | 12 | 11 | $16

2261 Shattuck Ave. (Kittredge St.), Berkeley, 510-548-8083

See review in San Francisco Directory.

Long Life Vegi House 🛱🆂🅼
13 | 8 | 12 | $13

*2129 University Ave. (Shattuck Ave.), Berkeley,
510-845-6072*

☑ "All sorts of odd people" come to this veggie house near UC Berkeley for the "cheap" prices on "big portions" of the "healthiest Chinese food in the area", with an emphasis on "faux meat and fish dishes"; although the "atmosphere is nil", that hasn't prevented this "real scene" from enjoying a long life (more than 25 years).

Mama's Royal Cafe 🛱🆂🅼⊅
20 | 14 | 14 | $16

4012 Broadway (40th St.), Oakland, 510-547-7600

■ "Wowza!" exclaim enthusiasts of this "Bay Area breakfast legend" in Oakland whipping up "omelets like no one makes" and the "best hollandaise bar none"; sure, there's a "huge wait on weekends" and, man, the "service is slow", but die-hard fans of this "funky" retro coffee shop ("don't miss the napkin art contest") predict "you'll wish she were your mama"; N.B. no dinner.

Max's Opera Café ⏢⬛Ⓜ | 16 | 15 | 16 | $22 |
1676 N. California Blvd. (bet. Civic Dr. & Cole Ave.),
Walnut Creek, 925-932-3434
See review in San Francisco Directory.

Mazzini Trattoria ⏢⬛Ⓜ | 21 | 20 | 19 | $35 |
2826 Telegraph Ave. (bet. Oregon & Stuart Sts.), Berkeley,
510-848-5599
◪ "A Tuscan oasis in Berkeley", this trattoria serving
"excellent Italian fare" ("try the fish stew") in a "stylish"
setting "with rich wood and good lighting" is the "new rising
star" of the area (it's "already hard to get a reservation");
however, the service gets mixed reviews – from "staff is
impeccable and thoughtful" to "rushed" and "untrained";
N.B. it's owned by Alice Waters' brother-in-law Jim Maser.

Mezze ⬛ | – | – | – | M |
3407 Lakeshore Ave. (Hwy. 580), Oakland, 510-663-2500
The Pan-Mediterranean dining trend has crossed the
bridge and is alive and cooking at this charming Oakland
newcomer; the diverse flavors of Italy and North Africa
emerge from the restaurant's open kitchen, in the guise of
meze and large plates.

Nan Yang Rockridge ⏢⬛ | 21 | 15 | 18 | $22 |
6048 College Ave. (Claremont Ave.), Oakland, 510-655-3298
■ Aficionados "adore this remarkably friendly", "very
original" Oakland ethnic eatery; after all, "how often do you
get to go Burmese?"; even foodies who "have never tasted
anything like this" develop a habit for the "excellent garlic
noodles" and "green tea salad"; while the flavors can be
"a revelation", the decor is best described as "plain."

Nizza La Bella ⬛Ⓜ | – | – | – | M |
825-827 San Pablo Ave. (Solano Ave.), Albany, 510-526-2552
La Côte d'Azur meets Albany at this stylish new bistro/
pizzeria featuring the sunny French and Italian flavors that
characterize *bella* Nice; there's a grand zinc-topped bar
and sidewalk seating, and while the wine list is limited to
French and Italian vintages, it's organized by varietals for
us California folk.

North Beach Pizza ◗⏢⬛Ⓜ | 18 | 9 | 13 | $16 |
1598 University Ave. (California St.), Berkeley, 510-849-9800
See review in San Francisco Directory.

Oak Town Cafe ⏢Ⓜ | ▽ 17 | 17 | 17 | $27 |
499 Ninth St. (Washington St.), Oakland, 510-763-4999
■ This "bright newcomer" sits in the epicenter of Jerry
Brown's effort to revitalize Downtown Oakland in a converted
120-year-old historic building; the kitchen turns out "simple
but well-prepared" American-Mediterranean fare, much
of it coming from the wood-fired oven; the few reviewers
who've discovered this "sleeper" say it "needs and is
worthy of encouragement."

Obelisque 🄢 | 16 | 16 | 17 | $38 |
5421 College Ave. (Hudson St.), Oakland, 510-923-9691
🄳 Oakland contender in restaurant-laden Rockridge that has a lot going for it – "interesting New French cuisine", "warm" mahogany decor "matched by an equally warm staff" and a "quiet atmosphere."

O Chamé 🄛🄼 | 22 | 21 | 19 | $28 |
1830 Fourth St. (Hearst Ave.), Berkeley, 510-841-8783
🄼 Surveyors seeking "Zen and the art of Japanese cuisine" head to this "unique", "beautiful", "minimalist" "treat" in Berkeley serving "simple but excellent food" in "serene surroundings"; it's "pancake paradise" for some and "noodle nirvana" for others trying to re-create a *Tampopo* experience with the "enormous bowls of broth."

OLIVETO | 24 | 21 | 21 | $45 |
CAFE & RESTAURANT 🄛🄢🄼
5655 College Ave. (Shafter Ave.), Oakland, 510-547-5356
🄳 "The subtle flavors of Tuscany come to life" at "master chef" Paul Bertolli's "outstanding" Oakland trattoria where he presents "extraordinary, rustic" Northern Italian fare in "spartan surroundings"; while many feel it's as "good as anything in Italy", critics complain the portions are "too small" for the "high prices"; perhaps they should try the more casual, moderately priced cafe downstairs.

Pasta Pomodoro 🄛🄢🄼 | 15 | 12 | 15 | $16 |
5500 College Ave. (Lawton Ave.), Oakland, 510-923-0900
See review in San Francisco Directory.

Phuping Thai Cuisine 🄛🄢🄼 ▽ | 19 | 17 | 18 | $21 |
Pacific East Mall, 3288 Pierce St. (Central Ave.), Richmond, 510-558-3242
🄼 "Great Thai comes to Richmond" thanks to the owners of Thep Phanom in SF, who launched this sib in the Pacific East Mall; fans are lapping up their brand of "well-prepared" "tasty stuff" and, despite the sterile location, find the restaurant "comfortable" and the service "friendly."

Piatti 🄛🄢🄼 | 18 | 19 | 18 | $32 |
100 Sycamore Valley Rd. W. (San Ramon Valley Blvd.), Danville, 925-838-2082
See review in North of San Francisco Directory.

Picante Cocina Mexicana 🄛🄢🄼 | 20 | 13 | 14 | $14 |
1328 Sixth St. (bet. Camelia & Gilman Sts.), Berkeley, 510-525-3121
🄼 Alice Waters' brother-in-law Jim Maser "does it again" at this "great little taqueria" "hidden" in the "warehousey Gilman Street district" in Berkeley; the "healthy", "high-quality food" (including tortillas made fresh daily) at "affordable" prices "draws quite a crowd" – especially "noisy families" that aren't fazed by the "no-nonsense service" and "cafeteria-like" interior.

Pizza Rustica L S M   19 | 11 | 13 | $17
5422 College Ave. (bet. Kales & Manila Aves.), Oakland,
510-654-1601

■ "Wonderfully fennel-y sausage pizza" and "innovative
vegetarian choices" (such as soy cheese) are the raison
d'être at this "easygoing" Oaklander that respondents
report is "more romantic than your average pizza place" and
also doles out "nice salads and great chicken"; although
some say the pies are "a little pricey", they "always go back."

Plearn Thai Cuisine L S M   19 | 13 | 16 | $19
2050 University Ave. (bet. Milvia St. & Shattuck Ave.),
Berkeley, 510-841-2148

☑ Diners are divided on this "standby" Berkeley Thai with
"hole-in-the-wall decor": advocates have "never been
disappointed after many visits", praising the "best pad Thai
in the East Bay", while the opposing camp has "never
understood why it's popular" and insists the food and
service have "headed south"; regardless, this "student
mecca" still offers the "best Thai lunch near UCB."

Postino S M   21 | 23 | 20 | $43
3565 Mt. Diablo Blvd. (Oak Hill Rd.), Lafayette, 925-299-8700

☑ Everyone "loves the decor" at this "charming" Northern
Italian in a "beautiful building" in Lafayette; while a few feel
the "food doesn't quite match" at this "wanna-be Tra Vigne
in the 'burbs"; most maintain that it's an "East Bay gem."

Prima L S M   21 | 21 | 20 | $39
1522 N. Main St. (bet. Bonanza & Lincoln Sts.), Walnut Creek,
925-935-7780

■ A "stunning" 1,600-plus label wine cellar and special
wine-tasting menus are the big draws at this "festive" (read:
"noisy") Northern Italian in Walnut Creek; voters assert that
the recent remodel, which enlarged the bar area, has made
it "better than ever" and are relieved to find the "food is
catching up to the wine list", thanks to the appointment of
a new chef.

Pyramid Alehouse L S M   12 | 15 | 12 | $19
901 Gilman St. (bet. 7th & 8th Sts.), Berkeley, 510-528-9880

☑ "It's fun to look at the equipment" at this "cool" Berkeley
brewpub, according to foam fans who confess they go for
the "great microbrews", not the "dismal" "bar food"; just
remember to "bring your hearing aid" ("what did you say?").

Red Tractor Cafe L S M   15 | 14 | 14 | $14
5634 College Ave. (bet. Keith Ave. & Ocean View Dr.),
Oakland, 510-595-3500

☑ "Cute" counter-service Oakland American that dishes up
"fast-and-filling" "comfort food"; "one of the best values
for the bucks", it's a "great place to take the kids" (the color-
it-yourself tractor placemats are an effective distraction),
even if cynics say the home cooking tastes "mass produced."

Restaurant Peony ⬛🅂🅼   19 | 15 | 13 | $25
Pacific Renaissance Plaza, 388 Ninth St. (bet. Franklin & Webster Sts.), Oakland, 510-286-8866
■ It's "noisy" and "crowded" and the service can be "a bit slapdash considering the expense", but that's the price you pay for the "best dim sum" in town according to admirers of this 400-seat "upscale" Cantonese in Downtown Oakland's Chinatown; it's also known for its "good presentation of high-quality" dinners, including Peking duck.

Rick & Ann's ⬛🅂🅼   21 | 16 | 17 | $19
2922 Domingo Ave. (bet. Ashby & Claremont Aves.), Berkeley, 510-649-8538
■ Vying for "best breakfast in the East Bay" status, this "quaint" Berkeley American that feels "like you're on a farm in Vermont" spawns "crazy waits" on weekends for its "unbelievably heavenly" omelets, pancakes and other "homestyle food" "like you wish your mom knew how to cook"; just "get there early" ("before the boomers") or at the very least "before you're hungry" – it's "worth the wait."

Rivoli 🅂🅼   26 | 21 | 23 | $39
1539 Solano Ave. (bet. Neilson St. & Peralta Ave.), Berkeley, 510-526-2542
■ This husband-and-wife-run Cal-Mediterranean is the "best-kept secret in Berkeley" whisper insiders who insist Wendy Brucker's "beautiful dishes" (try the "best portobello fritters") are "as delicious as anything in San Francisco"; add to that "a cooperative, generous staff" that "helps navigate the wine list" and a "lovely garden view" where you can "watch cats and raccoons" frolic "while you dine", and you end up "as close to perfection as a neighborhood restaurant can get."

Rue de Main ⬛🅼   ∇ 18 | 19 | 21 | $39
22622 Main St. (bet. B & C Sts.), Hayward, 510-537-0812
☑ "Wonderful murals", "dark ambiance" and a staff that "treats diners like royalty" win over traditionalists at this "surprise find" in Hayward serving "nicely prepared French dishes"; critics, however, claim this old-school haunt "is not what it used to be."

Salute Ristorante ⬛🅂🅼   19 | 22 | 19 | $31
Marina Bay, 1900 Esplanade Dr. (Melville Sq.), Richmond, 510-215-0803
☑ "Excellent views" of the harbor and San Francisco "make up for the ordinary food" offered at this "comfortable" Point Richmond Italian overlooking the marina; "friendly service" and "decent prices" are added bonuses; P.S. surveyors say the North Bay location, which lacks a view, is "getting better."

Santa Fe Bar & Grill 🅛🅢🅜   20 | 19 | 19 | $35
1310 University Ave. (bet. Acton & Chestnut Sts.),
Berkeley, 510-841-4740
☑ Downtown Berkeley "landmark" located in a former
Santa Fe Railroad station that serves "surprisingly good"
Californian food; despite a plethora of chef and ownership
changes over the years, the "awesome ambiance", "nice
jazz" and "great service" have remained constant draws.

Saul's Restaurant &   16 | 13 | 14 | $16
Delicatessen 🅛🅢🅜
1475 Shattuck Ave. (bet. Rose & Vine Sts.), Berkeley,
510-848-3354
☑ Matzo ball mavens and expats "from the five boroughs"
come to this "New York–style deli" in Berkeley when
they're "nostalgic for Jewish food" such as "mouth-filling
pastrami sandwiches", "good chicken soup" and "free
bowls of pickles"; dissenters insist "it's far from the real
thing", however, and kvetch that the eats have "taken a
long dive" since the recent expansion.

Scott's 🅛🅢🅜   18 | 17 | 17 | $34
2 Broadway (Embarcadero W.), Oakland, 510-444-3456
1333 N. California Blvd. (Mt. Diablo Blvd.), Walnut Creek,
925-934-1300
See review in San Francisco Directory.

Shen Hua 🅛🅢🅜   21 | 19 | 14 | $22
2914 College Ave. (bet. Ashby Ave. & Russell St.),
Berkeley, 510-883-1777
☑ "Very good" "off-the-beaten-track dishes" bathed in
"delectable sauces" and served in "an elegant modern
setting" are reasons to go to this "interesting" Chinese in
Berkeley's Elmwood district – and the "grumpy", "frantic
service" are reasons to go the "take-out" route.

Skates on the Bay 🅛🅢🅜   17 | 21 | 17 | $32
100 Seawall Dr. (University Ave.), Berkeley, 510-549-1900
■ "Go for the view, stay for the view" smirk samplers of this
Berkeley American, the area's "favorite" "setting for out-
of-town guests to ogle" the Bay Bridge, San Francisco Bay
and Golden Gate Bridge ("especially at sunset"); many
pony up the cash for the "overpriced" but "great drink
selection" and sit in the bar, skipping the "so-so seafood."

Soizic 🅛🅢   22 | 19 | 20 | $32
300 Broadway (3rd St.), Oakland, 510-251-8100
■ This "funky" Oakland bistro near Jack London Square, run
by a painter-turned-chef, has a heavy artistic slant, which
reveals itself in everything from the "Paris-meets-industrial-
chic" warehouse space to the "imaginative", "tasty" Cal-
French cuisine; the "rough neighborhood" notwithstanding,
it's a real "pearl for food and service" and, as a result,
"becoming more well-known and crowded."

Spenger's L S M
12 | 16 | 12 | $30

1919 Fourth St. (bet. Hearst & University Aves.), Berkeley, 570-845-7771
■ Nostalgists were relieved to see this "historic" "Berkeley institution" – a cavernous seafood shack crammed with kitschy shipwreck paraphernalia – "saved"; however, everyone seems "disappointed" with the "reincarnation": old-timers insist the remodel "has sucked out its soul", while modernists maintain the "upgrade in decor did not upgrade the food"; yet "it continues to be packed."

Spettro L S M
18 | 14 | 19 | $21

3359 Lakeshore Ave. (Mandana Blvd.), Oakland, 510-465-8320
■ An "inconsistent but daring" mishmash of Asian/Italian/ Mexican, with coconut-lime mussels sharing the menu with peanut-butter pizza, is the signature of this "noisy", "oddly charming neighborhood place" on Oakland's Lakeshore Avenue; the staff, "which is amazingly flexible with substitutions", is "friendly and casual" and assuages the "Gen X crowd" waiting on the "long lines" (no reservations) with Dixie cups of red wine.

Spiedini L S M
21 | 20 | 20 | $37

101 Ygnacio Valley Rd. (Oakland Blvd.), Walnut Creek, 925-939-2100
■ "Walnut Creek goes uptown and it works" confirm fans of this "consistent" Italian trattoria that's "excellent in every way except for the noise"; the smitten, especially fond of the "good grilled meats" and "pleasant atmosphere", admit "I want to keep it a secret, but it's too good."

Tachibana L S M
21 | 15 | 15 | $26

5812 College Ave. (bet. Birch Ct. & Chabot Rd.), Oakland, 510-654-3668
■ The wasabi contingent nominates this "friendly" Oaklander for "best sushi bar in the East Bay", but other admirers contend that it "covers all the bases of Japanese cuisine", including some very fine yakitori, "out-of-this-world soups" and "lots of sake selections"; the only flaw seems to be the pokey staff – "I got faster downloads of a gigabyte file @14.4k than service there."

Taiwan L S M
19 | 7 | 12 | $16

2071 University Ave. (Shattuck Ave.), Berkeley, 510-845-1456
See review in San Francisco Directory.

Thornhill Cafe L S
▽ 20 | 18 | 20 | $34

5761 Thornhill Dr. (Grisborne Ave.), Oakland, 510-339-0646
◪ Enthusiasts of this "elegant yet laid-back" Oakland French say it's a "culinary gem" with "wonderful creative food" and "beyond gracious service", but critics contend that it's a former neighborhood standby that's no longer "booming" and call the cooking merely "acceptable"; so it will have to be your call on this thorny matter.

Townhouse Bar & Grill L M   20 | 17 | 18 | $30
5862 Doyle St. (bet. 59th & Powell Sts.), Emeryville, 510-652-6151
■ A "good bar scene", "varied" but "reliable" New American menu and "nice patio" make this Emeryville "neighborhood joint" with a "rustic Northern California feel" "popular with locals" and a "tried-and-true" choice for "long business lunches."

Triple Rock Brewery L S M   12 | 12 | 12 | $16
1920 Shattuck Ave. (bet. Hearst & University Aves.), Berkeley, 510-843-2739
☑ Recently remodeled Berkeley hangout that was a "microbrewery before it was a fad"; it's a "must for all graduate students" who want to hang out, play shuffleboard, "watch sports" on the big screen or simply "relax with a beer on the roof deck"; less-than-stellar scores aside, some concede the "tasty array of sandwiches" and "interesting appetizers" "stand up to the liquid offerings."

Tropix L S M   ▽ 18 | 17 | 17 | $19
3814 Piedmont Ave. (MacArthur Blvd.), Oakland, 510-653-2444
■ This "quirky", "friendly" Caribbean-Creole "neighborhood place" serving up "great food" in a "cozy" space with "brightly painted rooms" may reside in Oakland, but islander-dreamers say "sitting on the patio you could be in a little cafe in Jamaica."

Uzen L M   24 | 17 | 18 | $28
5415 College Ave. (bet. Hudson St. & Kales Ave.), Oakland, 510-654-7753
■ Zealots "can't stop going back" to this "excellent" Oakland Japanese offering "sushi that makes you swoon for more" ("the most delicate and purest I've seen") and "warming bowls of udon" in a refreshingly "quiet" atmosphere; service is "friendly", the "lunch deals are great" and there's "almost always a seat" – all of which adds up to a "nice little place."

Venezia L S M   19 | 20 | 18 | $27
1799 University Ave. (Grant St.), Berkeley, 510-849-4681
■ The "clever" Venetian "piazza" decor, replete with "laundry hanging overhead from clotheslines", creates a "fun" ambiance at this "busy" Berkeley Italian serving "fabulous pastas" and "superbly executed fish" at "fair prices"; too bad you can't "bring your own laundry to hang up on the wall" while you wait for a table.

Vic Stewart's L S M   21 | 22 | 19 | $44
850 S. Broadway (bet. Mt. Diablo Blvd. & Newell Ave.), Walnut Creek, 925-943-5666
☑ Local carnivores claim this "true steakhouse" with "dark" railroad-motif decor in Walnut Creek is "the place to go in the East Bay for beef", scalloped potatoes ("a must") and other "above-average" American standards; unfortunately, the "expensive" tariff can derail the experience.

Vi's L S M ⊄   22 | 10 | 17 | $15
724 Webster St. (bet. 7th & 8th Sts.), Oakland, 510-835-8375
■ "Huge bowls" of "flavorful duck soup" and "Vietnamese noodles" at "rock-bottom prices" are the hallmark of this "Hanoi-style" hole-in-the-wall in Oakland's Chinatown; although the decor rating suggests otherwise, insiders say there are "amazing black-and-white photographs on the walls"; N.B. closed Thursday.

Voulez-Vous L S M   ▽ 14 | 16 | 15 | $22
2930 College Ave. (Ashby Ave.), Berkeley, 510-548-4708
☑ A relative newcomer to the restaurant scene in Berkeley's Elmwood district, this "very affordable, very French" brasserie wins points for its "authentic" bistro fare (such as "great" steak frites and dessert crêpes) and "live music during dinner", but a minority of critics gripes that the "loud" jazz "makes conversation difficult" and the kitchen "often runs out" of menu items; your call, mon ami.

Wente Vineyards L S M   24 | 26 | 23 | $44
5050 Arroyo Rd. (Wetmore Rd.), Livermore, 925-456-2450
■ "Outstanding Californian cuisine" (the "smoked pork chop will keep you coming back") served by a "well-trained staff" combines with "beautiful vineyard views", "perfect alfresco" dining and (naturally) a "great wine list" to make a jaunt to this "comfortably chic winery" restaurant in Livermore a "special" "day trip from San Francisco"; it's "well worth the drive" – "go!"

Xanadu L S M   18 | 21 | 17 | $33
700 University Ave. (4th St.), Berkeley, 510-548-7880
☑ George Chen's (of Betelnut, Long Life Noodle, Shanghai 1930 and Dragonfly fame) "eccentric" restaurant concept – relying on herbs and spices to provide not only flavor but also medicinal benefits to the Pan-Asian cuisine – seems perfectly suited to Berkeley, but it "doesn't quite deliver on the hype"; adherents adore the "beautiful decor" and suggest the "kitchen needs the same consistency."

Yoshi's at
Jack London Square L S M   17 | 19 | 17 | $32
510 Embarcadero W. (Washington St.), Oakland, 510-238-9200
☑ The "unorthodox yet fun combination" of a "world-class jazz club" and sushi bar may have played well at its original location, but since this "basic Japanese" moved to Jack London Square, many customers confess they mainly dine here "to get good seats at the 10 PM shows"; some raw fish fans, however, maintain the food "is better than it has to be" and the "hurried service" does a "decent job of getting diners to the shows on time."

Zachary's Chicago Pizza L S M ⌐ | 23 | 10 | 14 | $16 |
5801 College Ave. (Chabot Rd.), Oakland, 510-655-6385
1853 Solano Ave. (The Alameda), Berkeley, 510-525-5950
■ Dishing up "the best stuffed pizza this side of Chicago" (some argue "in the universe"), these "wildly popular" Italian twins inspire fierce loyalty from pie partisans; yes, prices are "a little on the steep side for pizza", but "it doesn't win all those awards for nothing"; if you're not willing to "brave the crowds" and "long waits for a seat", "call ahead" and "get it to go."

Zza's Trattoria L S M | 16 | 13 | 16 | $21 |
552 Grand Ave. (bet. Euclid Ave. & MacArthur Blvd.), Oakland, 510-839-9124
☑ "Take the kids" to this "friendly, noisy, affordable" Italian in Oakland (across the street from Lake Merritt); both the food and the space are "simple" and "adequate", but you "can show off your artistic skills on the tablecloths."

North of San Francisco

Acre Cafe & Lounge S⊟   ▽ 19 20 18 $30
420 Center St. (bet. North & Piper Sts.), Healdsburg,
707-431-1302
■ Small and "homey", this "newcomer on the Healdsburg
food scene" has impressed reviewers with its "clever"
Eclectic menu featuring what the owners call 'Sonoma
Kitchen Garden Cuisine' (i.e. local organic food); they also
offer "excellent wines", which should wash away any slights
from the "quirky service."

Albion River Inn S M   23 24 23 $42
3790 Hwy. 1 N., Albion, 707-937-1919
■ The "picture-postcard location" would make this
"romantic" hotel dining room "worth it alone for the
[ocean] view", but as it happens, the American coastal
"food's as good as the setting"; add in "excellent service"
and the "best wine list North of St. Helena" and the result
is a "great destination when in Mendocino."

Alfy's L S   – – – M
636 San Anselmo Ave. (Bridge St.), San Anselmo,
415-453-3407
This small town Contemporary French has big city culinary
ambitions, and considering the chef (ex 231 Ellsworth) and
manager's (ex Masa's) pedigrees, they should be able to
realize them; boasting one of San Anselmo's prettiest
outdoor patios with views of Mt. Tamalpais in the distance,
the newcomer is as long on ambiance as it is on talent.

Alta Mira L S M   14 22 17 $34
Alta Mira Hotel, 125 Bulkley Ave. (bet. Bridgeway &
Princess St.), Sausalito, 415-332-1350
■ At this Sausalito Californian-Continental, the "food is
forgettable, but sitting outside with that [Bay] view isn't";
surveyors recommend you "go for Sunday brunch on the
deck" – "a SF tradition since 1927" – but "nothing else."

Applewood Inn & Restaurant   ▽ 22 21 22 $39
13555 Hwy. 116 (Mays Canyon Rd.), Guerneville,
707-869-9093
■ Most reviewers discover this New French when they stay
at this Mediterranean-like resort near Guerneville, but with
its "fine" food and "friendly staff", the "beautiful" dining
room is becoming a "special-occasion" venue on its own.

Ara Wan Thai L S M   ▽ 21 | 17 | 18 | $25
47 Caledonia St. (Pine St.), Sausalito, 415-332-0882
■ Locals and pad Thai lovers flock to this "friendly neighborhood place" – the only Siamese in Sausalito – for "polite service" and must-have musamun curry; admittedly, it "isn't the best in the Bay Area, but it's great for Marin."

AUBERGE DU SOLEIL L S M   25 | 28 | 25 | $58
Auberge du Soleil Inn, 180 Rutherford Hill Rd. (Silverado Trail), Rutherford, 707-967-3111
■ It's just "a joy to be" at this "romantic" Rutherford "destination restaurant" where everything is "stunning": the "beautiful view of the Napa Valley" ("remember to request outdoor seating"), the "fabulous" French-Med fare ("just put your finger anywhere on the menu"), the vino selection (the "best list in California for American wines") and the "pleasant staff"; N.B. new chef Richard Reddington (ex Chapeau!) is expected to maintain the same high standards.

Avenue Grill S M   19 | 16 | 18 | $32
44 E. Blithedale Ave. (Sunnyside Ave.), Mill Valley, 415-388-6003
◪ "Hectic but happy", this "Mill Valley Californian combines hearty food with a party atmosphere" and a heaping "side order of noise"; while many find it's "fun", others feel it's "expensive" for an "extraordinarily ordinary" experience.

Bistro Don Giovanni L S M   24 | 22 | 22 | $40
4110 St. Helena Hwy./Hwy. 29 (bet. Oak Knoll & Salvador Aves.), Napa, 707-224-3300
■ Conveniently located at the "gateway to Napa Valley", Donna and Giovanni Scala's "loud but jolly" trattoria is a "must stop" before or "after hitting the wineries" for its "rustic Italian" cuisine (the fritto misto's a fave); despite a high-ceilinged, "handsome [dining] room", the place to be is on the "lovely patio" with its garden and vineyard views.

BISTRO JEANTY L S M   26 | 22 | 23 | $41
6510 Washington St. (Yount St.), Yountville, 707-944-0103
■ "Philippe Jeanty works his magic and the crowds come and come" at this "welcoming", "laid-back", Provençal bistro in Yountville, which serves "incredibly delicious" country French classics at relatively "reasonable" prices; followers insist "forget the fancy places" because this is one very "convincing" "slice of France" "and the place in Napa Valley to come back to."

Bistro Ralph L S M   23 | 17 | 21 | $38
109 Plaza St. (Healdsburg Ave.), Healdsburg, 707-433-1380
◪ Although Ralph Tingle's "cozy, dependable Sonoma find" is always filled with Healdsburg locals, many out-of-towners find it "fun to sit at the counter", order a specialty martini then dine on the "consistently excellent" New American cuisine ("go for the chicken liver appetizer!"), which showcases "fresh local ingredients."

Boonville Hotel 🆂🅼 21 ┃ 19 ┃ 20 ┃ $32 ┃
Hwy. 128 (Lambert Ln.), Boonville, 707-895-2210
◪ Chef-owner John Schmitt's "relaxed" Cal–New American in the beautifully restored historic Boonville Hotel surprises guests with its "short menu" of "very good", "unfussy" cuisine and "pretty", simple Shaker-style dining rooms; while you might not want to drive out to the boondocks for a meal, fans insist it's "a blessing on the way to Mendocino."

Bouchon ●🅻🆂🅼 23 ┃ 23 ┃ 21 ┃ $42 ┃
6534 Washington St. (Yount St.), Yountville, 707-944-8037
◪ "Don't feel bad if you can't get into the French Laundry" counsel the culinary police, because you can still experience some of Thomas Keller's magic at his French bistro up the street in Yountville; although the original general manager, Keller's brother Joseph, has left, the "gorgeous atmosphere" and "steak frites to die for" remain; however, critics of the "scene" complain that it's "overrated" with "cramped" seating and a noise level that "breaks the sound barrier."

Brannan's Grill 🅻🆂🅼 17 ┃ 20 ┃ 17 ┃ $37 ┃
1374 Lincoln Ave. (bet. Cedar & Washington Sts.), Calistoga, 707-942-2233
◪ A "real sleeper" in Calistoga for those looking for a "great" antique mahogany bar and a "hip and beautiful dining room" (Craftsman-style hardwood floors, a huge stone fireplace, hand-painted murals), this local hangout's New American food "doesn't always strike gold" but there are enough "interesting" dishes to warrant a meal.

Brava Terrace 🅻🆂🅼 19 ┃ 20 ┃ 19 ┃ $39 ┃
3010 St. Helena Hwy./Hwy. 29 (Lodi Ln.), St. Helena, 707-963-9300
◪ Fred Halpert's burgeoning restaurant empire, which now includes Livefire and Brazio, began with this St. Helena Cal outpost where diners can expect "wholesome, indigenous fare" and a "lovely" terrace that's an "absolute pleasure in the summer"; critics politely deem it "a good restaurant surrounded by great ones."

Brix 🅻🆂🅼 22 ┃ 23 ┃ 21 ┃ $42 ┃
7377 St. Helena Hwy./Hwy. 29 (Washington St.), Napa, 707-944-2749
■ "Yahoo!" exclaim "tourists and locals alike" after a meal at this Napa destination, which breaks the if-it's-wine-country-it-has-to-be-Mediterranean mold with "fabulous Asian fusion" cuisine matched by an equally "amazing" 450-label wine list; to make the most of the "incredible vineyard setting", be sure to "sit by the window" or, if weather permits, outside next to the "mesmerizing organic herb garden"; N.B. there's now a new maestro in the kitchen.

Bubba's Diner **L S M** | 21 | 15 | 17 | $20 |
566 San Anselmo Ave. (bet. Bridge & Magnolia Sts.),
San Anselmo, 415-459-6862

■ "Unpretentious" "down-home" American food in an
"upscale diner" format means permanent "crowds" at this
San Anselmo "hole-in-the-wall" famous for its "amazing
breakfasts" and legendary "fried chicken dinners"; however,
now that original chef Steve Simmons has moved on to
the Savanna Grill, locals are waiting to see how the new
chef will affect this Marin institution.

Buckeye Roadhouse **L S M** | 21 | 21 | 20 | $35 |
15 Shoreline Hwy./Hwy. 1 (west of Hwy. 101), Mill Valley,
415-331-2600

■ With a "grand old hunting lodge feel" and "convivial
watering-hole atmosphere", this Mill Valley Traditional
American attracts hipsters and yuppies who "drive up in
Beemers and Mercedes" for their fill of "finger-lickin' good
ribs", "to-die-for 'bingo' oysters" and "amazing burgers";
all in all, a "wonderful" end to a day of "hiking in Marin",
as long as you remember to reserve ahead.

Cactus Cafe **L S M** | 19 | 11 | 18 | $18 |
393 Miller Ave. (bet. Evergreen Ave. & LaGoma St.), Mill Valley,
415-388-8226

■ This Mill Valley taqueria "doesn't look like much but
boy" does it serve "fresh", "savory twists" on Mexican
and Tex-Mex grub shout modern-day cowboys; throw in
"friendly service" and you've got a winning "quick, cheap-
eats" option, handy before attending an event at the
Marin Theater Company or for takeout.

Cafe Beaujolais **L S M** | – | – | – | E |
961 Ukiah St. (bet. Evergreen & School Sts.), Mendocino,
707-937-5614

Changes are afoot at this "Mendocino gem", which
Margaret Fox put on the culinary map in 1977 with her
legendary New American breakfasts and later morphed
into an Eclectic dinner-only affair; in July 2000, Fox sold
the place, leaving the existing cooks and staff to carry on
the tradition, especially at the in-house bakery, which has
long been known for its "unforgettable breads."

Cafe Citti **L S M** | 19 | 11 | 15 | $22 |
9049 Sonoma Hwy./Hwy. 12 (Shaw Ave.), Kenwood,
707-833-2690

■ Dishing up "superb roasted chicken", "generous pasta
portions" and "garlicky Caesar salad", this "inexpensive"
Kenwood deli reminds Tuscan daydreamers of a "trattoria
in Italy"; the less romantic concede "there's no decor and
no service – you order at the counter" – but still consider
it a "cute, inexpensive place for a bite or takeout" in
swanky wine country.

Café La Haye S
25 | 17 | 22 | $35

140 E. Napa St. (bet. 1st & 2nd Sts.), Sonoma, 707-935-5994

■ How does the chef produce such "remarkable big flavors from such a tiny kitchen?" inquire adoring fans of this "unpretentious" Eclectic "favorite" in Sonoma, just off the town square; although the "charming" (read: "cramped") dining room might be "too cozy to be near so many wine snobs", there's nothing small-fry about "five-star food at three-star prices" or the "superb service."

Cafe Lolo L M
22 | 19 | 21 | $36

620 Fifth St. (bet. D St. & Mendocino Ave.), Santa Rosa, 707-576-7822

⊠ Locals insist this Cal-American haunt is the "top restaurant in Downtown Santa Rosa", so despite tables that are a "bit cramped", they return again and again for lunch and "business dinners" of "wonderfully fresh", "imaginative" food, a 200-label "killer wine list" and the "nicest staff."

California Cafe L S M
20 | 18 | 20 | $31

The Village, 1736 Redwood Hwy. (Paradise Dr.), Corte Madera, 415-924-2233

See review in East of San Francisco Directory.

Caprice, The S M
20 | 26 | 22 | $43

2000 Paradise Dr. (Mar West St.), Tiburon, 415-435-3400

⊠ Tiburon's "elegant" old standby boasts an "ethereal view of SF" that you can only get from outside the city; as ratings attest, the Cal-Continental cuisine doesn't quite reach the same heights, but "gracious" service and "romantic lighting" (especially at sunset) more than compensate.

Catahoula
Restaurant & Saloon S M
23 | 19 | 20 | $39

Mount View Hotel, 1457 Lincoln Ave. (bet. Fair Way & Washington St.), Calistoga, 707-942-2275

■ "After a mudbath" "leave the diet at the spa and check into full flavor" at Jan Birnbaum's American Calistoga outpost, which pays homage to the South with "creative, lighter Cajun food" (including "soulful", "spicy dishes" "hotter than the wood-fired oven") and photos of the famed Louisiana state dog, from whence the restaurant gets its name; P.S. this is a "fun place to sit at the counter."

Celadon L M
24 | 19 | 22 | $33

1040 Main St. (bet. 1st & Pearl Sts.), Napa, 707-254-9690

■ The love child of owner Greg Cole ("the most underrated chef in the Bay Area"), this "comfortable" Napa "secret" spot serves a "superb", albeit "limited", menu of Internationally influenced American cuisine; despite the down Valley address, the "caring" "waiters are way uptown" in "attentiveness", another reason why this is one "perfect neighborhood restaurant" that's "definitely worth the search", even if "the locals wish you hadn't."

Charcuterie L S M ▽ 21 | 16 | 19 | $32
335 Healdsburg Ave. (Plaza St.), Healdsburg, 707-431-7213
◼ If you're into the three little pigs, then you'll be in hog heaven at this little Healdsburg French bistro/charcuterie, which boasts a vast porcine collection made out of every imaginable material ranging from porcelain to resin; while there's only one pork dish on the menu, that doesn't mean you can't pig out with the portions ("go hungry").

CHATEAU SOUVERAIN CAFE AT THE WINERY L S M 23 | 27 | 21 | $37
400 Souverain Rd. (Hwy. 101, Independence Ln. exit), Geyserville, 707-433-3141
◼ For the ultimate wine-country experience, why not dine on the premises of a winery, as you can at this gorgeous Geyserville respite; expect solid Cal-French cuisine, a stunning dining room with a large fireplace, vaulted ceiling and view; savvy surveyors add that there's "nothing better than lunch on the patio during harvest" while drinking a bottle from the Chateau Souverain–dominated wine list.

Christophe S 22 | 19 | 22 | $32
1919 Bridgeway (Spring St.), Sausalito, 415-332-9244
◼ Dining at this "perfect-size" Sausalito bistro is like taking a "step back in time to good, basic" Gallic fare and "lower prices", specifically "early-bird specials" and "prix fixe menus" that are a "huge bargain"; moreover, the notion of "friendly French is not an oxymoron" here.

Cin Cin S ▽ 21 | 17 | 19 | $36
1440 Lincoln Ave. (Fair Way & Washington St.), Calistoga, 707-942-1008
◼ Run by alums of the girl & the fig, this "pleasant" Calistoga newcomer is a "terrific" Mediterranean bistro that impresses residents with its local organic fare, although nobody is toasting the "sparse" interior.

Cole's Chop House S – | – | – | E
1122 Main St. (bet. 1st & Pearl Sts.), Napa, 707-224-6328
Wine-country chef-restaurateur Greg Cole (owner of the nearby Celadon) shows his chops at this new Napa steakhouse, which features prime dry-aged steaks, the usual side-order suspects (creamed spinach, Caesar salad) and meaty, high-end California Cabs.

Cucina Jackson Fillmore S 22 | 18 | 20 | $34
337 San Anselmo Ave. (bet. Pine St. & Woodland Ave.), San Anselmo, 415-454-2942
◼ This boisterous spin-off of the popular SF trattoria is a "welcome addition" to the "restaurant wasteland" of "quaint" San Anselmo; although claustrophobics complain "there's too much togetherness" and the noise level is as explosive as Vesuvius, pasta lovers line up for "memorable down-home" Central and Southern Italian dishes.

Della Santina's L S M   20   18   19 $32
133 E. Napa St. (1st St.), Sonoma, 707-935-0576
■ "North Beach moves North" declare pasta fanatics and fans of the "good standard Northern Italian fare" found at this "unpretentious" Sonoma "standby" where the grilled meats rate as high as the "seasoned staff."

Deuce L S M   21   19   21 $36
691 Broadway (Andrieux St.), Sonoma, 707-933-3823
■ Breaking the monotony of "too many Italian" eateries in the Sonoma Plaza area, this American bistro in an old farmhouse features a menu with "something for everyone"; it's "what Sonoma is supposed to be" – a "comfortable" place where "mom and pop do fine dining" on a pleasant patio.

Dipsea Cafe, The L S M   17   15   16 $19
200 Shoreline Hwy./Hwy. 1 (Tennessee Valley Rd.), Mill Valley, 415-381-0298
☑ Overlooking a tidal inlet , this "hip" Mill Valley American diner is "very popular with locals" ("you sometimes see George Lucas") for its "satisfying portions" of "homey, basic" fare, especially at breakfast; phobes note the "terribly long waits" (no reservations) and ask "for what? I don't get it."

DOMAINE CHANDON L S M   26   26   25 $53
1 California Dr. (Hwy. 29), Yountville, 707-944-2892
■ "One of the greatest restaurant's in the Valley", this "pricey" "classic" on the "beautiful grounds" of the namesake Napa winery gets one big "wow" from surveyors for its "heaven-on-the-tongue" Cal-French fare, "staff that makes you feel like royalty" and "elegant", glass-walled interior overlooking a terrace; keep it in mind for that "special occasion" when you want a taste of "timeless quality."

Downtown   24   13   17 $13
Bakery & Creamery S M ⊄
308A Center St. (Matheson St.), Healdsburg, 707-431-2719
■ Wine tasters and day-trippers in the know "never go to Healdsburg without a stop" at this "fab-smelling" bakery known for "the world's best sticky buns"; pastries are half-off Monday–Thursday after 4:30 PM, and their products are also available at the SF Ferry Plaza Farmers' Market on Saturday.

Dragonfly   ▽   15   19   17 $28
Cafe & Jazz Bar L S M
Village at Corte Madera, 1546 Redwood Hwy. (Hwy. 101, Paradise Dr. exit), Corte Madera, 415-927-8889
■ Despite a snazzy look and "live jazz" Wednesday–Sunday night, surveyors "expected more from the experienced backers" (George Chen of Long Life Noodle, et al) of this "sophisticated oasis" in a Corte Madera strip mall; shortly after opening, the kitchen jettisoned its Asian-fusion fare for Chinese cuisine, which may assuage critics who feel they "spent all the money on the decor and forgot about the food."

Duck Club S M   20 20 20 $39
*Bodega Bay Lodge, 103 Coast Hwy. (Doran Beach exit),
Bodega, 707-875-3525*
See review in South of San Francisco Directory.

El Paseo S   23 25 24 $45
*17 Throckmorton Ave. (bet. E. Blithedale & Miller Aves.),
Mill Valley, 415-388-0741*
■ If Marinites were "giving out prizes for the most romantic
spot", this "intimate" Mill Valley "classic" would "definitely
win"; despite its "Spanish name" (and German owners), the
"very good" food is French, though the "awesome wine
list", with its "wonderful selection" of "older, less-known"
labels, makes space for California vintages.

Emporio Rulli L S M   26 25 20 $18
*464 Magnolia Ave. (bet. Cane & Ward Sts.), Larkspur,
415-924-7478*
■ After a cup of "great coffee" and a bite of the "peerless
panettone", "European wanna-bes" will think they've "died
and gone to Italy", but they'll simply be at this "real Italian
bakery" in Larkspur brimming with "cute, cute, cute", "old-
world atmosphere" and "fabulous" gelato, sandwiches
and homemade pastries; "a must stop when in Marin."

Feast L M   ▽ 22 16 20 $31
*98 Old Courthouse Sq. (bet. 4th St. & Mendocino Ave.),
Santa Rosa, 707-591-9800*
■ News hasn't traveled far or fast about this high-ceilinged,
celadon-colored Eclectic-American bistro overlooking the
courthouse square in Santa Rosa, but the few and the proud
who have discovered it call it an "excellent newcomer"
that's "sure to be a future hit", despite its "cramped quarters."

Felix & Louie's L S M   14 15 14 $31
106 Matheson St. (Healdsburg Ave.), Healdsburg, 707-433-6966
◪ Ralph Tingle's more casual Italian-American sib to his
nearby Bistro Ralph is called long on "homey atmosphere",
but short on culinary panache ("good, but not remarkable")
and service ("where's our waitress?"); still even comparison
shoppers who "can't believe Ralph owns it" talk up the
"great patio" and "extensive take-out possibilities."

Filou S   24 17 22 $41
*198 Sir Francis Drake Blvd. (Tunstead Ave.), San Anselmo,
415-256-2436*
■ This San Anselmo newcomer's "pleasant" staff serves
"excellent" Contemporary French fare prepared by chef-
owner Nikolaus Kaubisch, who cut his teeth at that daddy
of Gallic gastronomy, La Folie; the "intimate" setting makes
admirers feel like they're "dining at home with a gourmet
chef in their kitchen", though some find it's "a bit pricey"
for an "unadorned box of a room"; either way it may be
"the best restaurant in Marin county."

Foothill Cafe S　　　　24　14　19　$33
J&P Shopping Ctr., 2766 Old Sonoma Rd. (Foothill Blvd.),
Napa, 707-252-6178
☑ "Hidden" in a strip mall near the Napa outlet stores, this
California regional haunt wows locals with "outstanding
ribs" and oak-roasted fish; there's "no waiting area" and
the "small" room "can get crowded", which makes some
wonder: "aren't they doing well enough to move?"; P.S.
we're just going to ignore those residents who said "don't
tell the tourists about it."

Frantoio S M　　　　20　21　19　$36
152 Shoreline Hwy./Hwy. 1 (west of Hwy. 101), Mill Valley,
415-289-5777
☑ You'd never expect to find this "stylish", "trendy" Northern
Italian, replete with an active olive oil press, on the premises
of a "cavernous" former Howard Johnson's in Mill Valley,
but somehow the "cool" decor works; however, foodwise,
comments range from "unmemorable" to "well-crafted."

FRENCH LAUNDRY L S M　　29　27　27　VE
6640 Washington St. (Creek St.), Yountville, 707-944-2380
■ Once again voted No. 1 for Food in the *Survey*, and
moving up to No. 2 for Popularity and Service, Thomas
Keller's New American legend in Yountville is "more of an
event than a meal", from scoring reservations (doled out no
more or less than two months in advance) to "taking out a
mortgage" to pay for the "perfectly presented", "sublime"
tasting menu, delivered by an "impeccable" staff; an
"unforgettable experience", it may be "without equal in
the culinary firmament."

General's Daughter L S M　　20　23　21　$37
400 W. Spain St. (4th St.), Sonoma, 707-938-4004
■ "If you could eat the setting", this "elegant" Victorian
mansion-turned-Sonoma eatery would get high marks,
according to troop reports; unfortunately, the dispatches
also indicate that the "only-ok" Californian cuisine doesn't
"measure up to the decor" or to the "bright, cheery service";
still, there are worse fates than a "non-adventurous meal" in
"a wonderful country home."

Gira Polli S M　　　　19　13　16　$21
590 E. Blithedale Ave. (Camino Alto), Mill Valley, 415-383-6040
See review in San Francisco Directory.

girl & the fig, the S M　　22　19　21　$36
13690 Arnold Dr. (Warm Springs Rd.), Glen Ellen, 707-938-3634
■ This "laid-back country hangout" on "Glen Ellen's
restaurant row" showcases "interesting French bistro food
with character", but what really sets the "quaint" place
apart is its "unique" 'Rhône-Alone' wine list, consisting
exclusively of varietals made of the Rhône grape.

Glen Ellen Inn Restaurant ⑤Ⓜ   21 19 21 $36
13670 Arnold Dr. (Warm Springs Rd.), Glen Ellen, 707-996-6409
■ Make room at the inn for the "creative" Cal-Fusion cuisine prepared by the "darling couple that runs" this "romantic" Glen Ellen haunt; though it's "wonderful all-around", insiders recommend you "sit on the patio for the finest experience."

Gordon's Ⓛ⑤Ⓜ   23 18 19 $28
6770 Washington St. (Madison St.), Yountville, 707-944-8246
■ If you're not from Yountville, you might not know about this "locals' hangout" (more of a "diner than a restaurant"); while it whips up a "good, honest country" American breakfast or lunch every day, it's the "Friday night dinner that's a winner", and since it's only offered once a week, reservations are definitely recommended.

Green Valley Cafe Ⓛ   ▽ 19 14 19 $25
1310 Main St. (Hunt Ave.), St. Helena, 707-963-7088
■ "Simple, hearty Northern Italian food" makes this "casual and comfortable" St. Helena cafe a "local favorite" – and a well-kept secret; one reviewer reports: "I was told by a St. Helenan never to tell the tourists about this place" (sorry, but you just did).

Guaymas Ⓛ⑤Ⓜ   19 22 17 $29
5 Main St. (Tiburon Blvd.), Tiburon, 415-435-6300
☑ With a "view of the San Francisco skyline to die for", it's no wonder locals love to "wow out-of-towners" with a trip to this Tiburon spot that's practically "sitting on the dock of the bay"; but since the "beautiful setting" and fun "atmosphere overwhelm the ok Mexican fare", it's basically "best for its drinks and hors d'oeuvres" (just be sure to sit "outside or by the window").

Guernica ⑤Ⓜ   18 17 20 $31
2009 Bridgeway (Spring St.), Sausalito, 415-332-1512
■ There's "always a warm welcome from the affable chef-owner" of this "unpretentious" Sausalito spot, which after 25 years can be relied on for its "consistently good" classic French-Basque cuisine – especially the "fine paella."

Hana Japanese Ⓛ⑤   ▽ 26 18 22 $36
Doubletree Plaza, 101 Golf Course Dr. (Roberts Lake Rd.), Santa Rosa, 707-586-0270
■ "More people should know about" this "great" Japanese in Santa Rosa's Rhonert Park, which delights raw fish fans with an "astonishingly high quality" of "fresh, fresh, fresh" sushi and "fun maki", as well as a "huge sake list"; the credit goes to chef-owner Ken Tominaga, aka "the sashimi master of Sonoma" to his devoted subjects.

Heirloom Restaurant L S M ▽ 21 | 17 | 20 | $34
Sonoma Hotel, 110 W. Spain St. (1st St.), Sonoma, 707-939-6955
◪ Chef Michael Dotson is hoping to overcome this "jinxed corner" of the Sonoma Hotel with his "affordable" New American–French cuisine, but responses are mixed: while fans say "it's worthy of the big leagues" with its "careful service" and "nice outdoor patio", cons carp the food's "too fussy" and the wine list "needs repair."

Il Davide L S 20 | 18 | 19 | $31
901A St. (bet. 3rd & 4th Sts.), San Rafael, 415-454-8080
◪ A "handsome crowd" flocks to this "see-and-be-seen" spot in Downtown San Rafael, known for its "lively" (read: "noisy") ambiance; opinion is divided, however, over the Northern Italian fare: admirers say Michelangelo's "David himself would gladly lose an arm" for some of the specialties, while critics deem the food "lackluster" and "more expensive than comparable restaurants."

Il Fornaio L S M 19 | 21 | 19 | $31
Town Ctr., 222 Town Ctr., Corte Madera, 415-927-4400
See review in San Francisco Directory.

Insalata's Restaurant L S M 23 | 21 | 21 | $36
120 Sir Francis Drake Blvd. (Barber St.), San Anselmo, 415-457-7700
■ "Wonderful Cal-Med food in a simpatico setting" sums up this San Anselmo "scene" that "raises the bar for Marin County restaurants"; aside from the "fresh, creative" fare, fans are won by the "obvious [fact] that chef Heidi Krahling cares about her staff and customers"; N.B. don't leave without checking out the take-out section.

Jimtown Store L S M – | – | – | I
6706 State Hwy. 128 (1 mi. east of Russian River), Healdsburg, 707-433-1212
Situated among rolling vineyards and winding country roads, this kitschy Healdsburg American cafe/store is where insiders go to fuel up on breakfast pastries, haute salads, sandwiches or full box lunches before heading out for a day of Sonoma sightseeing; the shelves are also stocked with a whimsical selection of general store–style candies, toys and antiques.

Joe's Taco Lounge/Salsaria L S M 18 | 16 | 15 | $16
382 Miller Ave. (Montford Ave.), Mill Valley, 415-383-8164
■ "After a three-hour hike on Mt. Tam, nothing tastes better" than the "fresh Cal-Mex" at this "groovy, cheap" Mill Valley "dive" that "locals love"; sure, "service is minimal", but the experience is still "fun, tasty – and fast."

John Ash & Co. ⓁⓈⓂ 　 24 | 23 | 23 | $47
Vintners Inn, 4330 Barnes Rd. (River Rd.), Santa Rosa,
707-527-7687
■ This "pricey" Santa Rosa standby continues to be "worth every cent" surveyors say: its "creative" American regional fare, showcasing the "fresh, local ingredients" of Sonoma, is matched by "meticulous presentations", "great service" and a "beautiful setting (inside and out)"; no wonder it's a "favorite place to stop on the way to [or from] wine country."

Kasbah Moroccan Ⓢ 　 24 | 24 | 23 | $38
200 Merrydale Rd. (Willow St.), San Rafael, 415-472-6666
■ "Come to the Kasbah" – or at least to this "luxurious", carpeted facsimile: the "dreamy decor", "authentic" Moroccan fare (especially "excellent lamb dishes"), "gracefully courteous waiters" and "thrilling – not cheesy – belly dancers" all will make you feel "whisked away to another world" (though actually just to San Rafael).

Kenwood ⓁⓈ 　 23 | 21 | 22 | $40
9900 Sonoma Hwy./Hwy. 12 (Warm Springs Rd.),
Kenwood, 707-833-6326
■ To many reviewers, "this is California if any place is": "consistently fine" New French–American cuisine, "beautiful, classic presentation" and a chance "to sit outside, sipping a delicious selection of [local] wines"; though the "big priced, small portions" irritate a few, this Kenwood "retreat" is so nice that many locals sigh: "I should keep it a secret."

La Ginestra Ⓢ 　 18 | 12 | 18 | $24
127 Throckmorton Ave. (Miller Ave.), Mill Valley, 415-388-0224
■ This "good ole standby" in Mill Valley is a true "family-run restaurant for families", who stoically endure the "hectic service" and "terrible decor" to feast on the "rich" pizza and Southern Italian food ("homemade spinach-and-cheese ravioli – 'nuff said"); it's "still the same after 35 years – but who cares?"

Lark Creek Inn ⓁⓈⓂ 　 24 | 25 | 23 | $46
234 Magnolia Ave. (Madrone Ave.), Larkspur, 415-924-7766
■ Although Bradley Ogden has scattered his New American "comfort food" all around the Bay Area, his original Larkspur establishment – located in a "storybook" "Victorian home" – "maintains its well-earned reputation" as the "most elegant and delicious" place in Marin for "special occasions"; so, go on a lark and "dine under the redwoods on the patio" surveyors urge – "it doesn't get more adorable than this."

Las Camelias ⓁⓈⓂ 　 20 | 16 | 18 | $23
912 Lincoln Ave. (bet. 3rd & 4th Sts.), San Rafael, 415-453-5850
■ Reviewers moan for the "m-m-m-mole" and the rest of the "out-of-the-ordinary" food, presented with a "loving artistic touch" at this San Rafael Mexican; it's a casual *casa*, but "what it lacks in decor it makes up for in flavor" amigos say.

La Toque ●🅂　　25 | 23 | 26 | $74
1140 Rutherford Cross Rd. (Hwy. 29), Rutherford, 707-963-9770
■ "Wonderful tasting menus" showcase top toque Ken Frank's "superb" cooking at this New French, which surveyors claim is "almost as good as [its mighty neighbor] the French Laundry – and without the booking pains"; add in "very personable service" and the result is "a drop-dead dinner" in an "exquisitely romantic" Rutherford setting.

Le Bistro Cafe 🅂　　▽ 24 | 16 | 19 | $34
312 Petaluma Blvd. S. (bet. D & E Sts.), Petaluma, 707-762-8292
■ Though little-known outside the neighborhood, this French bistro is a "local Petaluma favorite"; the "lovely food" (prepared by a California Culinary Academy alum) and "hard-working staff" provide all-around "good value", especially for "intimate occasions."

Leford House 🅂　　▽ 23 | 23 | 23 | $42
3000 N. Highway 1, Albion, 707-937-0282
■ For a "perfect dinner on the coast", traveling gourmets head to this spot just south of Mendocino, where a multi-windowed dining room offers "gorgeous Pacific Ocean vistas" and "outstanding" Cal-Med fare with vegetarian options that some would "crawl up a mountain for"; try to time your visit to catch the "romantic sunset."

Left Bank 🅛🅢🅜　　21 | 21 | 19 | $37
507 Magnolia Ave. (Ward St.), Larkspur, 415-927-3331
■ "You'll swear you're in Paris" at this "fun and lively" French bistro, judging from its "authentic fare and authentic noise and attitude" to match; although the Larkspur locale "attracts an affluent Marin crowd", admirers point out it's a *très bonne* way of experiencing chef Roland Passot's (of SF's pricey La Folie) master touch at a "value price"; N.B. there's also a branch in Menlo Park.

Livefire
Grill & Smokehouse 🅛🅢🅜　　15 | 17 | 15 | $33
6518 Washington St. (Yount St.), Yountville, 707-944-1500
☑ Fred Halpert's (Brava Terrace, Brazio) American "barbecue place" in Yountville may use real wood to cook its food, but reviewers aren't terribly stoked about the results; while to some "fire + meat + wine = good life", to others "lousy food" plus "dismal atmosphere" plus "poor service" equals "big disappointment"; N.B. a San Francisco sib recently opened.

Lotus Cuisine of India 🅛🅢🅜　　▽ 19 | 15 | 19 | $23
704 Fourth St. (Tamalpais Ave.), San Rafael, 415-456-5808
■ "When the craving for good Indian food strikes", San Rafael *masala* mavens head for this newcomer, which offers dining under a retractable skylight; reviewers single out the "fresh lunch buffet", which will leave your stomach and wallet in happy shape.

Lucy's Cafe L S M ▽ 20 | 15 | 18 | $21
110 N. Main St. (Bodega Ave.), Sebastopol, 707-829-9713
■ "A haven in the kooky west Sonoma country town" of
Sebastopol, this "relaxed" Cal-Eclectic cafe scores with
"the best pizza for miles around", baked in a brick-oven
and topped with lots of local produce; there are "yummy"
organic soups and salads too.

MacCallum House S M ▽ 23 | 23 | 23 | $38
*MacCallum House Inn, 45020 Albion St. (Lansing St.),
Mendocino, 707-937-5763*
☑ "Another reason to visit Mendocino" say advocates of this
Californian, located in a Victorian house-turned-inn; while
most like the organically oriented menu, a vocal minority finds
the "fare fairly unoriginal"; even the critics, however, admit
the two firelit rooms provide a truly "beautiful atmosphere."

Madrona Manor S M 21 | 24 | 21 | $48
*Madrona Manor Hotel, 1001 Westside Rd. (W. Dry Creek Rd.),
Healdsburg, 707-433-4231*
☑ "Elegant" grounds and "breathtaking decor" (think
candlelit dinners) set this "serene" Healdsburg Victorian
inn apart from its more casual wine-country brethren; the
service can be "slow" and the New French–American fare
"inconsistent", but since it's such a "lovely setting", you'll
be tempted to "spend the night after dinner" anyway.

Manka's Inverness Lodge S M 25 | 25 | 22 | $47
30 Callendar Way (Argyle St.), Inverness, 415-669-1034
■ Surrounded by the Point Reyes Peninsula, this "romantic
getaway" – a 1917 Arts and Crafts–style hunting lodge –
offers an "awesome" American–Coastal Marin menu that's
"as gamey" as it gets and a "great" wine list; although the
sticker-shocked gripe that "prices are getting out of sight",
most still feel the place "makes a wonderful woodsy retreat."

Marin Joe's ◑ L S M 18 | 12 | 18 | $27
1585 Casa Buena Dr. (Tamalpais Dr.), Corte Madera, 415-924-2081
■ Drive your "'51 Plymouth" to this Corte Madera "classic"
that provides a "slice of old Marin" – from the "huge
portions" of "consistent" "old-school Italian" food to the
"servers that are fixtures"; you "don't go here for the
atmosphere", but the "huge local following" feels "it can't
be beat for grilled meat" at "honest prices."

MARIPOSA 26 | 20 | 23 | $43
275 Windsor River Rd. (Bell Rd.), Windsor, 707-838-0162
■ "Heaven near the highway" exclaim enthusiasts of this
"great newcomer" to Windsor (just south of Healdsburg)
set in an "tiny", "charming cottage"; husband-and-wife
team Raymond and Shawn Tang have won over locals with
their "inventive", "beautifully prepared" wine-country cuisine,
"warm and friendly service" and "good wine list", making
it a contender for "best new restaurant in Sonoma County."

Maya L S M   20 | 21 | 20 | $28
101 E. Napa St. (1st St.), Sonoma, 707-935-3500
■ "Fun", "interesting" Southern Mexican dishing up "delicious", "adventurous" Yucatan specialties and "excellent" hand-shaken margaritas in an "upbeat" dining room (with "great outdoor seating" as well); it's a "good addition" to the town of Sonoma.

Meadowood Grill L S M   22 | 23 | 22 | $42
Meadowood Resort, 900 Meadowood Ln. (bet. Howell Mtn. Rd. & Silverado Trail), St. Helena, 707-963-3646
■ The more casual (yet still pricey) dining option at this posh St. Helena resort and golf course "scores big points" for its "peaceful, serene" atmosphere, "unsurpassed" outdoor seating and Californian bistro fare that's "as fantastic as the surroundings"; surveyors say the "excellent country-club place" is a "perfect post-croquet gathering spot" and the "most pleasant luncheon [venue] in the Valley."

Meritage L S M   ▽ 20 | 19 | 19 | $36
522 Broadway (W. Napa St.), Sonoma, 707-938-9430
■ "A bright spot in the Sonoma fine dining" scene, according to oenophiles who've uncorked this "friendly" wine-oriented Northern Italian–New French that replaced the short-lived Freestyle; reviewers report "so far so good", calling the rookie a "welcome addition."

Mikayla at the Casa Madrona S M   22 | 26 | 22 | $41
Casa Madrona, 801 Bridgeway (El Monte Ln.), Sausalito, 415-331-5888
■ It doesn't get better than "Sunday brunch overlooking the Golden Gate and San Francisco Bay" swoon admirers of this "romantic" Californian in the Casa Madrona hotel tucked in the hills of Sausalito; no doubt the "fabulous view" is the major attraction here, but the kitchen produces "exciting, intense flavors" that stand up to the setting.

Mixx Restaurant L S M   22 | 19 | 21 | $36
Historic Railroad Sq., 135 Fourth St. (Davis St.), Santa Rosa, 707-573-1344
☑ The name of this Santa Rosa Med-Eclectic could easily refer to the mixed reaction of voters: adherents adore the "lovely old bar", "very good" Sonoma County–slanted wine list and "excellent desserts" ("the star here"), while the less impressed insist it's "not as good as everyone says"; still, it's a "comfortable, friendly" "local place" to discover.

Model Bakery L S   18 | 12 | 13 | $12
1357 Main St. (bet. Adams & Spring Sts.), St. Helena, 707-963-8192
■ This model bakery in Downtown St. Helena, specializing in artisanal breads and "great sweets", "can hold its own among giants for what it is" claims the carbo crowd; there are also "freshly prepared sandwiches" and "good pizza."

Moosse Cafe L S M   ▽ 20 | 18 | 20 | $29
Blue Heron Inn, 390 Kasten St. (Albion St.), Mendocino,
707-937-4323
■ It seems that the secret is out about this "understated"
Californian bistro that samplers swear is "better than the
'name' places in Mendocino", but still leverages that Mendo
charm with "lovely gardens", "homey atmosphere" and
"very good food and service."

Mucca S   – | – | – | M
Jack London Village, 14301 Arnold Dr. (north of Madrone Rd.,
off Sonoma Hwy.), Glen Ellen, 707-938-3451
The dynamic duo behind San Francisco's Globe, owners
Joseph Manzare and Mary Klingbell, have brought the cow
town of Glen Ellen their own 'mucca' (Italian for 'cow'); the
American menu revolves around meat, while the modest
wine list leans heavily toward local bottlings; set in a
restored historic grist mill, the newcomer also offers an
outdoor deck overlooking the lovely Sonoma Creek; N.B.
dinner only, Thursday–Saturday.

Mustards Grill L S M   24 | 19 | 21 | $37
7399 St. Helena Hwy./Hwy. 29 (Yount Mill Rd.), Napa,
707-944-2424
■ "Tourists" and "locals" "never tire" of Cindy Pawlcyn's
"electric" Napa New American, considered a "signature
of wine country"; although plebeians protest that "seating
is limited by local politics", even they admit the "outstanding"
fare ("they do magical things with a pork chop") is "worth
the aggravation"; N.B. reservations can be tough, but you
can eat at the "tiny bar" without them.

Napa Valley Grille L S M   21 | 20 | 20 | $36
Washington Sq., 6795 Washington St. (Madison St.),
Yountville, 707-944-8686
◪ Chef "Bob Hurley has a good thing going" at this
Yountville Californian – "great food and drink" combined
with "nicely redone" decor; a pocketful of wallet-watchers
grill it for being "pricey for what you get" and point out
there are "better choices" in the area, but most agree
that "lunch on the deck" is "lovely."

Napa Valley Wine Train L S M   18 | 25 | 20 | $52
1275 McKinstry St. (bet. 1st St. & Soscol Ave.), Napa,
707-253-2111
◪ Wining and dining your way through the Napa Valley at
40 miles per hour while glimpsing the passing vineyards is
the appeal of this "costly" Californian; scores suggest that
the "trip is more memorable than the food", particularly if
you're seated in the "delightful dome car", yet it's a "fun
way to spend a day" "with out-of-towners."

955 Ukiah ⑤Ⓜ ▽ | 23 | 21 | 22 | $37 |
955 Ukiah St. (Lansing St.), Mendocino, 707-937-1955
■ "Pleasant" French-American, hidden away on "a rustic Mendocino side street", featuring "sophisticated and well-presented food" and a great local wine list, both of which are a "good bang for the buck", prompting patrons to beg "please don't tell everyone about it."

Olema Inn Ⓛ⑤Ⓜ | 19 | 20 | 19 | $29 |
10000 Sir Francis Drake Blvd. (Hwy. 1), Olema, 415-663-9559
☑ "Surprise!" this "homey" Olema New American set in a "charming" bed-and-breakfast offers guests "on the way back from a hike" in Point Reyes a "quiet", "romantic" place for "better-than-average" food in a "beautiful setting"; "where else can you go" in these parts, anyway?

ONDINE ⑤Ⓜ | 25 | 27 | 23 | $56 |
558 Bridgeway (Princess Ave.), Sausalito, 415-331-1133
■ "A classic reborn" is the consensus on this Sausalito waterfront spot resuscitated by chef Seiji Wakabayashi's "highly sophisticated fusion of Eastern and Western cuisines" whose flavors and presentations are as "striking" as the "drop-dead views of San Francisco"; while a few find it "too expensive", fans warn "when word gets out about this place it will be difficult to get a reservation."

101 Main Bistro ⑤ ▽ | 22 | 20 | 22 | $31 |
101 S. Main St. (Bodega Ave.), Sebastopol, 707-829-3212
■ "You can bank on the duck" served at this "underrated" yet "outstanding" Sebastopol French bistro set in a 1907 bank building; the handful who've happened upon it call it a "foodie's delight" and a "gem" in a restaurant-bereft area.

Pasta Pomodoro Ⓛ⑤Ⓜ | 15 | 12 | 15 | $16 |
421 Third St. (Irving St.), San Rafael, 415-256-2401
See review in San Francisco Directory.

Pearl Ⓛ ▽ | 23 | 17 | 21 | $27 |
1339 Pearl St. (Franklin & Polk Sts.), Napa, 707-224-9161
■ This "small", "undiscovered treat" (dare we say pearl?) boasting a globe-trotting Eclectic menu is "where smart locals eat in the city of Napa", thanks to "great food", "good prices" and "comfort to spare" (the "patio is nice" too.)

Piatti Ⓛ⑤Ⓜ | 18 | 19 | 18 | $32 |
625 Redwood Hwy./Hwy. 101 (Seminary Dr. exit), Mill Valley, 415-380-2525 ◐
El Dorado Hotel, 405 First St. W. (Spain St.), Sonoma, 707-996-2351
6480 Washington St. (Oak Circle), Yountville, 707-944-2070
☑ "Pleasant Italian chain" proffering "consistently good" if "rarely ever great" food in "casual", "kid-friendly" settings; service can be "slow" and you may "not rush to return", but it's "priced right" and "one of the better chains out there."

Piazza D'Angelo L S M   18 | 19 | 18 | $31
22 Miller Ave. (Throckmorton Ave.), Mill Valley, 415-388-2000
☑ Arguably the "most happening restaurant in Mill Valley", this "chic" yet "reasonably priced" "neighborhood trattoria" attracts a "lively bar crowd" (read: "noise"), along with locals looking for "hearty portions" of "dependable" Italian dishes; critics claim the food is "mediocre" and "service can be a problem", but that hasn't prevented it from becoming "the scene" in Marin.

Pinot Blanc L S M   22 | 23 | 21 | $45
641 Main St. (Grayson St.), St. Helena, 707-963-6191
☑ Admirers of LA-based superchef Joachim Splichal's "gorgeous" St. Helena New French outpost report that the menu (under the supervision of Sean Knight) is "terrific" and "daring" at times, the "wine list rocks" and the outdoor patio is "the loveliest"; while casual customers consider it "too stuffy" and "dressy" "for the Valley", the "upscale" set says it's a "real sleeper."

PlumpJack Cafe L S M   25 | 21 | 23 | $45
PlumpJack Squaw Valley Inn, 1920 Squaw Valley Rd.,
Olympic Valley, 530-583-1576
See review in San Francisco Directory.

Ravenous L S ⊄   25 | 17 | 22 | $34
117 North St. (bet. Center & Healdsburg Sts.), Healdsburg,
707-431-1770
■ Located next door to the Raven Theater, this "tiny" "hangout" is the "best in Healdsburg – if you can get in"; "lucky locals" concede that the "space is tight and cramped" and the Californian-Eclectic menu is "limited" (albeit "fabulous"), but that just "adds to the experience"; N.B. closed Monday and Tuesday.

Restaurant at   24 | 24 | 24 | $54
Meadowood, The S M
Meadowood Resort, 900 Meadowood Ln. (bet. Howell
Mtn. Rd. & Silverado Trail), St. Helena, 707-963-3646
■ You don't have to be a golf pro to "delight" in the "innovative" wine-country cuisine and be coddled by the "excellent" service at this "gracious" resort dining room situated in a "beautiful, serene setting" – you just need to be prepared for the price; supporters say it's "worth a visit even if you're not staying at the Meadowood" – "sit on the deck", "relax" and "enjoy the food and the views."

Rice Table S   ▽ 18 | 16 | 19 | $28
1617 Fourth St. (G St.), San Rafael, 415-456-1808
■ While "not as good as being there", this "cozy" San Rafael cafe specializing in multicourse rice table dinners prepares the "best Indonesian food outside that country" and "the service couldn't be nicer" according to world travelers who've discovered it.

Ristorante Fabrizio ▮M　　20 | 16 | 19 | $30
455 Magnolia Ave. (Cane St.), Larkspur, 415-924-3332
■ Although "lost in the shadow of the Lark Creek Inn" for outsiders, "locals know" this "dependable" Larkspur Northern Italian is "a find" for "simple food" at "reasonable prices" and "personalized care" from owner Fabrizio; N.B. lobster lovers can indulge their cravings on Monday nights.

Robata Grill & Sushi ▮S▮　　20 | 16 | 17 | $28
591 Redwood Hwy./Hwy. 101 (Seminary Dr. exit), Mill Valley, 415-381-8400
■ As the name implies, both the cooked and the raw are doled out at this "fine" Mill Valley Japanese; fans of the former opt for the "great grilled" items from the open-fire robata, while afishionados of the latter lap up the "very good sushi"; both camps can end their meal with the not-so-authentic but luscious-sounding green tea brûlée.

Royal Thai ▮S▮　　22 | 16 | 19 | $23
610 Third St. (Irwin St.), San Rafael, 415-485-1074
■ "Still the best in Marin", "still a favorite" sum up reviewer reaction to this "authentic" San Rafael Thai (with a sib in the city) that "consistently gets it right" – from the "delicious" dishes to the "congenial" service and "bargain" prices.

Rutherford Grill ▮S▮　　20 | 19 | 20 | $31
1180 Rutherford Rd. (Hwy. 29), Rutherford, 707-963-1792
■ The "ample portions" of "good old-fashioned American food" ("ribs to die for") served at this "unpretentious" Rutherford steakhouse (a spin-off of the Houston's chain) win over "local" carnivores who consider it "a nice break from the oh-so-precious Napa dining scene"; it can be "too crowded" and the "no-reservations policy means long waits", yet (mostly) "everybody loves this place."

Salute Ristorante ▮S▮　　19 | 22 | 19 | $31
706 Third St. (Tamalpais Ave.), San Rafael, 415-453-7596
See review in East of San Francisco Directory.

Sam's Anchor Cafe ▮S▮　　13 | 19 | 14 | $24
27 Main St. (Tiburon Blvd.), Tiburon, 415-435-4527
☒ Boaters, "weekend athletes" and "tank tops" flock to this "funky", "wildly popular" American "watering hole" in Tiburon for the "best babe-watching in the Bay area"; "drinks on the deck in the sun" served by "friendly, scantily clad waitresses" are de rigueur, but "eat only if you must."

Sand Dollar ▮S▮　　▽ 13 | 13 | 14 | $21
3458 Shoreline Hwy./Hwy. 1 (Calle Del Mar), Stinson Beach, 415-868-0434
☒ Practically the "only game in town", this hangout survives on landlocked locals and day-trippers refueling "after a day at Stinson Beach"; while critics call the American fare "mediocre" and "overpriced" and the staff "spaced out", a recent change in ownership may draw a new line in the sand.

Santi L S M
_| − | − | − | M |_

21047 Geyserville Ave. (Hwy. 101), Geyserville, 707-857-1786
Former Jordan Winery chefs Thomas Oden and Franco Dunn jettisoned their cushy corporate gigs to open this new Italian trattoria situated in a historic building in Downtown Geyserville; the seasonally driven menu is informed by their extensive experience cooking in over 22 restaurants in Italy, and it focuses on hearty Northern specialties in the winter and Southern dishes in the warmer months.

Savanna Grill L S M
_| − | − | − | M |_

Marketplace, 55 Tamalvista Blvd. (Tamalpais Dr.), Corte Madera, 415-924-6774
Steve Simmons (longtime right-hand man of Bradley Ogden), who perfected his brand of down-home fare at Bubba's Diner, and his partner Steve Grant (ex SF's mc^2) have revamped the menu (giving it a Southern slant) and interior of this 14-year-old Pat Kuleto–designed American grill in Corte Madera; N.B. live jazz augments the mood on most nights.

Scoma's L S M
| 19 | 17 | 17 | $35 |

588 Bridgeway (Princess St.), Sausalito, 415-332-9551
See review in San Francisco Directory.

Sonoma Mission Inn Grille S M
| 22 | 20 | 20 | $43 |

Sonoma Mission Inn, 18140 Sonoma Hwy./Hwy. 12 (Boyes Blvd.), Sonoma, 707-939-2415
■ Although this "excellent", "upscale" Californian is located on the grounds of Sonoma's swank hotel and spa, the menu ranges from "healthy to binge fare"; "beautiful decor", "impeccable service" and a "great wine list" make it the "most formal dining in Sonoma Valley", so come expecting to shed some money along with those pounds.

Station House Cafe L S M
| 19 | 16 | 17 | $25 |

11180 Hwy. 1 (2nd St.), Point Reyes Station, 415-663-1515
■ A "great, reliable dining oasis in West Marin", this "very mellow" New American seafooder ("the oysters are a must!") is an "ideal destination after a Point Reyes hike"; it's "not fancy", but it's "affordable" and "loved by locals as well as weekenders" who welcome dining in the "beautiful garden" and listening to "live music" on weekends.

St. Orres S M ⧸
| 24 | 26 | 24 | $51 |

36601 S. Hwy. 1 (2 miles north of Gualala), Gualala, 707-884-3303
■ Visiting this "unique", "romantic" Mendocino County hotel and restaurant noted for its "fantastic" Russian Orthodox architecture is "like being transported to a foreign world" ("maybe it's what heaven is like"); while "the decor carries the day", chef Rosemary Campiformio's Californian "food with an attitude" (specializing in wild game and foraged mushrooms) is a close "match"; the circuitous trip to the "middle of nowhere" is "worth it", but do yourself a favor and book a room in the inn.

SUSHI RAN L S M   26 | 18 | 20 | $34
107 Caledonia St. (bet. Pine & Turney Sts.), Sausalito,
415-332-3620
■ It's "the place to go in Sausalito" for the "best Japanese food", including "amazingly fresh" and "beautifully presented sushi" and "well-prepared tempuras"; "it will cost a big eater an arm and a leg", but you can drown your financial sorrows with a selection from the "wonderful sake list" or "new wine bar"; P.S. "make reservations" or "wait."

Sushi to Dai For S M   ▽ 19 | 12 | 17 | $27
869 Fourth St. (bet. Cijos St. & Lootens Pl.), San Rafael,
415-721-0392
☑ It's a good thing fans of San Rafael's "no-frills sushi joint" ("could do with a revamp") like to "sit at the bar" and watch the "personable sushi chefs" slice and dice their dinner, 'cause there's "little else" going on here.

Syrah L   ▽ 22 | 19 | 21 | $37
205 Fifth St. (Davis St.), Santa Rosa, 707-568-4002
■ This Santa Rosa rookie is "still on trial", but early samplers say it is "improving nicely" and "aims to please" with a "pleasant atmosphere" and "creative" Cal-French bistro menu; it's a "great addition" to the area and some surveyors' "first choice for a romantic evening out."

TERRA S M   27 | 24 | 25 | $54
1345 Railroad Ave. (bet. Adams & Hunt Sts.), St. Helena,
707-963-8931
■ Chef-owner "Hiro is a hero" in the kitchen and his wife Lissa works small miracles in the "romantic", "stone-walled" dining room; together they keep this "just about perfect" St. Helena Cal-French (with strong Asian accents) on terra firma, although reviewers report they "feel like their eating in heaven"; professional service and a formidable wine list also prompt patrons to rate it "one of the best anywhere."

Tomales Bay Foods L S   24 | 16 | 18 | $18
80 Fourth St. (B St.), Point Reyes Station, 415-663-8153
■ Savvy shoppers can put together "the ultimate beach picnic" composed of the "freshest organic take-out foods", "wonderful bread and cheese" and "famous homemade ice cream" at this "incredible" Point Reyes Station food purveyor run by ex–Chez Panisse chef Peggy Smith; it's "not a restaurant", but it's a "delightful discovery" nevertheless.

Tomatina L S M   17 | 13 | 13 | $20
Inn at Southbridge, 1016 Main St. (bet. Charter Oak Ave. &
Pope St.), St. Helena, 707-967-9999
■ "Finally, an unpretentious Napa Valley spot that serves fabulous food at great prices" say fans of this Real Restaurants–run Southern Italian specializing in "wonderful" thin pizzas and panini; the only downsides are "stand-in-line-to-order" service and "too many kids."

TRA VIGNE L S M   25 | 26 | 22 | $43
1050 Charter Oak Ave. (Hwy. 29), St. Helena, 707-963-4444
■ Surveyors smitten with Michael Chiarello's "gorgeous"
St. Helena Italian swear it's "like eating in a villa", with its
"vaulted ceilings to the sky", "sublime" food that's "always
scaling new heights" and "idyllic" outdoor space; although
you may have to "brave the lines" and some "attitude" to
enjoy this "wine-country classic", amici admit that it was "so
wonderful we bought the cookbook"; N.B. don't miss the
Cantinetta, an Italian-style deli/gourmet shop on the premises.

Tuscany S M   – | – | – | M
1005 First St. (Main St.), Napa, 707-258-1000
Bustling, new Napa trattoria that's winning over locals with
its Tuscan pastas and meats cooked in an exhibition kitchen
that features a wood-burning pizza oven, grill and rotisserie.

Uva, Trattoria Italiana L S M   – | – | – | M
1040 Clinton St. (Main St.), Napa, 707-255-6646
This easy-on-the-wallet Downtown Napa trattoria run by
Puglian chef-owner Candido DiTerlizzi has quickly earned
a following for its homemade gnocchi, crackling-hot pizzas,
freshly made breads and desserts; *uva* is Italian for 'grape',
and the restaurant tries to live up to its namesake by offering
a fairly extensive wine list of Italian and Napa vintages.

Wappo Bar Bistro L S M   23 | 19 | 20 | $34
1226 Washington St. (Lincoln Ave.), Calistoga,
707-942-4712
■ The name comes from a local Native American tribe, but
the culinary inspiration for the "fantastic" menu comes from
all around the world at this "small", "hidden" Eclectic-
International in Calistoga; respondents recommend: "take a
soak, a walk and then mangia" out on the "pretty patio."

Willowside Cafe S   24 | 17 | 22 | $44
3535 Guerneville Rd. (Willowside Rd.), Santa Rosa,
707-523-4814
■ "Don't be put off" by the "dilapidated roadhouse" exterior
of this "off-the-beaten-path" Santa Rosa Californian that
reminds voters of a "truck stop" until they "taste the vittles";
despite a recent chef and ownership change, loyalists
insist the fare is still "inventive" and "totally satisfying"
and the staff's as "friendly" as ever.

Willow Wood Market Cafe L M ▽ 23 | 16 | 20 | $21
9020 Graton Rd. (bet. Eddison & Ross Sts.), Graton,
707-522-8372
■ "Delightful", "relaxed" Californian serving a "limited"
but "imaginative" range of entrees and sandwiches in a
"country store setting" near Sebastopol; it's the perfect
place for refueling before shopping for imported groceries.

Wine Spectator Greystone L S M 22 | 23 | 20 | $41
Culinary Institute of America, 2555 Main St. (Deer Park Rd.), St. Helena, 707-967-1010
■ Set in a "beautiful old building" on the West Coast campus of the Culinary Institute of America, this "marvelous" New American specializing in wine-country cuisine is "finally" "where it should be", thanks to the arrival of chef Todd Humphries (ex Campton Place); voyeurs feel it's "fun to watch your meal being cooked" in the open kitchen, while romantics prefer to "eat outside and enjoy the views" of the valley; either way, the food is "fab", "service is wonderful" and "wine is king."

Yankee Pier L S M – | – | – | M
286 Magnolia Ave. (bet. William Ave. & King St.), Larkspur, 415-924-7676
Everything should be Yankee doodle dandy in Larkspur this fall when Bradley Ogden is scheduled to open his casual California-meets-New England seafood shack; his Lark Creek Inn chef-partner Jeremy Sewall will oversee a menu featuring fried clams, fish 'n' chips and steamed lobsters, as well as more sophisticated seasonal seafood dishes.

Zin L S M 20 | 18 | 18 | $37
344 Center St. (North St.), Healdsburg, 707-473-0946
■ It's no sin to love Zin, according to early supporters of this Healdsburg rookie offering a "limited" menu of "gourmet comfort food" with a California twist and "one of the best wine lists", which leans heavily on — what else? — California Zinfandels.

South of San Francisco

	F	D	S	C

Amber India 🅛🅢🅜   23 | 18 | 19 | $27
Olive Tree Shopping Ctr., 2290 El Camino Real (Rengstorff Ave.), Mountain View, 650-968-7511
◼ "Don't let the strip mall location fool you" caution curry lovers, 'cause this Mountain View restaurant serves "hands down the best Indian cuisine on the Peninsula"; "well-balanced flavors" ("the butter chicken is addictive") enhanced by "charming decor" make it a top "ethnic food" choice for "venture capitalists" who queue up with the regular folk for the lunch buffets.

Anton & Michel   ▽ 21 | 25 | 22 | $46
Restaurant 🅛🅢🅜
Mission St. (bet. Ocean & 7th Aves.), Carmel, 831-624-2406
◪ Surveyors are split on this venerable Carmel institution: supporters say a "beautiful" setting is the backdrop for "classy food and service", but since critics counter that it's an "overrated" "dinosaur" serving "your grandma's French food", it will have to be your call.

A.P. Stump's 🅛🅢🅜   24 | 24 | 22 | $48
163 W. Santa Clara St. (Almaden Ave.), San Jose, 408-292-9928
◼ Jim Stump's "noisy but inviting" and "upscale" New American rookie is where San Jose's "elite meet to eat", thanks to his "creative", "gloriously presented" cuisine, "ooh la la" decor and "well-chosen wines", all of which "meet SF standards"; "Silicon Valley yuppies" aren't stumped by the "pricey" tabs, shrugging "you get what you pay for."

Aqui Cal-Mex Grill 🅛🅢🅜   22 | 16 | 14 | $14
1145 Lincoln Ave. (bet. Minnesota Ave. & Willow St.), San Jose, 408-995-0381
◼ "When you want high-quality", "creative", "tasty" and "fresh" Cal-Mexican fare at "affordable prices", "look no further" say local fans of this *muy bueno*, "self-serve" spot in San Jose; the best place to savor the flavor is on the "lovely outside patio."

Avanti 🅛🅢🅜   ▽ 24 | 16 | 23 | $27
Palm Ctr., 1711 Mission St. (Bay St.), Santa Cruz, 831-427-0135
◼ The few who know this "quaint", "homey" Californian in Santa Cruz, with a "great neighborhood feel" and a kitchen that's dedicated to organic produce, praise its "outstanding fish and pasta", "excellent wines" and "good service"; moderate prices are another reason for hying here.

Bacchanal ⬛Ⓜ   ▽ 17 | 16 | 16 | $37
265 Grand Ave. (Linden Ave.), South San Francisco, 650-742-6600
☑ Downtown South SF isn't exactly a hotbed of wine consumption or fine dining, but that hasn't dissuaded owner Ken Taylor from opening this American (in a former speakeasy) showcasing a "huge" and "incredible wine selection" (with 80 choices by the glass); while oenophiles appear to be over the moon, some foodies feel that what's on the plate doesn't hit the same heights.

Basque Cultural Center ⬛Ⓢ   18 | 14 | 18 | $26
599 Railroad Ave. (bet. Orange & Spruce Aves.),
South San Francisco, 650-583-8091
■ "Be prepared to eat" enthuse respondents about this "unique and slightly anachronistic" South SF "gem" known for "huge portions" of "very good", "family-style" Basque cooking at "cheap prices"; even if you're not looking for cultural enlightenment, it's a convenient spot for a "near-the-airport, waiting-for-rush-hour-to-clear meal."

Bella Vista Ⓜ   21 | 23 | 22 | $50
13451 Skyline Blvd. (Ware Rd., 5 mi. south of I-92),
Woodside, 650-851-1229
☑ "Breathtaking views of the Silicon Valley" (albeit "only on clear nights") are the appeal of this "old-fashioned" Woodside Continental (remember Steak Diane?); request a table by the window or the fireplace to make the most of your romantic experience, since cynics say the "spotty", "expensive" food ranges from "excellent to mediocre."

Bistro Vida ⬛ⓈⓂ   20 | 19 | 20 | $34
641 Santa Cruz Ave. (El Camino Real), Menlo Park, 650-462-1686
■ "Authentic" Menlo Park French bistro that warms hearts and stomachs with its "good preparation of classic dishes" like cassoulet; a "pleasant owner" who "knows your name" makes it a "very friendly place."

Bittersweet   ▽ 24 | 22 | 21 | $41
Bistro & Cafe ⬛ⓈⓂ
787 Rio Del Mar Blvd. (bet. Clubhouse Dr. & Hwy. 1), *APTOS*
Aptos, 831-662-9799
■ "Elegant" Eclectic with "sophisticated ambiance for the Santa Cruz–Aptos area" that gets kudos for its "great little pizzas", but it's the "desserts to die for" that sweeten the deal; N.B. there's live jazz every Friday night.

Blue Chalk Cafe ⬛ⓈⓂ   15 | 15 | 14 | $25
630 Ramona St. (bet. Forest & Hamilton Aves.), Palo Alto,
650-326-1020
■ "Calling all frat boys (and Silicon geeks who wish that they had been"), "you're table is ready" mock foes of this Palo Alto cafe , where the pub food is an afterthought; pool sharks "enjoy a game" of billiards with their booze, but warn: "friends don't let friends eat" here.

Buca di Beppo 🆂Ⓜ   14 | 18 | 16 | $23
Pruneyard Shopping Ctr., 1875 S. Bascom Ave. (Campbell Ave.),
Campbell, 408-377-7722
643 Emerson St. (bet. Forest & Hamilton Aves.), Palo Alto,
650-329-0665
☑ Supporters say "bring your family or someone else's"
to this "outrageously fun", "cheesy" Southern Italian
chain that's notorious for serving "big, falling-off the-plate
portions" in a "high-kitsch" setting; while foes fume about
the "heavy", "Chef Boyardee"—quality food geared to a
"hogs-to-the-trough" clientele, groups giggle: "it's hard to
stay depressed here."

Buck's Ⓛ🆂Ⓜ   15 | 18 | 17 | $23
3062 Woodside Rd. (Cañada Rd.), Woodside, 650-851-8010
■ "Don't forget to wear $500 Italian loafers and a polo shirt"
to this "funky" Woodside American (sporting a campy
Wild West ambiance) where "Silicon Valley moguls meet
to eat", and "let's make a deal" is heard as frequently as
'you want fries with that?'; although it serves three square
meals, it's known as the "best breakfast hot spot around."

Buffalo Grill Ⓛ🆂Ⓜ   18 | 19 | 18 | $33
Hillsdale Mall, 66 31st Ave. (El Camino Real), San Mateo,
650-358-8777
☑ "Red-meat fans" say this San Mateo standby is "handy
if you're shopping at the Hillsdale Mall", but while some
call the American "comfort food" "good", gourmets gripe
it's the "epitome of average."

Cafe Borrone Ⓛ🆂Ⓜ   18 | 17 | 15 | $17
1010 El Camino Real (Santa Cruz Ave.), Menlo Park,
650-327-0830
■ "Lattes for the laptop set" and desserts are the draws
at this "stylish European sidewalk cafe" in Menlo Park
that's the "perfect place to soak up the sun while you
watch the world go by"; it's also a popular spot to relax
"after shopping at Kepler's Books."

Cafe Marcella Ⓛ🆂   24 | 19 | 22 | $40
368 Village Ln. (Santa Cruz Ave.), Los Gatos, 408-354-8006
■ "Cozy" French bistro, "brimming with laughter, good
smells", "great wine and food", that's the toast of Los
Gatos; however, "you have to like lots of noise to survive."

Cafe Torre ⓁⓂ   – | – | – | M
St. Joseph Place, 20343 Stevens Creek Blvd. (bet. DeAnza
Blvd. & Torre Ave.), Cupertino, 408-257-2383
Ok, it's in a "strip mall", but surveyors say that congenial
host and restaurateur Vince Torre's (ex Cafe Marcella)
Cupertino Cal-Ital rookie features "well-crafted", "tasty
food", including "excellent pasta", at reasonable prices.

California Cafe L S M   20 | 18 | 20 | $31
Old Town Shopping Ctr., 50 University Ave. (Main St.), Los Gatos,
408-354-8118
Stanford Barn, 700 Welch Rd. (Quarry St.), Palo Alto,
650-325-2233
Valley Fair Shopping Ctr., 2855 Stevens Creek Blvd. (Hwy. 280),
Santa Clara, 408-296-2233
See review in East of San Francisco Directory.

Camranh Bay L S M   ▽ 20 | 18 | 18 | $26
201 E. Third Ave. (Ellsworth Ave.), San Mateo,
650-342-7577
■ You won't find any foes of the "good pho" or the signature
scallops at chef-owner Son Truong's "excellent" Vietnamese
with "refined flavors", which fans rave is a "great addition to
San Mateo"; N.B. there's live jazz every Thursday night.

Capellini L S M   20 | 20 | 20 | $34
310 Baldwin Ave. (S. B St.), San Mateo, 650-348-2296
◪ Surveyors seem to be splitting hairs over this San Mateo
tri-level Northern Italian designed by Pat Kuleto: admirers
insist that it offers "solid, predictable" "quality" food and a
"happy bar scene", but critics complain the fare is "boring"
and the atmosphere is "too noisy"; in any case, it's best to
"eat downstairs where you can hear yourself think."

Carpaccio L S M   21 | 19 | 19 | $34
1120 Crane St. (Santa Cruz Ave.), Menlo Park,
650-322-1211
■ Older, smaller Menlo Park sibling of Capellini serving
"consistent", "traditional" Northern Italian food in a
"pleasant", "comfortable" setting; its popular bar is also a
long-standing "locals' hangout."

Casanova L S M   22 | 24 | 22 | $46
Fifth Ave. (bet. Mission & San Carlos Sts.), Carmel,
831-625-0501
◪ "Charming" Carmel stalwart, operating since 1977, that
continues to lure a steady stream of romantics with its
"quaint", "cozy" interior, "lovely outdoor patio", "delicious"
French-Italian fare and a "fabulous wine list"; however, a
vocal contingent insists it's "touristy", "pricey for what
you get" and "needs some punch."

Charlie Hong Kong L S M   ▽ 21 | 9 | 13 | $10
1141 Soquel Ave. (Seabright Ave.), Santa Cruz,
831-426-5664
6249 Hwy. 9 (Graham Hill Rd.), Felton, 831-335-9770
■ "Fast and filling", this creative Santa Cruz joint relies on
mostly organic produce and serves up "big portions" of
"yummy", "healthy" Asian noodles that also make for the
"best takeout"; N.B. the Felton branch is new and unrated.

Chef Chu's L S M 19 14 17 $24
1067 N. San Antonio Rd. (El Camino Real), Los Altos, 650-948-2696
■ This Los Altos Chinese "institution" is overseen by Lawrence Chu, a "great personality and chef" (as the profusion of national and "local celeb" photos on the walls seemingly attests to); however, while supporters say it serves "consistent", "always enjoyable" fare, foes feel that it's "no longer one of the best", citing "expensive", "flavorless, Americanized dishes" and "depressing decor."

Chez T.J. 24 23 24 VE
938 Villa St. (bet. Castro St. & Shoreline Blvd.), Mountain View, 650-964-7466
■ "For an evening of culinary delights", "Silicon Valley stock-option millionaires" and normal folks celebrating a "special occasion" splurge at this Mountain View American-French in a "Victorian house setting"; diners can choose from three "creative", "delicious" tasting menus (priced from $42-$65) prepared by new chef Kirk Bruderer (a prodigy of the French Laundry's Thomas Keller); "excellent service" also helps make for a "nicely paced meal."

Cielo L S M ∇ 21 23 22 $52
Ventana Inn & Spa, Hwy. 1, Big Sur, 831-667-4242
■ Loyalists "love to lunch on the outdoor patio" of this "pricey" New American at the Ventana Inn & Spa in Big Sur because it offers "the most beautiful view in the world"; cynics say "like the resort itself, the decor feels a little dated", but there's nothing more timeless than watching the Pacific Ocean crash over the cliffs while you're wining and dining.

5C **Clouds Downtown** L S M ∇ 21 16 19 $29
110 Church St. (bet. Chestnut St. & Pacific Ave.), Santa Cruz, 831-429-2000
■ "Bustling bistro with good service" and a "varied menu" of Continental dishes that's located in Downtown Santa Cruz; its popular bar also makes for a "good after-work hangout."

Club XIX L S M 24 27 24 $58
Lodge at Pebble Beach, 17 Mile Dr. (Hwy. 1), Pebble Beach, 831-625-8519
■ Probably "no more famous view exists" than the one at this "elegant" New French overlooking Carmel Bay and Pebble Beach's legendary 18th-hole gush golfers; factor in the "chic atmosphere", "beautifully prepared food" and "solid service" and its "hard to do better."

5C **Convivio Trattoria** S ∇ 21 21 21 $34
655 Capitola Rd. (7th Ave.), Santa Cruz, 831-475-9600
■ Convivial Cal-Ital that strikes a chord with local gourmets, who rave about its "excellent food" and "friendly, welcoming service"; a few complain that the "preparations can border on fussy", which almost amounts to a misdemeanor in this laid-back college town, but most welcome this new addition.

Covey, The ⓁⓈⓂ   23 | 24 | 24 | $52
*Quail Lodge Resort & Golf Club, 8205 Valley Greens Dr.
(Carmel Valley Rd.), Carmel, 831-620-8860*
☑ Pricey Carmel institution (operating since 1963) providing
a "classic country-club atmosphere" and "tranquil",
"beautiful surroundings" overlooking the lake at Quail Lodge
Resort; however, while fans feel it's a "treat" that features
"solid" Californian cooking, modernists maintain that "it
tries hard", but it's "lost its edge" and needs an "update."

Crow's Nest ⓁⓈⓂ   16 | 19 | 16 | $27
2218 E. Cliff Dr. (5th Ave.), Santa Cruz, 831-476-4560
☑ The eagle-eyed time their visit to this "fun" Santa Cruz
steak-and-seafood joint "on the water" so that they can
"watch the sunset"; most say "forget the food", but drinks
"on the porch on a summer day can't be beat."

Dal Baffo ⒧Ⓜ   22 | 20 | 23 | $53
*878 Santa Cruz Ave. (bet. Crane St. & University Dr.),
Menlo Park, 650-325-1588*
☑ Opinion is divided on this Menlo Park French-Italian:
supporters say it's a "class act" with "excellent" cuisine,
"old-world charm" and "superb service", but cons call
the "inconsistent" food "overpriced" and the "waiters
stuffy"; N.B. jackets required.

Duarte's Tavern ⓁⓈⓂ   20 | 13 | 18 | $24
202 Stage Rd. (Pescadero Rd.), Pescadero, 650-879-0464
■ This "funky" American "roadhouse" set in an "old tavern"
in the sleepy town of Pescadero (between SF and Santa
Cruz) is famous for "artichoke anything" (don't miss the
"soup") and "fabulous homemade pies"; "it's old California
at its best" and "worth the trip on the Pacific Coast Highway."

Duck Club ⓁⓈⓂ   20 | 20 | 20 | $39
*Stanford Park Hotel, 100 El Camino Real (University Ave.),
Menlo Park, 650-330-2790*
■ Everything's ducky (from the paintings on the walls to the
"well-prepared food" on your plate) at this "enjoyable"
American in Menlo Park; resembling a "gracious" "men's
club", it offers a "deal-closing ambiance" that makes it a
popular spot for business lunches; N.B. there's also a
branch North of San Francisco in the Bodega Bay Lodge.

E&O Trading Co. ⓁⓈⓂ   19 | 21 | 17 | $31
96 S. First St. (San Fernando St.), San Jose, 408-938-4100
See review in San Francisco Directory.

El Palomar ⓁⓈⓂ   ▽ 18 | 17 | 16 | $21
*Palomar Hotel, 1336 Pacific Ave. (Soquel Ave.), Santa Cruz,
831-425-7575*
☑ "Lively" Mexican in the historic Palomar Hotel that's a
major spot in the local scene; although the food ranges
from "mediocre" to "decent", revelers agree that the
"ambiance is right on", especially at the "noisy bar."

Emile's
26 ┃ 22 ┃ 25 ┃ $55

545 S. Second St. (bet. Reed & William Sts.), San Jose, 408-289-1960

☑ For a "dining experience that is near perfect", South Bay connoisseurs come to this "classy" stalwart noted for its "consistently wonderful", "Classic French" fare and "excellent service"; a few cynics sniff that it's "dated" and "overrated", but more maintain it's "great for San Jose."

Empire Grill & Tap Room L S M
19 ┃ 21 ┃ 18 ┃ $30

651 Emerson St. (Hamilton Ave.), Palo Alto, 650-321-3030

■ Its "idyllic" "garden setting" seems to exert a "magnetic appeal", so a "young" crowd braves "long waits" at this Palo Alto eatery; although the American cuisine (with a smattering of French and Italian) here is "consistent", some oenophiles opt to have "wine on the patio" with an appetizer.

ERNA'S
ELDERBERRY HOUSE S M
27 ┃ 26 ┃ 27 ┃ $70

48688 Victoria Ln. (Hwy. 41), Oakhurst, 559-683-6800

■ For those lucky reviewers who "can find it and afford it" (it's in tiny Oakhurst, "close to Yosemite"), this Cal–New French is "unforgettable in every way", with its "absolutely flawless service", dreamy "castle-like atmosphere" and "exquisite" cuisine that'll put you in "culinary heaven"; since Erna conveniently owns the equally lavish Château du Sureau resort next door, visitors are fully equipped for "a romantic weekend away."

Eulipia S
19 ┃ 18 ┃ 19 ┃ $38

374 S. First St. (bet. San Carlos & San Salvador Sts.), San Jose, 408-280-6161

☑ This Cal-Continental garners a mixed response: one camp claims the "consistent food and service" "rank with San Jose's best", while the other insists the "pricey" place has "lost it"; the fact that "they change chefs a little too often" could explain the lack of consensus.

Evvia L S M
24 ┃ 23 ┃ 21 ┃ $40

420 Emerson St. (bet. Lytton & University Aves.), Palo Alto, 650-326-0983

■ "You could well be in Greece" say worshippers of this Hellenic hot spot in Palo Alto, which boasts a "stunning tavern setting" and "rustic, lusty food" that's "the best this side of the Mediterranean"; the combination makes dining here a "culinary Odyssey" – and "getting a table" like the Twelve Labors of Hercules.

Fandango L S M
21 ┃ 21 ┃ 21 ┃ $38

223 17th St. (Lighthouse Ave.), Pacific Grove, 831-372-3456

☑ "Lovely, lovely, lovely" ambiance, "creative" cooking and a "wonderful staff" make this Pacific Grove Mediterranean one of the "better dining experiences" on the South coast, though a handful of hedgers warn of a "hit-or-miss" menu.

Faz L S M
| 18 | 17 | 17 | $29 |

1108 N. Mathilda Ave. (Hwy. 237/Moffett Park Dr.), Sunnyvale, 408-752-8000
See review in San Francisco Directory.

Flea St. Cafe L S
| 21 | 18 | 21 | $37 |

3607 Alameda de las Pulgas (Avy St.), Menlo Park, 650-854-1226
■ "Jesse Cool reigns in her original court" as her loyal subjects swoon over "inventive", "truly wonderful" "organic fare", "served with pizazz" at this "cozy and inviting" Menlo Park American-Californian; even the vegetarian vanguard attests "they take care of you", and there's now a full bar.

Flying Fish Grill S M
∇ | 24 | 21 | 23 | $31 |

Carmel Plaza (bet. Ocean & 7th Aves.), Carmel, 831-625-1962
■ Vividly painted papier-mâché fish float across the ceiling, but it's chef-owner Kenny Fukumoto's "wonderfully inventive" Asian-Californian seafood that really soars at this "intimate" (ok, tiny) eatery, an "all-around pleasant" place sited just off the side entrance to the Carmel Plaza.

Fook Yuen L S M
| 22 | 12 | 14 | $25 |

195 El Camino Real (Millbrae Ave.), Millbrae, 650-692-8600
■ The "array and quality" of the "wonderful dim sum" keep this "enormous", highly "authentic" Millbrae Chinese "packed" despite the "stark decor" and "brusque" service; patrons need not speak Cantonese to order, but be sure "not to mispronounce" the name of the restaurant itself.

Fresh Cream S M
| 26 | 24 | 24 | $53 |

Heritage Harbor, 99 Pacific St. (Scott St.), Monterey, 831-375-9798
■ This "old standby in Monterey" is the cream of the crop according to admirers of the "beautiful setting" ("ask for a table by the water"), "rich", "meticulously" prepared French fare and "polished service"; "flawless from start to finish", it's a "special-occasion" destination where diners arrive ready to "spend the bankroll."

Gabriella Cafe L S M
∇ | 22 | 18 | 18 | $28 |

910 Cedar St. (bet. Church & Locust Sts.), Santa Cruz, 831-457-1677
■ "Consistently excellent" Cal-Ital cuisine "prepared with fresh local ingredients" and served in a "romantic setting" nourishes the rep of this "cute" (albeit "a little cramped") cafe, "one of the best" in Santa Cruz.

Gayle's
Bakery & Rosticceria L S M
| 25 | 15 | 17 | $15 |

504 Bay Ave. (Capitola Ave.), Capitola, 831-462-1200
■ "Wow" sums up the response to this "casual" Capitola bakery/deli and its "unbelievable panoply" of "world-class breads", "baked items to die for" and "fabulous" Californian comfort food; supporters sigh it's "just like grandma's cooking", though grandma never gave you "counter service."

Gaylord India L S M   17 | 16 | 16 | $32
1706 El Camino Real (Encinal Ave.), Menlo Park, 650-326-8761
See review in San Francisco Directory.

Gordon Biersch Brewery L S M   13 | 15 | 14 | $24
*640 Emerson St. (bet. Forest & Hamilton Aves.), Palo Alto,
650-323-7723*
*33 E. San Fernando St. (bet. 1st & 2nd Sts.), San Jose,
408-294-6785*
■ "Nirvana" for devotees of "beer and garlic fries", this
area "brewpub" chain is the place where the suds "surpass
the norm" even when the "so-so" American fare doesn't;
it's your "typical pickup scene" in a "corporate" setting,
favored by those who can cope with "frat-boy central."

Grandview L S M   ▽ 21 | 13 | 20 | $25
*1107 Howard Ave. (bet. Highland & Lorton Aves.),
Burlingame, 650-348-3888*
■ "Top-notch" food and service "to match" compensate
for the "cafeteria" decor at this Burlingame Asian; though
there's no grand view in sight, the "excellent" chow has
loyalists labeling it the "best Chinese nobody knows about."

Grasing's Coastal Cuisine L S M ▽ 24 | 21 | 22 | $38
Sixth & Misson Sts., Carmel, 831-624-6562
■ "What a find!" exclaim enterprising enthusiasts who
seek out this "charming" Carmel Californian where "great
seasonal menus" showcasing "fine local ingredients"
make for "delicious" grazing; an "accommodating" staff
and a "pleasant" setting round out the experience.

Grill on the Alley, The L S M   ▽ 22 | 24 | 20 | $48
*Fairmont Hotel, 172 S. Market St. (bet. San Carlos &
San Fernando Sts.), San Jose, 408-294-2244*
◪ A "masculine meat house done right", this scene for
"movers and shakers" in San Jose's Fairmont Hotel is a
spin-off of a Beverly Hills powerhouse; it's known for its
"prime" cuts and "clubby" ambiance, though a few foes
find the food "boring" and the room "stuffy"; N.B. name
notwithstanding, the locale is the epicenter of Silicon
Valley, *not* Silicon Alley.

Hong Kong Flower Lounge L S M 22 | 16 | 15 | $28
51 Millbrae Ave. (El Camino Real), Millbrae, 650-692-6666
560 Waverly St. (Hamilton St.), Palo Alto, 650-326-3830
◪ The "classic" menu and "fantastic dim sum" are the
calling cards of this "premium" (and "pricey") Chinese
chainlet where the "bustling dining rooms look like Hong
Kong"; supporters say the food is so "fabulous" that they're
willing to "overlook the shoddy service" and "tacky" decor.

Iberia 🄻🅂🅜 | 19 | 19 | 17 | $41 |
Ladera Country Shopper, 3130 Alpine Rd. (La Cuesta Dr.),
Portola Valley, 650-854-1746
☑ Despite its "suburban mini-mall" location, this Portola
Valley Spaniard provides some "wonderful" dishes and
offers one of the area's "loveliest" patios, making it a
"natural setting" for "warm evening dining"; however,
contras complain of "snooty" service and food that's
"expensive for what you get."

Il Fornaio 🄻🅂🅜 | 19 | 21 | 19 | $31 |
327 Lorton Ave. (bet. Burlingame Ave. & California St.),
Burlingame, 650-375-8000
The Pine Inn (Ocean Ave. & Monte Verde), Carmel, 831-622-5100
520 Cowper St. (bet. Hamilton St. & University Ave.), Palo Alto,
650-853-3888
Hyatt Sainte Claire, 302 S. Market St. (San Carlos St.),
San Jose, 408-271-3366
See review in San Francisco Directory.

Isobune Sushi 🄻🅂🅜 | 18 | 14 | 15 | $23 |
1451 Burlingame Ave. (El Camino Real), Burlingame,
650-344-8433
See review in San Francisco Directory.

JoAnn's Cafe 🄻🅂🅜⇴ | 22 | 12 | 18 | $16 |
1131 El Camino Real (Westborough Blvd.),
South San Francisco, 650-872-2810
■ "For a better breakfast, you'd have to make it yourself"
claim "cult followers" of JoAnn di Lorenzo, "terrific hostess"
and owner of this "down-to-earth" South San Francisco
coffee shop; early risers agree the "sublime omelets" and
"hearty" flapjack stacks are well "worth the ride"; N.B.
closes at 2:30 PM.

Jocco's Restaurant 🄻🅂🅜   ▽ | 22 | 16 | 20 | $39 |
236 Central Plaza (bet. 2nd & 3rd Sts.), Los Altos, 650-948-6809
■ This "great little" Los Altos New American has plenty
to pride itself on: a "delicious, hearty" menu (courtesy of
chef-owner Jaime Carpenter), "outstanding service" and
displays of "great artwork" from area talents; the "cozy"
room may grow "noisy", but that doesn't deter locals from
returning "again and again."

John Bentley's 🄻 | 26 | 20 | 24 | $47 |
2991 Woodside Rd. (bet. Cañada & Whiskey Hill Rds.),
Woodside, 650-851-4988
■ Chef-owner John Bentley's eponymous "romantic
hideaway" in Woodside disarms admirers "in all respects",
from the "charming little" dining room set in a 1920s firehouse
to the master's "creative touch" with the "outstanding"
New American menu ("don't miss dessert"); it's one of
the Peninsula's popular "special-occasion" spots, so be
prepared to pay prices to match.

Juban 🗏🖸🖻 19 19 17 $27
1204 Broadway (bet. California Dr. & El Camino Real),
Burlingame, 650-347-2300
712 Santa Cruz Ave. (bet. El Camino Real & Santa Cruz Ave.),
Menlo Park, 650-473-6458
■ Head to this upscale Japanese pair in Burlingame and
Menlo Park for fresh fish or meat that "melts in your mouth"
after you've grilled it yourself at the table; while a few whine
about working "at these prices", most find it's all "such fun" –
especially if you "go bankrupt and order the Kobe beef."

JZ Cool 🗏🖸 ▽ 20 15 17 $19
827 Santa Cruz Ave. (bet. Crane St. & University Dr.),
Menlo Park, 650-325-3665
■ Casual newcomer (operated by Jesse Cool, chef-owner
of the Flea St. Cafe) that's "what Menlo Park needed
most", since almost all of its wide range of comfort food –
from the "fresh breads" to the adventurous "variety of
salads" – is prepared from scratch; P.S. the organic fare
is also a "good choice for healthy-style take-home."

Kathmandu West 🗏🖸🖻 ▽ 19 13 18 $20
20916A Homestead Rd. (Hollenbeck Ave.), Cupertino,
408-996-0940
■ Strip-mall spot serving "authentic and varied Nepalese"
cuisine (kind of like "Indian food for people who can't
take the heat"); despite the "very plain room", the "calm
environment", "superfriendly staff" and "bargain prices"
all make you "feel you've left the U.S for dinner" –though
in fact the trek's only been to Cupertino.

Koi Palace 🗏🖸🖻 24 16 14 $31
365 Gellert Blvd. (Hickey Blvd.), Daly City, 650-992-9000
■ With a lobby that's a literal zoo – containing "huge
aquariums packed with oversized" crustaceans and crowds
of humans waiting for tables – this Daly City cavern is no
place to be coy; however, it does "set the standard for
Chinese seafood" (straight from those tanks) and "startlingly
delicious" dim sum; so gird your loins, ignore the "tacky"
decor, and "go early to avoid the awful wait."

Kuleto's Trattoria 🗏🖸🖻 18 19 18 $35
1095 Rollins Rd. (Broadway), Burlingame, 650-342-4922
◪ While the "dependable" Italian fare at this Burlingame
trattoria strikes most surveyors as "nothing special, it
can be a godsend when you're looking for a nice venue"
in between San Francisco and Palo Alto, especially one
"right by the airport."

La Cumbre Taqueria 🗏🖸🖻 20 9 14 $10
28 N. B St. (bet. 1st & Tilton Aves.), San Mateo,
650-344-8989
See review in San Francisco Directory.

La Fondue 🅢🅜   21 | 21 | 20 | $41

14510 Big Basin Way (bet. 3rd & 4th Sts.), Saratoga, 408-867-3332

■ Saratoga Swiss where you "do fondue" (with "great choices" that range from wild turkey to teriyaki sirloin); though "pricey", the place is "so in demand" with couples and "large parties" that "it's hard to get reservations" – so whether "you go for the food or the fun", don't plan on just dipping in unannounced.

L'Amie Donia   24 | 19 | 20 | $45

530 Bryant St. (bet. Hamilton & University Aves.), Palo Alto, 650-323-7614

☑ Donia Bijan's "soulful bistro fare" –a real "slice of Provence" in Palo Alto – is "still great" to its many admirers and the "dot-com millionaires who feel they've arrived", but even Donia's *amis* deplore the "small, tight space" ("tables are so close together that I could eat off my neighbor's plate") and "sky-high prices"; insiders say for the best time "sit at the counter and watch the talented kitchen crew" at work.

La Pastaia 🅛🅢🅜   23 | 21 | 21 | $37

Hotel De Anza, 233 W. Santa Clara St. (Almaden Blvd.), San Jose, 408-286-8686

■ "The food seems to have improved" at this Italian, a "favorite hangout" in Downtown San Jose; regulars recommend you "stick with the pasta dishes", "huge portions" of which are served in a "beautiful" room.

Lark Creek 🅛🅢🅜   22 | 21 | 21 | $38

Benjamin Franklin Hotel, 50 E. Third Ave. (El Camino Real), San Mateo, 650-344-9444

See review in East of San Francisco Directory.

La Taqueria 🅛🅜⊅   23 | 8 | 13 | $11

15 S. First St. (Santa Clara St.), San Jose, 408-287-1542

See review in San Francisco Directory.

Left at Albuquerque 🅛🅢🅜   13 | 15 | 14 | $22

1100 Burlingame Ave. (California Ave.), Burlingame, 650-401-5700
Pruneyard Shopping Ctr., 1875 S. Bascom Ave. (bet. Campbell & Hamilton Aves.), Campbell, 408-558-1680
445 Emerson St. (bet Lytton & University Aves.), Palo Alto, 650-326-1011

☑ The "ongoing post-college frat party" that indulges in "awesome" "fishbowl margaritas" and a lively "pickup" scene at this Tex-Mex chainlet "doesn't seem to care" that the Southwestern eats are "predictable"; the disgruntled argue the kitchen has "taken a wrong turn" and deem it "better for happy hour than dinner" hour.

Left Bank 🅛🅢🅜 21 | 21 | 19 | $37
635 Santa Cruz Ave. (Doyle St.), Menlo Park, 650-473-6543
See review in North of San Francisco Directory.

Le Mouton Noir 🅛🅢🅜 25 | 23 | 24 | $54
14560 Big Basin Way (bet. 4th & 5th Sts.), Saratoga,
408-867-7017
■ There's a "grandmotherly feel" – in a good way – to this
recently redecorated Saratoga classic, "a special spot
for [over] 20 years"; the "sublime French" food and "very
polite, very unhurried" service make for an experience
that's "expensive but worth it."

LE PAPILLON 🅛🅢🅜 27 | 24 | 25 | $55
410 Saratoga Ave. (Kiely Blvd.), San Jose, 408-296-3730
■ "Catering to Silicon Valley money", this South Bay
butterfly isn't cheap, but it does offer some "superb haute
New French cuisine" (the "herb-crusted halibut is amazing")
and a sense of "cosseted comfort"; although some say
"the atmosphere can be a little stuffy", to most it's "one of
San Jose's best."

Linda's ▽ 23 | 14 | 22 | $23
Seabreeze Cafe 🅛🅢🅜⊜
542 Seabright Ave. (Logan St.), Santa Cruz, 831-427-9713
■ Although original owner Linda sold her share to her
partner in '99, this cream-and-mauve colored "true beach
cafe" remains ground central for breakfast (and lunch) for
Santa Cruz students and "hippies"; moreover, it continues to
get morning lines "around the block", so be prepared to wait.

Lion & Compass 🅛🅜 21 | 20 | 20 | $37
1023 N. Fair Oaks Ave. (Weddell Dr.), Sunnyvale,
408-745-1260
◪ "High-energy Silicon Valley action" permeates this
Sunnyvale American, for nearly two decades the "perfect
place for a business lunch or dinner"; while critics dismiss
the "forgettable food at premium prices", more tolerant
reviewers report it's "improved – if you haven't been there
recently, give it a try."

Los Gatos Brewing Co. 🅛🅢🅜 19 | 17 | 18 | $27
130G N. Santa Cruz Ave. (Grays Ln.), Los Gatos,
408-395-9929
■ "A winning combo of great fresh beer" with "better
New American food than you'd think" turns this Los Gatos
hangout – a big barn of a place – into a real "see-and-be-
seen scene" for the "twenty- and thirtysomething" crowd
that seems oblivious to the "noisy", "upscale setting."

MacArthur Park 🅛🅢🅜 17 | 17 | 17 | $30
27 University Ave. (bet. Alma St. & El Camino Real), Palo Alto,
650-321-9990
See review in San Francisco Directory.

Manuel's ❶ⓁⓈⓂ ▽ 21 | 14 | 19 | $21

261 Center Ave. (Hwy. 1), Aptos, 831-688-4848

■ "Take a tourist for some local flavor" suggest amigos of this Aptos hole-in-the-wall; "warm friendly service" and "good margaritas" help make it a "Mexican standout."

Marinus ⓁⓈⓂ ▽ 27 | 27 | 24 | $67

Bernardus Lodge, 415 W. Carmel Valley Rd.
(Laureles Grade Rd.), Carmel Valley, 831-658-3500

■ Top toque Cal Stamenov, formerly of Pacific's Edge, has steered this luxury Cal-French yearling into an "impressively flawless restaurant" where "spectacular food", a winning wine list and "lovely setting" overlooking nearby mountains all combine into an experience that's "heaven on earth" (or at least in Carmel Valley).

Max's Opera Café 16 | 15 | 16 | $22

1250 Old Bayshore (Airport Blvd.), Burlingame,
650-342-6297 ⓁⓂ
711 Stanford Shopping Ctr. (El Camino Real), Palo Alto,
650-323-6297 Ⓢ

See review in San Francisco Directory.

Mei Long ⓁⓈⓂ ▽ 26 | 22 | 24 | $36

867 E. El Camino Real (Bernardo Ave.), Mountain View,
650-961-4030

■ "Elegance in a strip mall" might seem like an oxymoron, but this "distinctive" Mountain View spot serves some of the most "innovative", "beautifully presented" Chinese fare around; longtime admirers wonder why this "gem" isn't more crowded – it "would be mobbed in Palo Alto."

Mezza Luna ⓁⓈⓂ – | – | – | M

459 Prospect Way (Capistrano Rd.), Princeton by the Sea,
650-728-8108

Convivial Southern Italian "getaway" near Half Moon Bay that's a write-in fave noted for its "great grilled seafood", "lovely room" and "fabulous waiters", making it an ideal "place to stop for lunch or dinner along the coast"; N.B. live music and dancing on the weekend are an added bonus.

Mio Vicino ⓁⓈⓂ 19 | 12 | 17 | $24

1290 Benton St. (Monroe St.), Santa Clara, 408-241-9414
384 E. Campbell Ave. (Central Ave.), Campbell,
408-378-0335

1140-8 Lincoln Ave. (bet. Meredith Ave. & Willow St.),
San Jose, 408-286-6027

◪ "Good, basic Italian food" – mainly pastas and pizzas – at "very reasonable prices" is enough to turn this trattoria trio into "regular hangouts" for some; but factors such as the "bare surroundings" and "service that needs work" cause others to vow "never again."

Mojo ⑤Ⓜ ▽ 20 19 19 $34
543 Emerson St. (bet. Hamilton & University Aves.), Palo Alto, 650-323-7700

◪ This "recent addition to Palo Alto" offers New American cuisine with a "trendy Southern" twist (highly recommended: the BBQ gulf shrimp) in a mirrored "no-frills atmosphere"; while foes feel it's "inconsistent", fans of chef Donald Link (ex sous-chef at New Orleans' famed Bayona) are convinced he has the mojo to make the place a "winner."

Montrio Ⓛ⑤Ⓜ 23 21 21 $42
414 Calle Principal (Franklin St.), Monterey, 831-648-8880

■ Eclectic charmer (the menu includes French, Northern Italian and "California cuisine at its best") that's a "favorite" among reviewers, who say its "lively atmosphere" and "old firehouse" setting make it a "not-to-be-missed" stop when visiting historic Downtown Monterey.

Moss Beach Distillery Ⓛ⑤Ⓜ 13 20 15 $29
Beach Way & Ocean Blvd. (off Hwy. 1), Moss Beach, 650-728-5595

■ The "cliffside location" and the resident Blue Lady phantom (star of an *Unsolved Mysteries* episode) make this old Moss Beach "roadhouse" "popular"; sure, the American cuisine is "a joke" (the "ghost could probably cook better"), the "service amateurish" and the "atmosphere run-down", but it's still a "really cool place" to "cuddle under a blanket" with "a drink on deck" at sunset.

Nepenthe Ⓛ⑤Ⓜ 15 25 16 $29
Hwy. 1, Big Sur, 831-667-2345

■ "No words can describe the awesome, breathtaking view of Big Sur" that you get at this rustic spot perched over the Pacific Ocean; the treehouse-like "setting is so fabulous, it doesn't matter" that the American fare, featuring "passable burgers", is largely "incidental" – "anyone driving the coast must stop", even if it's only for a drink.

Nola Ⓛ⑤Ⓜ 20 20 16 $28
535 Ramona St. (bet. Hamilton & University Aves.), Palo Alto, 650-328-2722

■ It's Bayou-by-the-Bay time at this "hip and hot" spot in Palo Alto, whose balconied courtyard conjures up New Orleans about as well as the Cajun-Creole menu does; "primarily a party place", it gets totally "swamped" at happy hour by – what else? – a "young dot-com crowd."

Omei Ⓛ⑤Ⓜ ▽ 24 15 18 $28
2316 Mission St. (King St.), Santa Cruz, 831-425-8458

■ "You'd never know it from the outside", but this "Santa Cruz institution" – tucked away in a "weird strip mall setting" – serves "some of the tastiest Chinese food" in the area; however, some "bad attitude" on the staff's part prompts reviewers to recommend trying takeout.

Osteria ⬛Ⓜ | 21 | 16 | 18 | $31 |
Cardinal Hotel, 247 Hamilton Ave. (Ramona St.), Palo Alto, 650-328-5700

■ "To have a comfortable, reliable meal without breaking the bank", locals head to this "old-style" Northern Italian in Palo Alto, where the "perfectly done pasta" never lets them down; unfortunately, two other things are equally certain: the "service will be a bit off" and "you have to like your neighbors, as they're practically in your lap."

Oswald's Ⓢ | ▽ 23 | 18 | 21 | $37 |
1547 Pacific Ave. (Cedar St.), Santa Cruz, 831-423-7427

■ For "stellar dining" in Santa Cruz, locals head to this "quiet gem of a place hidden in an alley" where they uncover "creative yet down-to-earth" Californian cuisine "done with a deft touch."

Pacific's Edge ⓈⓂ | 25 | 27 | 24 | $59 |
Highlands Inn, 120 Highland Dr. (Hwy. 1), Carmel, 831-622-5445

■ "Luxury and more luxury" is the byword at this Cal – New French dining room where "a superb coast view is the excellent decor"; while a few feel the food's lost its edge, plenty of others rave over the "yummy, unique creations"; for "those who travel on their stomachs", this is still "an elegant Carmel treasure" and – for you romantics – "a nice place to propose"; N.B. jackets are required.

Palace, The | ▽ 22 | 23 | 17 | $38 |
146 S. Murphy Ave. (bet. Evelyn & Washington Aves.), Sunnyvale, 408-739-5179

■ You'll be royally entertained at this Sunnyvale restaurant/ nightclub, a perfect place for "a dinner-and-dancing date", with "great jazz" that swings every night amidst the "out-of-this-world decor" of a remodeled art deco movie house; the "imaginative and appetizing" Eclectic cuisine provides a refreshing pause between sets.

Paolo's ⬛Ⓜ | 23 | 23 | 22 | $45 |
River Park Tower, 333 W. San Carlos St. (Woz Way), San Jose, 408-294-2558

☑ "A San Jose landmark", this Italian continues to offer "excellent food and professional service"; although some say "they liked it better in the old days" (deeming it now "pricey for the quality"), it remains a "Downtown fave."

Pasta Moon ⬛ⓈⓂ | 22 | 17 | 20 | $32 |
315 Main St. (Mill St.), Half Moon Bay, 650-726-5125

■ Located within shouting distance of the beach, this South Coast Nouvelle Italian offers a "wonderful wine selection", along with plenty of "inventive pizza" and you-know-what; although the service can be "homespun" and the dining room "short on elbow room", surveyors say it's "worth the long, winding trip" to the sleepy town of Half Moon Bay.

SC

Pearl Alley Bistro L S M   ▽ 20 19 20 $33
110 Pearl Alley (Cedar St.), Santa Cruz, 831-429-8070
☑ Marc Westburg's affordable Downtown Santa Cruz
bistro features an ever-changing Eclectic menu that plays
ethnic riffs ranging from French to Asian; although the dining
room has a "woody", old-world interior, it's countered by
a "fun" modern bar scene, which is "still the best place
in town for wines by the glass"; N.B. partyers at the
happening Club Dakota downstairs can order from the
restaurant's bar menu.

Piatti L S M   18 19 18 $32
Sixth & Junipero Aves., Carmel, 831-625-1766
2 Stanford Shopping Ctr. (El Camino Real), Palo Alto,
650-324-9733
See review in North of San Francisco Directory.

PISCES L S M   26 21 23 $50
1190 California Dr. (Broadway), Burlingame, 650-401-7500
■ "Another Charles Condy success" declare devotees, who
are already calling this "great newcomer" with its "amazing
seafood creations" "the Aqua of the South Bay" (which
Condy owns, along with SF's Charles Nob Hill); although
they deplore the "crowded and noisy" dining room ("should
be in a larger space" – already!), locals "thank God" that
there's "finally an upscale restaurant in Burlingame."

Plumed Horse M   22 21 23 $53
14555 Big Basin Way (4th St.), Saratoga, 408-867-4711
☑ This "high-priced" Saratoga veteran woos diners the
old-fashioned way – with a "most gracious host", "top-
notch service", "an extraordinary wine list" and strains of
"soft jazz" in the background; but while fans loyally deem
the New French fare "excellent", critics say the "stuffy"
place is now "more of an institution than a great restaurant."

Pluto's L S M   18 11 12 $14
482 University Ave. (Cowper St.), Palo Alto, 650-853-1556
See review in San Francisco Directory.

Ramen Club L   ▽ 21 10 18 $16
723 California Dr. (Oak Grove Ave.), Burlingame,
650-347-3690
■ Join the club – this Burlingame hole-in-the-wall is "a
great place to slurp" good, "cheap ramen"; although there is
other Japanese fare, card-carrying members urge you to
"go for the noodles."

Red Tractor Cafe L S M   15 14 14 $14
El Paseo Shopping Ctr., 1320 El Paseo De Saratoga (bet.
Campbell & Saratoga Aves.), San Jose, 408-374-2222
See review in East of San Francisco Directory.

Rio Grill 🇱🇸🇲 22 | 19 | 20 | $36

Crossroads Shopping Ctr., 101 Crossroads Blvd. (Rio Rd.), Carmel, 831-625-5436

■ This "open, airy" Cal-Southwestern remains an "extremely popular" Carmel standby, partly because the "imaginative menu" is "always delicious" and partly because of the "funky, fun atmosphere"; while there's a "high, high noise level", it's still "the kind of place where you could come regularly, because they make you feel at home" – even the "kids are always welcome."

Robert's Bistro 🇸🇲 24 | 23 | 23 | $42

Crossroads Shopping Ctr., 217 Crossroads Blvd. (Rio Rd.), Carmel, 831-624-9626

■ The name's changed, but everything else remains the same at this "cozy and romantic" Carmel eatery, which offers not only "classic French bistro food done extremely well", but also "better atmosphere" and lower prices (especially if you have the early-bird special) than many of the tourist spots in town.

Roy's at Pebble Beach 🇱🇸🇲 25 | 26 | 24 | $47

The Inn at Spanish Bay, 2700 17 Mile Dr. (Congress Rd.), Pebble Beach, 831-647-7423

■ Fans "cannot say enough wonderful things about" the "impeccable standards" of this "spectacular spot" where the "breathtaking view of the ocean" is nearly matched by peripatetic chef Roy Yamaguchi's "inventive" Euro-Asian fare and the staff's "attentive service"; P.S. "cocktails and appetizers at sunset are not to be missed."

San Benito House 🇸 ▽ 20 | 19 | 19 | $31

356 Main St. (bet. Correas & Filbert Sts.), Half Moon Bay, 650-726-3425

■ Tucked away in a historic country inn of the same name, this small, charming Half Moon Bay Victorian-style dining room ("doily central") serves a solid monthly-changing Cal-Med menu, which features local produce, seafood and meat.

Santa Barbara Grill 🇱🇸🇲 14 | 16 | 16 | $31

10745 N. De Anza Blvd. (bet. Hwy. 280 & Valley Green Dr.), Cupertino, 408-253-2233

☑ This "watering hole for Apple Computer" worker bees offers "large portions" of "decent" American edibles and provides "cheerful service", not that everyone notices "amid the cell-phone action"; cynics say this neighborhood spot is "only good because it's in Cupertino."

Scott's 🇱🇸🇲 18 | 17 | 17 | $34

2300 E. Bayshore Rd. (Embarcadero Rd.), Palo Alto, 650-856-1046
185 Park Ave. (bet. Almaden Blvd. & Market St.), San Jose, 408-971-1700
See review in San Francisco Directory.

SENT SOVI ⑤   27 | 22 | 24 | $61
14583 Big Basin Way (5th St.), Saratoga, 408-867-3110
■ Chef-owner David Kinch's "romantic" Saratoga "jewel" features "beautifully presented, creative" New French–American cuisine and employs a "knowledgeable staff" that "treats you very well"; a copper-topped bar and Oriental rugs add to this "heaven-sent" choice that you may "never want to leave."

71 Saint Peter ⓛ Ⓜ   24 | 18 | 23 | $39
71 N. San Pedro St. (bet. Santa Clara & St. John Sts.), San Jose, 408-971-8523
■ Disciples of this San Jose bistro find solace in its "reliable", "soulful" Mediterranean fare (prepared by CIA grad Mark Tabak) and "excellent service"; although the interior is "very small", "you can eat outside on warm nights."

Sierra Mar ⓛⓈⓂ   ▽ 27 | 29 | 28 | $64
Post Ranch Inn, Hwy. 1 (30 mi. south of Carmel), Big Sur, 831-667-2800
■ For a "breathtaking experience" where the "Cal-French food" and the "stunning views of the Pacific Ocean" "run neck-in-neck", check into this rustic but luxurious "hideaway" in Big Sur's Post Ranch Inn; the prices are as high as its 1,200 foot perch above the ocean, "but you're in heaven, so who cares?"

Spago Palo Alto ⓛⓈⓂ   24 | 24 | 22 | $51
265 Lytton Ave. (Bryant St.), Palo Alto, 650-833-1000
■ "Another home run in the Wolfgang Puck Spago series", this "big, high-style" Californian (which features an original Rauschenberg) is a perfect fit for the "powerful" "Silicon Valley crowd" that "comes to network" and to show off their "trophy wives"; despite the hype, surveyors concede chef Michael French's "inventive" fare is "fabulous" and the staff "treats you like royalty" ("and charges you like it too").

Stillwater Bar & Grill ⓛⓈⓂ   ▽ 22 | 26 | 22 | $43
Lodge at Pebble Beach, 17 Mile Dr. (Hwy. 1), Pebble Beach, 831-625-8524
■ "Anything would taste good with that view" declare surveyors commenting on this Pebble Beach seafooder with a "beautiful" setting looking out onto the famed golf course's 18th hole; hungry duffers and "tourists" also add that it's "fun to sit at the raw bar and eat oysters."

Stokes Adobe ⓛⓈⓂ   23 | 22 | 22 | $44
500 Hartnell St. (bet. Madison & Polk Sts.), Monterey, 831-373-1110
■ Set in a "historical adobe" in Monterey with a "magnificent interior" with two fireplaces, this "destination dining spot" boasts an "equally unusual" Cal-Med bistro menu crafted by "well-regarded chef" Brandon Miller; "gracious service" adds to the "consistently satisfying experience."

Straits Cafe L S M   22 | 18 | 18 | $29
3295 El Camino Real (Lambert Ave.), Palo Alto, 650-494-7168
See review in San Francisco Directory.

Sushi Ya M   ▽ 18 | 10 | 16 | $26
380 University Ave. (Waverley St.), Palo Alto, 650-322-0330
■ Only known by a small band of sushi fanatics, this "quiet",
Japanese "hole-in-the-wall" in Palo Alto serves super
fresh fish that some swear is "still moving" when it's
served; "fairly cheap" prices add to its appeal.

Swagat Indian Cuisine S M   18 | 11 | 14 | $21
*2700 W. El Camino Real (bet. Los Altos Ave. & San Antonio Rd.),
Mountain View, 650-948-7727*
☑ "It's nothing fancy" but this Mountain View Indian stalwart
has a lunch buffet that remains a popular choice for Silicon
Valley diners looking for a "good, inexpensive meal"; the
kitchen also prepares many "hard-to-find South Indian
dishes" such as *dosai*, which are lacy lentil-flour crêpes.

Tapestry L M   23 | 21 | 22 | $43
11 College Ave. (E. Main St.), Los Gatos, 408-395-2808
■ A relatively recent addition to the Los Gatos dining scene,
this "hidden charmer" weaves together a monthly changing
menu of "awesomely presented" Cal-Eclectic fare with
"very friendly service" and a "quaint" ("almost too quaint")
cottage-style decor to create a terrific dining tapestry;
P.S. don't pass up the "outdoor" eating in warm weather.

Tarpy's Roadhouse L S M   22 | 21 | 21 | $37
*2999 Monterey-Salinas Hwy. (Canyon Del Rey), Monterey,
831-647-1444*
■ "Hearty eaters with discriminating taste" know to "grab a
table on the patio" of this "isolated roadhouse", which is
located in a "whimsically decorated" historic Monterey
building; expect a "diversified" lineup of "wonderful"
American "comfort food" (which includes a different game
dish every week) enhanced by a "great wine list."

Tarragon L M   ▽ 20 | 23 | 19 | $37
*140 S. Murphy Ave. (bet. Evelyn & Washington Aves.),
Sunnyvale, 408-737-8003*
☑ This narrow, "crowded" Sunnyvale Californian serves a
constantly evolving menu of very respectable cuisine; with
"CEO prices" and a "plush"interior with comfy booths and
handmade hourglass-shaped lamps, it's not surprising that it
attracts an upscale clientele.

Taste Cafe and Bistro L S   ▽ 23 | 17 | 22 | $35
1199 Forest Ave. (Prescott Ave.), Pacific Grove, 831-655-0324
■ Now under new ownership, this "tiny", rustic Pacific
Grove New American is called a "sleeper" for its compact
menu of dishes "that never fail to please the palate", like
the "fabulous" signature salmon in parchment.

Viaggio Ristorante L S
20 | 21 | 20 | $40

14550 Big Basin Way (bet. 3rd & 4th Sts.), Saratoga, 408-741-5300

◪ Bustling, "noisy" and capacious, this eatery along Saratoga's restaurant row is noted for its "pretty room", "attentive staff" and "very good" Mediterranean fare, which embraces a diverse collection of classics from paella Valenciana to bouillabaisse to chicken tagine; the extensive wine list includes many nearby Santa Cruz Mountain vintages.

Viognier L S M
24 | 21 | 22 | $45

Draeger's Mkt., 222 E. Fourth Ave. (bet. B St. & Ellsworth Ave.), San Mateo, 650-685-3727

◼ Considered a foodie favorite in San Mateo, this impressive, globally influenced Mediterranean is "not what you'd expect" to find "above a grocery store", but Draeger's gourmet market is a standout in its category and so is the restaurant; moreover, regulars report that despite the departure of opening chef Gary Danko, the cuisine is still at the same high level, as is the "gracious service."

Wild Hare L S M
22 | 22 | 21 | $46

1029 El Camino Real (bet. Menlo & Santa Cruz Aves.), Menlo Park, 650-327-4273

◼ "Joey Altman has a hit" (and we're not talking about his local TV show *Bay Cafe*) at this "ambitious" Menlo Park American rookie, which specializes in "unusual wild" game such as ostrich, kangaroo and "out-of-this-world" grilled bison steak; a "very well-trained" staff presides over the upscale lodge setting.

Zao Noodle Bar L S M
15 | 14 | 15 | $17

261 University Ave. (Ramona St.), Palo Alto, 650-328-1988
See review in San Francisco Directory.

Zibibbo L S M
20 | 21 | 18 | $39

430 Kipling St. (bet. Lytton & University Aves.), Palo Alto, 650-328-6722

◼ "A faithful recreation of SF's LuLu" (its sister restaurant), this bi-level, "hyper-trendy Palo Alto scene" serves "family-style" portions of "lusty" Mediterranean cuisine ("excellent" iron skillet–roasted mussels) to a "young", "polished" "post-IPO" crowd that ignores the "way-too-noisy" acoustics.

CUISINES*

Afghan

Helmand

American (New)

A.P. Stump's/S
Avenue Grill/N
Avenue 9
Bacar
Big Four
Bistro Ralph/N
Boonville Hotel/N
Brannan's Grill/N
Cafe Beaujolais/N
Cafe Kati
Café La Haye/N
Cafe Lolo/N
Carnelian Room
Celadon/N
Chaz
Chez T.J./S
Cielo/S
Cobalt Tavern
Cosmopolitan Cafe
Cypress Club
Deuce/N
DINE
Dot
Duck Club/N
Duck Club/S
Ella's
Feast/N
First Crush
Flea St. Cafe/S
French Laundry/N
Gary Danko
Ginger Island/E
Globe
Harry Denton's Starlight
Heirloom/N
Indigo
Infusion
Jack's
Jianna
Jocco's/S
John Bentley's/S
Johnfrank
Kenwood/N
Lark Creek Inn/N
La Scene
Liberty Café
Lion & Compass/S
Los Gatos Brewing/S

Madrona Manor/N
Mecca
Meetinghouse
Miss Millie's
Mojo/S
Mustards Grill/N
955 Ukiah/N
Occidental Grill
Olema Inn/N
One Market
Paragon
Park Grill
Perlot
P.J. Mulhern's
Rick's
Ricochet
Rotunda
Rouge
Santa Barbara Grill/S
Sent Sovi/S
Skates on the Bay/E
Slow Club
Sno-Drift
Station Hse. Cafe/N
Taste Café/S
Tomales Bay Foods/N
Townhouse B&G/E
Town's End
Universal Cafe
Wild Hare/S
Wine Spectator/N
Woodward's Garden
Zin/N

American (Regional)

Catahoula/N
Connecticut Yankee
Crescent City Cafe
Duarte's Tavern/S
Eastside West
Mojo/S
PJ's Oyster Bed
Savanna Grill/N
Yankee Pier/N

American (Traditional)

Academy Grill
Anzu
Autumn Moon Cafe/E
Balboa Cafe

---

* All restaurants are in the City of San Francisco unless otherwise noted (E=East of San Francisco; N=North of San Francisco; and S=South of San Francisco).

Beach Chalet
Bette's Oceanview/E
Bill's Place
Bitterroot
Bix
Blue
Blue Chalk Cafe/S
Boulevard
Brazen Head
Bubba's Diner/N
Buckeye Roadhse./N
Buck's/S
Buffalo Grill/S
Cafe For All Seasons
Casa Orinda/E
Cheesecake Factory
Chloe's Cafe
Clement St. B&G
Cliff House
Delancey Street
Dipsea Cafe/N
Doidge's Cafe
Dottie's True Blue
Empire Grill/S
FatApple's/E
Felix & Louie's/N
Firewood Cafe
Fly Trap
Fog City Diner
Gordon Biersch
Gordon Biersch/S
Gordon's/N
Grill on the Alley/S
Hamburger Mary's
Hard Rock Cafe
Hayes St. Grill
It's Tops
Jimtown Store/N
John's Grill
Kate's Kitchen
Kelly's Mission Rock
Lark Creek/E
Lark Creek/S
Lark Creek Inn/N
Linda's Seabreeze/S
Livefire
Livefire/N
Liverpool Lil's
MacArthur Park
MacArthur Park/S
Magnolia Pub
Mama's/Washington Sq.
Mama's Royal Cafe/E
Mel's Drive-In
MoMo's

Moss Beach/S
Mucca/N
Nepenthe/S
Northstar
Oak Town Cafe/E
Original Joe's
Perry's Downtown
Pier 23 Cafe
Planet Hollywood
Pluto's
Pluto's/S
Pork Store Cafe
Potrero Brewing
Pyramid Alehouse/E
Red Tractor Cafe/E
Red Tractor Cafe/S
Rick & Ann's/E
Rosamunde
Rutherford Grill/N
Sam's Anchor Cafe/N
Sam's Grill
Sand Dollar/N
Sears Fine Food
Tarpy's Roadhse./S
Tommy's Joynt
Triple Rock Brewery/E
Twenty Four
2223 Restaurant
Vic Stewart's/E

Asian
AsiaSF
Azie
Betelnut Pejiu Wu
Bridges/E
Brix/N
Charlie Hong Kong/S
E&O Trading
E&O Trading/S
Eos
Flying Fish Grill/S
Grandview/S
House
Ma Tante Sumi
Ne O
Oritalia
Ponzu
Silks
Spettro/E
Straits Cafe
Straits Cafe/S
Tin-Pan
Tonga Room
Venture Frogs
Watergate

Xanadu/E
Zao Noodle Bar
Zao Noodle Bar/S

Bakery

Cheeseboard/E
Citizen Cake
Downtown Bakery/N
Emporio Rulli/N
Gayle's/S
Liberty Café
Model Bakery/N
Northstar
Town's End

Barbecue

Brother-in-Law's
Brother's
Buckeye Roadhse./N
Foothill Cafe/N
Hahn's Hibachi
Koryo/E
Livefire
Livefire/N
MacArthur Park
MacArthur Park/S
Memphis Minnie's BBQ

Brazilian

Terra Brazilis

Burmese

Irrawaddy
Mandalay
Nan Yang Rockridge/E

Cajun/Creole

Catahoula/N
Crescent City Cafe
Elite Cafe
Mojo/S
Nola/S
PJ's Oyster Bed
Tropix/E

Californian

Acre Café/N
Albion River Inn/N
Alta Mira/N
Aqui/S
Avanti/S
Avenue Grill/N
Bacchanal/S
Backflip
Bay Wolf/E
Bistro Viola/E

Blackhawk Grille/E
Boonville Hotel/N
Brava Terrace/N
Bridges/E
Cafe Lolo/N
Cafe Monk
Cafe Torre/S
California Cafe/E
California Cafe/N
California Cafe/S
Caprice/N
Charles Nob Hill
Chateau Souverain/N
Cheers
Chez Panisse/E
Chez Panisse Cafe/E
Christopher's/E
Cin Cin/N
Citizen Cake
Convivio Trattoria/S
Covey/S
Domaine Chandon/N
Duarte's Tavern/S
Emma
Erna's Elderberry/S
Eulipia/S
Farallon
Flea St. Cafe/S
Flying Fish Grill/S
Food Inc.
Foothill Cafe/N
Fournou's Ovens
Gabriella Cafe/S
Garden Court
Garibaldis
Garibaldis/E
Gayle's/S
General's Daughter/N
Glen Ellen Inn/N
Grasing's/S
Hawthorne Lane
Insalata's/N
Italian Colors/E
Jardinière
Jimmy Bean's/E
Joe's Taco/N
John Ash/N
Jordan's/E
Julie's Supper Club
Leford House/N
London Wine Bar
Lucy's Cafe/N
MacCallum House/N
Manka's Inverness/N
Marinus/S

168   www.zagat.com

Mariposa/N
mc^2
Meadowood Grill/N
Mikayla/Casa Madrona/N
Montage
Moose's
Moosse Cafe/N
Mucca/N
Napa Valley Grille/N
Napa Valley Wine Train/N
Oritalia
Oswald's/S
Pacific
Pacific's Edge/S
Palomino
paul K
Pier 40
Postrio
Presidio Cafe
Ravenous/N
Rest. at Meadowood/N
Rio Grill/S
Rivoli/E
Rubicon
San Benito House/S
Santa Fe B&G/E
Sierra Mar/S
Silks
Soizic/E
Sonoma Mission Inn/N
Spago Palo Alto/S
Stars
Stokes Adobe/S
St. Orres/N
Syrah/N
Tadich Grill
Tapestry/S
Tarragon/S
Terra/N
Top of the Mark
Tortola
Waterfront
Wente Vineyards/E
Willowside Cafe/N
Willow Wood Mkt. Café/N
Xyz
Zin/N
Zinzino
Zodiac Club

Cambodian
Angkor Borei
Angkor Wat
Battambang/E
Cambodiana/E

Caribbean
Cha Cha Cha
Charanga
Primo Patio Cafe
Tropix/E

Chinese
Alice's
Brandy Ho's
Chef Chu's/S
Dragonfly Café/N
Dragon Well
Eliza's
Empress of China
Eric's
Firecracker
Fook Yuen/S
Fountain Court
Gourmet Carousel
Grandview/S
Great Eastern
Harbor Village
Hong Kong Flower/S
House of Nanking
Hunan
Hunan Home's
Jade Villa/E
Koi Palace/S
Lichee Garden
Long Life Noodle
Long Life Noodle/E
Long Life Vegi/E
Mandarin
Mayflower
Mei Long/S
Omei/S
R & G Lounge
Rest. Peony/E
Shanghai 1930
Shen Hua/E
Taiwan
Taiwan/E
Tommy Toy's
Ton Kiang
Yank Sing
Yuet Lee
Zao Noodle Bar
Zao Noodle Bar/S

Coffeehouse
Cafe Borrone/S
Caffe Centro
Circadia

Coffee Shop/Diner
Bagdad Cafe
Bette's Oceanview/E
Bubba's Diner/N
Dipsea Cafe/N

It's Tops
JoAnn's Cafe/S
Mama's Royal Cafe/E
Mario's Bohemian
Max's Diner
Mel's Drive-In
Sears Fine Food

Continental

Alta Mira/N
Bella Vista/S
Caprice/N
Clouds Downtown/S
Compass Rose
Eulipia/S
Hotel Mac/E
Ovation
Rocco's
Schroeder's

Deli/Sandwich Shop

Arlequin Food to Go
Cafe Citti/N
David's Deli
Gayle's/S
Jimtown Store/N
JZ Cool/S
Max's on Square
Max's Opera Café
Max's Opera Café/E
Max's Opera Café/S
Moishe's Pippic
Rosamunde
Saul's/E
Vivande Porta Via

Dim Sum

Fook Yuen/S
Harbor Village
Hong Kong Flower/S
Jade Villa/E
Koi Palace/S
Lichee Garden
Mayflower
Rest. Peony/E
Ton Kiang
Yank Sing

Eclectic/International

Acre Café/N
Bittersweet Bistro/S
Blue Plate
Britt-Marie's/E
Bubble Lounge
Cafe Beaujolais/N
Cafe Flore

Café La Haye/N
Caffe Proust
Careme Room
Carta
Celadon/N
Chow
Crepevine
Crepevine/E
Feast/N
Firefly
Flying Saucer
Fog City Diner
Frascati
Fuzio
Glen Ellen Inn/N
Gordon's Hse.
Hayes & Vine
Lalime's/E
Lucy's Cafe/N
Mixx/N
Montrio/S
Northstar
Ondine/N
Palace/S
Park Chow
Pearl/N
Pearl Alley Bistro/S
Ravenous/N
Rick's
Rooster
Tapestry/S
Three Ring
Wappo Bar/N

English

Lovejoy's

Eritrean

Massawa

Ethiopian

Blue Nile/E
Rasselas

French (Bistro)

Absinthe
Alamo Square
Anjou
Baker St. Bistro
Belon
Bistro Clovis
Bistro Jeanty/N
Bistro Vida/S
Bistro Viola/E
Bizou
Black Cat

Bocca Rotis
Bouchon/N
Brasserie Savoy
Butler & the Chef
Cafe Bastille
Café Claude
Café de la Presse
Cafe de Paris
Cafe Marcella/S
Cafe Rouge/E
Chapeau!
Charcuterie/N
Christophe/N
Clementine
Florio
Fringale
girl & the fig/N
Hyde St. Bistro
L'Amie Donia/S
La Note/E
Le Bistro Cafe/N
Le Central Bistro
Le Charm
Left Bank/N
Left Bank/S
Luna Park
Nizza La Bella/E
101 Main Bistro/N
Pastis
Piaf's
Plouf
Robert's Bistro/S
Savor
Scala's Bistro
Soizic/E
South Park Cafe
Syrah/N
Three Ring
Voulez-Vous/E
Zazie

French (Classic)
Anton & Michel/S
Auberge du Soleil/N
Basque Cultural Ctr./S
Cafe Jacqueline
Cafe Mozart
Campton Place
Casanova/S
Chateau Souverain/N
Christophe/N
Citron/E
Dal Baffo/S
El Paseo/N
Emile's/S

Foreign Cinema
Gary Danko
Guernica/N
Heirloom/N
Jojo/E
Le Mouton Noir/S
L'Olivier
Masa's
Ne O
Rue de Main/E
Ti Couz
Waterfront

French (New)
Alfy's/N
Applewood Inn/N
Aux Delices
Azie
Cafe Fanny/E
Charles Nob Hill
Chaya Brasserie
Chez T.J./S
Club XIX/S
Domaine Chandon/N
Elisabeth Daniel
Erna's Elderberry/S
Fifth Floor
Filou/N
Fleur de Lys
Flying Saucer
Fresh Cream/S
Grand Cafe
Jack's
Jardinière
Kenwood/N
La Folie
La Toque/N
Le Papillon/S
Madrona Manor/N
Marinus/S
Ma Tante Sumi
mc^2
Meritage/N
955 Ukiah/N
Obelisque/E
Ovation
Pacific's Edge/S
Pastis
Pinot Blanc/N
Plumed Horse/S
Ritz-Carlton Din. Rm.
Rubicon
Sent Sovi/S
Sierra Mar/S
Sno-Drift

Stars
Terra/N
Thornhill Cafe/E
Watergate
Xyz

Fusion

Azie
butterfly
Eos
House
Ondine/N
Oritalia
Roy's
Roy's at Pebble Beach/S

German

Schroeder's
Suppenküche
Tommy's Joynt
Walzwerk

Greek

Evvia/S
Kokkari Estiatorio

Hamburger

Balboa Cafe
Barney's
Barney's/E
Bill's Place
Connecticut Yankee
Hamburger Mary's
Hard Rock Cafe
Liverpool Lil's
Mel's Drive-In
Mo's Burgers
Nepenthe/S
Perry's Downtown

Hawaiian

Tita's

Hungarian

Hungarian Sausage

Indian

Ajanta/E
Amber India/S
Breads of India/E
Ganges
Gaylord India
Gaylord India/S
Indian Oven
Lotus/N
Maharani
North India
Shalimar
Swagat/S

Indonesian

Jakarta
Rice Table/N

Irish

O'Reilly's

Italian

(N=Northern; S=Southern;
N&S=Includes both)
Acquerello (N)
Albona Rist. (N)
Allegro (N&S)
Antica Trattoria (N&S)
Aperto (N&S)
Baldoria (N&S)
Bella Trattoria (N&S)
Bistro Don Giovanni/N (N&S)
Bocca Rotis (N&S)
Bocce Cafe (N&S)
Bontà Rist. (N&S)
Brazio/E (N)
Bruno's (S)
Buca di Beppo (S)
Buca di Beppo/S (S)
Buca Giovanni (N&S)
Cafe Citti/N (N)
Cafe 817/E (N)
Cafe Niebaum Coppola (S)
Cafe Riggio (N&S)
Cafe Tiramisu (N)
Cafe Torre/S (N&S)
Caffe Delle Stelle (N)
Caffe Greco (N&S)
Caffe Macaroni (S)
Caffe Proust (N&S)
Caffe Sport (S)
Capellini/S (N)
Capp's Corner (N&S)
Carpaccio/S (N)
Casanova/S (N)
Convivio Trattoria/S (N&S)
Cucina Jackson Fillmore/N (S)
Dal Baffo/S (N&S)
dalla Torre (N)
Delfina (N&S)
Della Santina's/N (N)
E'Angelo (N)
Emma (N&S)
Emporio Rulli/N (N&S)
Enrico's (S)
Felix & Louie's/N (N&S)
Fior d'Italia (N)
Florio (N&S)
Frantoio/N (N)
Frascati (N&S)

Gabriella Cafe/S (N)
Gira Polli (N&S)
Gira Polli/E (N&S)
Gira Polli/N (N&S)
Green Valley Cafe/N (N)
I Fratelli (N&S)
Il Davide/N (N)
Il Fornaio (N)
Il Fornaio/E (N)
Il Fornaio/N (N)
Il Fornaio/S (N)
Il Porcellino/E (N)
Iron Horse (N)
Italian Colors/E (N&S)
Jackson Fillmore (S)
Julius' Castle (N)
Kuleto's (N&S)
Kuleto's Trattoria/S (N&S)
La Felce (N)
Laghi (N)
La Ginestra/N (S)
La Pastaia/S (N&S)
La Villa Poppi (N)
Little City (N&S)
Little Italy (S)
Little Joe's (N&S)
L'Osteria Del Forno (N)
Luna Park (N&S)
Macaroni Sciue Sciue (S)
Mangiafuoco (N)
Marin Joe's/N (N&S)
Mario's Bohemian (N)
Maye's Oyster Hse. (N)
Mazzini/E (N&S)
Meritage/N (N)
Mescolanza (N)
Mezza Luna/S (S)
Michelangelo Cafe (N&S)
Mio Vicino/S (N&S)
New Pisa (N&S)
Nizza La Bella/E (N&S)
Nob Hill Cafe (N)
North Bch. Rest. (N&S)
Oliveto/E (N)
Original Joe's (N&S)
Osteria (N)
Osteria/S (N)
Palio d'Asti (N&S)
Pane e Vino (N)
Paolo's/S (N&S)
Parma (N)
Pasta Moon/S (N&S)
Pasta Pomodoro (N&S)
Pasta Pomodoro/E (N&S)
Pasta Pomodoro/N (N&S)

Pazzia (N&S)
Piatti/E (N&S)
Piatti/N (N&S)
Piatti/S (N&S)
Piazza D'Angelo/N (N&S)
Postino/E (N)
Prego (N&S)
Prima/E (N)
Puccini & Pinetti (N&S)
Radicchio (N)
Rist. Bacco (N&S)
Rist. Ecco (N&S)
Rist. Fabrizio/N (N)
Rist. Ideale (N&S)
Rist. Milano (N)
Rist. Umbria (N&S)
Rose Pistola (N)
Rose's Cafe (N)
Salute Ristorante/E (N&S)
Salute Ristorante/N (N&S)
Santi/N (N&S)
Scala's Bistro (N&S)
Spettro/E (N&S)
Spiedini/E (N&S)
Splendido (N&S)
Stars (N&S)
Stelline (N&S)
Stinking Rose (N)
Tavolino (N)
Tomatina/N (N&S)
Tommaso's (N&S)
Trattoria Contadina (N&S)
Tra Vigne/N (N&S)
Tuscany/N (N)
Uva/N (N&S)
Venezia/E (N&S)
Venticello (N)
Via Vai (N&S)
Vicolo (N&S)
Vivande Porta Via (N&S)
Zachary's/E (N&S)
Zinzino (N&S)
Zuni Cafe (N)
Zza's Trattoria/E (N&S)

Japanese
Ace Wasabi's
Anzu
Blowfish, Sushi
Chaya Brasserie
Ebisu
Godzila Sushi
Grandeho's Kamekyo
Hamano Sushi
Hana/N

Hotei
Iroha
Isobune Sushi
Isobune Sushi/E
Isobune Sushi/S
Juban
Juban/S
Kabuto Sushi
Kirala/E
Kyo-Ya
Maki
Matsuya
Mifune
Murasaki
Nippon Sushi
O Chamé/E
Osaka Grill
Osome
Ramen Club/S
Robata/N
Sanppo
Sanraku
Sushi Groove
Sushi Ran/N
Sushi to Dai For/N
Sushi Ya/S
Tachibana/E
Ten-Ichi
Tokyo Go Go
Uzen/E
We Be Sushi
Yoshida-Ya
Yoshi's/Jack London Sq./E

Jewish

David's Deli
Max's Diner
Max's on Square
Max's Opera Café
Max's Opera Café/E
Max's Opera Café/S
Moishe's Pippic
Saul's/E

Korean

Brother's
Coriya Hot Pot City
Hahn's Hibachi
Koryo/E
New Korea Hse.

Latin American

Cafe de la Paz/E
Charanga

Mediterranean

Aram's
Arlequin Food to Go

Auberge du Soleil/N
Bay Wolf/E
Bistro Aix
Bistro Zaré
Blackhawk Grille/E
Bucci's/E
Caffe Museo
Chez Nous
Chez Panisse/E
Chez Panisse Cafe/E
Cin Cin/N
Enrico's
Fandango/S
Faz
Faz/E
Faz/S
Food Inc.
42°
Fournou's Ovens
Garibaldis
Garibaldis/E
Insalata's/N
Lalime's/E
La Mediterranée
La Mediterranée/E
Lapis
Leford House/N
LuLu
Metropol
Mezze/E
Mixx/N
Moose's
Oak Town Cafe/E
Palomino
paul K
PlumpJack Cafe
PlumpJack Cafe/N
Postrio
Ritz-Carlton Terrace
Rivoli/E
San Benito House/S
Savor
71 Saint Peter/S
Stokes Adobe/S
Truly Mediterranean
Viaggio/S
Viognier/S
Waterfront
Zaré on Sacramento
Zax
Zibibbo/S
Zodiac Club
Zuni Cafe

Mexican/Tex-Mex

Aqui/S
Cactus Cafe/N
Cactus Taqueria/E
Cafe Marimba

Casa Aguila
Doña Tomás/E
El Balazo
El Palomar/S
Guaymas/N
Joe's Taco/N
Juan's Place/E
La Cumbre
La Cumbre/S
La Palma
La Rondalla
Las Camelias/N
La Taqueria
La Taqueria/S
Left at Albuquerque
Left at Albuquerque/S
Manuel's/S
Maya
Maya/N
Mom is Cooking
Pancho Villa
Picante Cocina/E
Roosevelt Tamale
Spettro/E
Taqueria Cancun
Tortola
Wa-Ha-Ka Oaxaca

Middle Eastern
Aram's
Kan Zaman
La Mediterranée
La Mediterranée/E
Maykedah
Truly Mediterranean
Ya-Ya Cuisine

Moroccan
Kasbah/N

Nepalese
Kathmandu West/S

Noodle Shop
Charlie Hong Kong/S
Citrus Club
Hotei
Iroha
Long Life Noodle
Long Life Noodle/E
Mifune
Zao Noodle Bar
Zao Noodle Bar/S

Pakistani
Shalimar

Persian
Maykedah

Pizza
Bittersweet Bistro/S
Bucci's/E
Cafe Niebaum Coppola
Cheeseboard/E
Firewood Cafe
Il Fornaio
Il Fornaio/E
Il Fornaio/N
Il Fornaio/S
La Ginestra/N
Lucy's Cafe/N
Mio Vicino/S
Model Bakery/N
Nizza La Bella/E
Nob Hill Cafe
North Bch. Pizza
North Bch. Pizza/E
Pasta Moon/S
Pauline's
Pazzia
Pizza Rustica/E
Pizzetta 211
Tomatina/N
Tommaso's
Uva/N
Via Vai
Vicolo
Zachary's/E
Zinzino

Russian
Katia's

Seafood
Alamo Square
Alioto's
Aqua
A. Sabella's
Belon
Crow's Nest/S
Crustacean
Eastside West
Farallon
Flying Fish Grill/S
Hayes St. Grill
Koi Palace/S
Maye's Oyster Hse.
McCormick & Kuleto's
Nonna Rose
Pacific Cafe
Pier 23 Cafe
Pisces/S
PJ's Oyster Bed
Red Herring

Rocco's
Rose Pistola
Sam's Grill
Scoma's
Scoma's/N
Scott's
Scott's/E
Scott's/S
Skates on the Bay/E
Spenger's/E
Station Hse. Cafe/N
Stillwater B&G/S
Swan Oyster Depot
Tadich Grill
Waterfront
Yabbies
Yankee Pier/N

Singaporean
Straits Cafe
Straits Cafe/S

South African
Joubert's

Southern/Soul
Biscuits & Blues
Catahoula/N
Crescent City Cafe
Memphis Minnie's BBQ
Mojo/S
Nola/S
PJ's Oyster Bed
Powell's Place

Southwestern
Left at Albuquerque
Left at Albuquerque/S
Rio Grill/S

Spanish
Alegrias
Barcelona
Basque Cultural Ctr./S
B44
Cafe de la Paz/E
César/E
Esperpento
Guernica/N
Iberia/S
Picaro
Pintxos
Thirsty Bear
Timo's
Zarzuela

Steakhouse
Alfred's Steak Hse.
Bighorn Grill/E
Brazio/E
Cole's/N
Crow's Nest/S
Grill on the Alley/S
Harris'
House of Prime Rib
Izzy's
John's Grill
Morton's of Chicago
Rutherford Grill/N
Scott's
Scott's/E
Scott's/S
Vic Stewart's/E

Swiss
La Fondue/S
Matterhorn Swiss

Taiwanese
Coriya Hot Pot City
Taiwan
Taiwan/E

Tapas
Alegrias
Alfy's/N
AsiaSF
Barcelona
Cafe de la Paz/E
César/E
Cha Cha Cha
Charanga
Chez Nous
Esperpento
Picaro
Pintxos
Tavolino
Thirsty Bear
Timo's
Zarzuela

Thai
Ara Wan/N
Basil
Cha Am Thai
Cha Am Thai/E
Dusit Thai
Khan Toke
King of Thai
Manora's
Marnee Thai
Narai
Neecha Thai

Phuping/E
Plearn/E
Royal Thai
Royal Thai/N
Thai House
Thanya & Salee
Thep Phanom
Yukol Place

Tibetan

Lhasa Moon

Vegetarian

(Most Chinese, Indian and
Thai restaurants)
Flea St. Cafe/S
Fleur de Lys
Ganges
Greens
Herbivore

Joubert's
Leford House/N
Long Life Vegi/E
Millennium
Valentine's Cafe

Vietnamese

Ana Mandara
Aux Delices
Camranh Bay/S
Crustacean
Golden Turtle
La Vie
Le Cheval/E
Le Colonial
Le Soleil
Slanted Door
Thanh Long
Tu Lan
Vi's/E

LOCATIONS

SAN FRANCISCO

Bernal Heights
Angkor Borei
Blue Plate
Dusit Thai
Hungarian Sausage
Liberty Café
Taqueria Cancun

Castro
Bagdad Cafe
Blue
Cafe Flore
Chow
Crepevine
Firewood Cafe
Fuzio
La Mediterranée
Ma Tante Sumi
Pasta Pomodoro
Thai House
Tin-Pan
Tita's
2223 Restaurant
Zao Noodle Bar

Chinatown
Brandy Ho's
Empress of China
Great Eastern
House of Nanking
Hunan Home's
Lichee Garden
R & G Lounge
Yuet Lee

Civic Center
Indigo
Max's Opera Café
Millennium
Stars
Venture Frogs

Cow Hollow
Baker St. Bistro
Balboa Cafe
Betelnut Pejiu Wu
Bontà Rist.
Brazen Head
Cafe de Paris
Doidge's Cafe
Eastside West

Left at Albuquerque
Liverpool Lil's
Osome
Pane e Vino
Perry's Downtown
PlumpJack Cafe
Prego
Radicchio
Rose's Cafe
Via Vai
Wa-Ha-Ka Oaxaca
Yoshida-Ya

Downtown
Alfred's Steak Hse.
Anjou
Anzu
Aqua
Barcelona
B44
Biscuits & Blues
Bix
Boulevard
Brasserie Savoy
Bubble Lounge
Cafe Bastille
Café Claude
Café de la Presse
Cafe Niebaum Coppola
Cafe Tiramisu
Campton Place
Carnelian Room
Cha Am Thai
Cheesecake Factory
Compass Rose
Cypress Club
David's Deli
Dottie's True Blue
E&O Trading
Elisabeth Daniel
Farallon
Faz
Fifth Floor
First Crush
Fleur de Lys
Fuzio
Garden Court
Gaylord India
Globe
Grand Cafe
Harbor Village

Harry Denton's Starlight
Hunan
Il Fornaio
Iron Horse
Jack's
John's Grill
Kokkari Estiatorio
Kuleto's
La Scene
Le Central Bistro
Le Colonial
L'Olivier
London Wine Bar
MacArthur Park
Masa's
Max's on Square
mc²
Metropol
Morton's of Chicago
Occidental Grill
Oritalia
Pacific
Palio d'Asti
Park Grill
Pastis
Perry's Downtown
Planet Hollywood
Plouf
Ponzu
Postrio
Puccini & Pinetti
Rotunda
Rubicon
Sam's Grill
Sanraku
Scala's Bistro
Schroeder's
Scott's
Sears Fine Food
Silks
Tadich Grill
Taqueria Cancun
Tommy Toy's
Tortola
Yank Sing
Ya-Ya Cuisine
Zaré on Sacramento

Embarcadero
Cosmopolitan Cafe
Delancey Street
Fog City Diner
Lapis
Long Life Noodle
One Market

Palomino
Pier 23 Cafe
Red Herring
Splendido
Town's End
Waterfront

Excelsior
Mom is Cooking
North Bch. Pizza

Haight-Ashbury/ Cole Valley
Cha Cha Cha
Citrus Club
Crescent City Cafe
El Balazo
Eos
Grandeho's Kamekyo
Kan Zaman
Magnolia Pub
Massawa
North Bch. Pizza
Pork Store Cafe
Truly Mediterranean
Zazie

Hayes Valley
Absinthe
Arlequin Food to Go
Bistro Clovis
Caffe Delle Stelle
Citizen Cake
Hayes & Vine
Hayes St. Grill
Jardinière
Moishe's Pippic
Ovation
paul K
Piaf's
Powell's Place
Stelline
Suppenküche
Terra Brazilis
Vicolo
Zuni Cafe

Inner Richmond
Angkor Wat
Bella Trattoria
Brother's
Cafe Riggio
Cheers
Clementine
Clement St. B&G
Coriya Hot Pot City

Fountain Court
Jakarta
Katia's
King of Thai
Le Soleil
Mandalay
Mel's Drive-In
Murasaki
Royal Thai
Straits Cafe
Taiwan
We Be Sushi

Inner Sunset

Avenue 9
Crepevine
Ebisu
Ganges
Hahn's Hibachi
Hotei
House
Park Chow
PJ's Oyster Bed
Pluto's
Tortola
We Be Sushi

Japantown

Cafe Kati
Dot
Iroha
Isobune Sushi
Juban
Maki
Mifune
New Korea Hse.
Pasta Pomodoro
Perlot
Sanppo

Lower Haight

Hahn's Hibachi
Indian Oven
Kate's Kitchen
Memphis Minnie's BBQ
Rosamunde
Thep Phanom

Marina

Ace Wasabi's
Alegrias
Barney's
Bistro Aix
Cafe Marimba
Chaz
Dragon Well

E'Angelo
Fuzio
Greens
Hahn's Hibachi
Irrawaddy
Izzy's
Lhasa Moon
Mel's Drive-In
North India
Parma
Pasta Pomodoro
Pluto's
Yukol Place
Zao Noodle Bar
Zinzino

Mission

Bitterroot
Blowfish, Sushi
Bruno's
butterfly
Cha Cha Cha
Charanga
Circadia
Delfina
Esperpento
Firecracker
Flying Saucer
Foreign Cinema
Gordon's Hse.
Herbivore
La Cumbre
La Palma
La Rondalla
La Taqueria
La Villa Poppi
Luna Park
Mangiafuoco
Ne O
Pancho Villa
Pauline's
Picaro
Pintxos
Potrero Brewing
Roosevelt Tamale
Rooster
Slanted Door
Slow Club
Taqueria Cancun
Three Ring
Ti Couz
Timo's
Tokyo Go Go
Truly Mediterranean
Universal Cafe
Walzwerk
Watergate

We Be Sushi
Woodward's Garden

Nob Hill

Big Four
Cafe Mozart
Charles Nob Hill
Fournou's Ovens
Nob Hill Cafe
Ritz-Carlton Din. Rm.
Ritz-Carlton Terrace
Tonga Room
Top of the Mark
Venticello

Noe Valley

Alice's
Barney's
Chloe's Cafe
Eric's
Firefly
Hahn's Hibachi
Hamano Sushi
Little Italy
Lovejoy's
Matsuya
Miss Millie's
Rist. Bacco
Savor
Valentine's Cafe

North Beach

Albona Rist.
Black Cat
Bocce Cafe
Brandy Ho's
Buca Giovanni
Cafe Jacqueline
Caffe Greco
Caffe Macaroni
Caffe Sport
Capp's Corner
Cobalt Tavern
dalla Torre
Emma
Enrico's
Fior d'Italia
Gira Polli
Helmand
House
Jianna
Julius' Castle
La Felce
Little City
Little Joe's
L'Osteria Del Forno

Macaroni Sciue Sciue
Mama's/Washington Sq.
Mario's Bohemian
Maykedah
Michelangelo Cafe
Moose's
Mo's Burgers
New Pisa
North Bch. Pizza
North Bch. Rest.
O'Reilly's
Pasta Pomodoro
P.J. Mulhern's
Rist. Ideale
Rose Pistola
Stinking Rose
Taiwan
Tavolino
Tommaso's
Trattoria Contadina
Zax

Pacific Heights

Eliza's
Food Inc.
Godzila Sushi
Gourmet Carousel
Laghi
Meetinghouse
Neecha Thai
Rasselas

Potrero Hill

Aperto
Connecticut Yankee
Eliza's
42°
Kelly's Mission Rock
Northstar
Sno-Drift
Thanya & Salee

Presidio Heights

Aram's
Ella's
Garibaldis
Osteria
Presidio Cafe
Tortola

Richmond

Beach Chalet
Bill's Place
Chapeau!
Cliff House
Kabuto Sushi

Khan Toke
La Vie
Mayflower
Mescolanza
Narai
Pacific Cafe
Pizzetta 211
Ton Kiang

Russian Hill

Allegro
Frascati
Hyde St. Bistro
I Fratelli
Rist. Milano
Sushi Groove
Zarzuela

SoMa

AsiaSF
Azie
Bacar
Basil
Bizou
Buca di Beppo
Cafe Monk
Caffe Museo
Cha Am Thai
Chaya Brasserie
DINE
Firewood Cafe
Fly Trap
Fringale
Gordon Biersch
Hamburger Mary's
Hawthorne Lane
Hunan
Julie's Supper Club
Kyo-Ya
Le Charm
Long Life Noodle
LuLu
Manora's
Max's Diner
Maya
Montage
Mo's Burgers
North Bch. Pizza
Pazzia
Primo Patio Cafe
Rist. Umbria
Roy's
Sanraku
Shanghai 1930
Sushi Groove
Thirsty Bear
Tu Lan
Wa-Ha-Ka Oaxaca

Xyz
Yank Sing

South Beach/
Pacific Bell Park

Butler & the Chef
Caffe Centro
Infusion
Livefire
MoMo's
Paragon
Pier 40
Rist. Ecco
South Park Cafe
Twenty Four

Stonestown

Tortola

Sunset

Casa Aguila
Cha Am Thai
Joubert's
Little Joe's
Marnee Thai
Pasta Pomodoro
Rick's
Thanh Long

Tenderloin

Academy Grill
Backflip
Belon
Careme Room
Maharani
Original Joe's
Shalimar

Twin Peaks/West Portal

Bocca Rotis
Cafe For All Seasons
Ricochet

Upper Fillmore

Chez Nous
Elite Cafe
Florio
Jackson Fillmore
La Mediterranée
Ten-Ichi
Vivande Porta Via
Zao Noodle Bar

Upper Market/
Church Street

Carta
It's Tops
Johnfrank

Mecca
Nippon Sushi
Zodiac Club

Van Ness/Polk

Acquerello
Antica Trattoria
Aux Delices
Baldoria
Bistro Zaré
Crustacean
Golden Turtle
Hahn's Hibachi
Hard Rock Cafe
Harris'
House of Prime Rib
La Folie
Mario's Bohemian
Matterhorn Swiss
Maye's Oyster Hse.
Osaka Grill
Rocco's

Rouge
Swan Oyster Depot
Tommy's Joynt
Yabbies

Western Addition

Alamo Square
Brother-in-Law's
Caffe Proust
Rasselas

Wharf

Alioto's
Ana Mandara
A. Sabella's
Gary Danko
Gaylord India
Grandeho's Kamekyo
Mandarin
McCormick & Kuleto's
Nonna Rose
Scoma's

EAST OF SAN FRANCISCO

Albany

Britt-Marie's
Christopher's
Nizza La Bella

Berkeley

Ajanta
Barney's
Bette's Oceanview
Bistro Viola
Blue Nile
Breads of India
Cactus Taqueria
Cafe de la Paz
Cafe Fanny
Cafe Rouge
Cambodiana
César
Cha Am Thai
Cheeseboard
Chez Panisse
Chez Panisse Cafe
FatApple's
Ginger Island
Jimmy Bean's
Jordan's
Juan's Place
Kirala
Lalime's
La Mediterranée
La Note

Long Life Noodle
Long Life Vegi
Mazzini
North Bch. Pizza
O Chamé
Picante Cocina
Plearn
Pyramid Alehouse
Rick & Ann's
Rivoli
Santa Fe B&G
Saul's
Shen Hua
Skates on the Bay
Spenger's
Taiwan
Triple Rock Brewery
Venezia
Voulez-Vous
Xanadu
Zachary's

Danville

Blackhawk Grille
Brazio
Bridges
Faz
Piatti

El Cerrito
FatApple's

Emeryville
Bucci's
Townhouse B&G

Hayward
Rue de Main

Lafayette
Postino

Livermore
Wente Vineyards

Oakland
Autumn Moon Cafe
Barney's
Battambang
Bay Wolf
Cactus Taqueria
Cafe 817
Citron
Crepevine
Doña Tomás
Garibaldis
Il Porcellino
Isobune Sushi
Italian Colors
Jade Villa
Jojo
Koryo
Le Cheval
Mama's Royal Cafe
Mezze
Nan Yang Rockridge
Oak Town Cafe
Obelisque
Oliveto
Pasta Pomodoro

Pizza Rustica
Red Tractor Cafe
Rest. Peony
Scott's
Soizic
Spettro
Thornhill Cafe
Tropix
Uzen
Vi's
Yoshi's/Jack London Sq.
Zachary's
Zza's Trattoria

Orinda
Casa Orinda
Tachibana

Pleasanton
Faz

Richmond
Hotel Mac
Phuping
Salute Ristorante

San Ramon
Bighorn Grill

Walnut Creek
California Cafe
Gira Polli
Il Fornaio
Lark Creek
Max's Opera Café
Prima
Scott's
Spiedini
Vic Stewart's

NORTH OF SAN FRANCISCO

Calistoga
Brannan's Grill
Catahoula
Cin Cin
Wappo Bar

Corte Madera
California Cafe
Dragonfly Café
Il Fornaio
Marin Joe's
Savanna Grill

Geyserville
Chateau Souverain
Santi

Glen Ellen/Kenwood
Cafe Citti
girl & the fig
Glen Ellen Inn
Kenwood
Mucca

Guerneville
Applewood Inn

Healdsburg

Acre Café
Bistro Ralph
Charcuterie
Downtown Bakery
Felix & Louie's
Jimtown Store
Madrona Manor
Ravenous
Zin

Lake Tahoe

PlumpJack Cafe

Larkspur

Emporio Rulli
Lark Creek Inn
Left Bank
Rist. Fabrizio
Yankee Pier

Mendocino County

Albion River Inn
Boonville Hotel
Cafe Beaujolais
Leford House
MacCallum House
Moosse Cafe
955 Ukiah
St. Orres

Mill Valley

Avenue Grill
Buckeye Roadhse.
Cactus Cafe
Dipsea Cafe
El Paseo
Frantoio
Gira Polli
Joe's Taco
La Ginestra
Piatti
Piazza D'Angelo
Robata

Napa

Bistro Don Giovanni
Brix
Celadon
Cole's
Foothill Cafe
Mustards Grill
Napa Valley Wine Train
Pearl
Tuscany
Uva

Olema

Olema Inn

Petaluma

Le Bistro Cafe

Rutherford

Auberge du Soleil
La Toque
Rutherford Grill

San Anselmo

Alfy's
Bubba's Diner
Cucina Jackson Fillmore
Filou
Insalata's

San Rafael

Il Davide
Kasbah
Las Camelias
Lotus
Pasta Pomodoro
Rice Table
Royal Thai
Salute Ristorante
Sushi to Dai For

Santa Rosa

Cafe Lolo
Feast
Hana
John Ash
Mariposa
Mixx
Syrah
Willowside Cafe

Sausalito

Alta Mira
Ara Wan
Christophe
Guernica
Mikayla/Casa Madrona
Ondine
Scoma's
Sushi Ran

Sebastopol/Valley Ford

Lucy's Cafe
101 Main Bistro
Willow Wood Mkt. Café

Sonoma

Café La Haye
Della Santina's

Deuce
General's Daughter
Heirloom
Maya
Meritage
Piatti
Sonoma Mission Inn

Sonoma Coast
Duck Club

St. Helena
Brava Terrace
Green Valley Cafe
Meadowood Grill
Model Bakery
Pinot Blanc
Rest. at Meadowood
Terra
Tomatina
Tra Vigne
Wine Spectator

Tiburon
Caprice
Guaymas
Sam's Anchor Cafe

West Marin
Manka's Inverness
Sand Dollar
Station Hse. Cafe
Tomales Bay Foods

Yountville
Bistro Jeanty
Bouchon
Domaine Chandon
French Laundry
Gordon's
Livefire
Napa Valley Grille
Piatti

SOUTH OF SAN FRANCISCO

Burlingame
Grandview
Il Fornaio
Isobune Sushi
Kuleto's Trattoria
Left at Albuquerque
Max's Opera Café
Pisces
Ramen Club

Campbell
Buca di Beppo
Left at Albuquerque
Mio Vicino

Cupertino
Cafe Torre
Kathmandu West
Santa Barbara Grill

Half Moon Bay/Coast
Duarte's Tavern
Mezza Luna
Moss Beach
Pasta Moon
San Benito House

Los Altos
Chef Chu's
Jocco's

Los Gatos
Cafe Marcella
California Cafe

Los Gatos Brewing
Tapestry

Menlo Park
Bistro Vida
Cafe Borrone
Carpaccio
Dal Baffo
Duck Club
Flea St. Cafe
Gaylord India
Juban
JZ Cool
Left Bank
Wild Hare

Millbrae
Fook Yuen
Hong Kong Flower

Monterey/Carmel
Anton & Michel
Casanova
Cielo
Club XIX
Covey
Fandango
Flying Fish Grill
Fresh Cream
Grasing's
Il Fornaio
Marinus
Montrio

Nepenthe
Pacific's Edge
Piatti
Rio Grill
Robert's Bistro
Roy's at Pebble Beach
Sierra Mar
Stillwater B&G
Stokes Adobe
Tarpy's Roadhse.
Taste Café

Mountain View
Amber India
Chez T.J.
Mei Long
Swagat

Palo Alto
Blue Chalk Cafe
Buca di Beppo
California Cafe
Empire Grill
Evvia
Gordon Biersch
Hong Kong Flower
Il Fornaio
L'Amie Donia
Left at Albuquerque
MacArthur Park
Max's Opera Café
Mojo
Nola
Osteria
Piatti
Pluto's
Scott's
Spago Palo Alto
Straits Cafe
Sushi Ya
Zao Noodle Bar
Zibibbo

San Jose
A.P. Stump's
Aqui
E&O Trading
Emile's
Eulipia
Gordon Biersch
Grill on the Alley
Il Fornaio
La Pastaia
La Taqueria
Le Papillon
Mio Vicino
Paolo's
Red Tractor Cafe

Scott's
71 Saint Peter

San Mateo
Buffalo Grill
Camranh Bay
Capellini
La Cumbre
Lark Creek
Viognier

Santa Clara
California Cafe
Mio Vicino

Santa Cruz/Aptos
Avanti
Bittersweet Bistro
Charlie Hong Kong
Clouds Downtown
Convivio Trattoria
Crow's Nest
El Palomar
Gabriella Cafe
Gayle's
Linda's Seabreeze
Manuel's
Omei
Oswald's
Pearl Alley Bistro

Saratoga
La Fondue
Le Mouton Noir
Plumed Horse
Sent Sovi
Viaggio

South San Francisco/ Daly City
Bacchanal
Basque Cultural Ctr.
JoAnn's Cafe
Koi Palace

Sunnyvale
Faz
Lion & Compass
Palace
Tarragon

Woodside
Bella Vista
Buck's
Iberia
John Bentley's

Yosemite-Oakhurst
Erna's Elderberry

SPECIAL FEATURES AND APPEALS*

Breakfast
(All hotels and the following standouts)
Absinthe
Autumn Moon Cafe/E
Bagdad Cafe
Bette's Oceanview/E
Bocca Rotis
Bubba's Diner/N
Café de la Presse
Cafe 817/E
Cafe Fanny/E
Cafe Flore
Caffe Centro
Caffe Greco
Casa Aguila
Chloe's Cafe
Citizen Cake
Crescent City Cafe
Dipsea Cafe/N
Doidge's Cafe
Dottie's True Blue
Downtown Bakery/N
Duarte's Tavern/S
Ella's
Emporio Rulli/N
FatApple's/E
Hamburger Mary's
Harbor Village
Hong Kong Flower/S
Il Fornaio/N
It's Tops
Jimmy Bean's/E
JoAnn's Cafe/S
Kokkari Estiatorio
La Mediterranée
La Note/E
Lark Creek Inn/N
Mama's Royal Cafe/E
Mama's/Washington Sq.
Mel's Drive-In
Metropol
Miss Millie's
Model Bakery/N
Oliveto/E
Pacific
Park Grill
Pluto's
Pork Store Cafe

Red Tractor Cafe/E
Rick & Ann's/E
Rose's Cafe
Savor
Sears Fine Food
Station Hse. Cafe/N
Swan Oyster Depot
Ton Kiang
Town's End
Universal Cafe
Yank Sing
Zazie

Brunch
(Best of many)
Absinthe
Alamo Square
Aperto
Autumn Moon Cafe/E
Avenue 9
Bagdad Cafe
Bette's Oceanview/E
Buckeye Roadhse./N
Cafe Marimba
California Cafe/E
California Cafe/N
California Cafe/S
Caprice/N
Careme Room
Cheers
Chloe's Cafe
Connecticut Yankee
Doidge's Cafe
Dottie's True Blue
Duck Club/S
Ella's
Empire Grill/S
FatApple's/E
Flea St. Cafe/S
Frascati
Garden Court
General's Daughter/N
Harbor Village
Il Fornaio/E
Il Fornaio/S
Insalata's/N
Jimmy Bean's/E
Kate's Kitchen
La Mediterranée (Noe St.)

---

* All restaurants are in the City of San Francisco unless otherwise noted (E=East of San Francisco; N=North of San Francisco; and S=South of San Francisco).

La Note/E
Lark Creek Inn/N
LuLu
Mama's/Washington Sq.
Mazzini/E
Mel's Drive-In
Mikayla/Casa Madrona/N
Miss Millie's
MoMo's
Moose's
Moss Beach/S
Napa Valley Grille/N
Pacific
Pasta Moon/S
Piazza D'Angelo/N
Postrio
Prego
Primo Patio Cafe
Rick & Ann's/E
Rio Grill/S
Sam's Anchor Cafe/N
Saul's/E
Swan Oyster Depot
Thornhill Cafe/E
Ton Kiang
Tortola
Town's End
Universal Cafe
Valentine's Cafe
Wente Vineyards/E
Yank Sing
Zazie
Zibibbo/S
Zuni Cafe

Buffet Served
(Check prices, days
and times)
Amber India/S
Anzu
Brannan's Grill/N
Cliff House
Duck Club/S
Empress of China
Garden Court
Gaylord India
Gaylord India/S
Hunan
Hunan Home's
Il Davide/N
Irrawaddy
Jakarta
Jordan's/E
Julie's Supper Club
Kathmandu West/S

Le Soleil
Little Joe's
Lotus/N
MacArthur Park/S
Maharani
Maye's Oyster Hse.
Meadowood Grill/N
Mom is Cooking
Pacific
Pasta Moon/S
Piatti/N
Rest. at Meadowood/N
Ritz-Carlton Terrace
Robata/N
Salute Ristorante/E
Santa Barbara Grill/S
Santa Fe B&G/E
Scoma's/N
Stinking Rose
Swagat/S
Thornhill Cafe/E
Tommy's Joynt
Top of the Mark
Wappo Bar/N

Business Dining
Academy Grill
Alfred's Steak Hse.
Anzu
Aqua
Azie
Big Four
Bizou
Boulevard
Brasserie Savoy
Campton Place
Carnelian Room
Cha Am Thai
Charles Nob Hill
Chaya Brasserie
Cole's/N
Cypress Club
dalla Torre
DINE
Emile's/S
Faz
Fior d'Italia
Flea St. Cafe/S
Fly Trap
Fournou's Ovens
Gordon's Hse.
Grill on the Alley/S
Hawthorne Lane
House of Prime Rib
Il Fornaio/S

Infusion
Izzy's
Jack's
John's Grill
Julius' Castle
Kokkari Estiatorio
Kuleto's
Kyo-Ya
Le Central Bistro
Lion & Compass/S
LuLu
Masa's
Max's Diner
Maya
mc²
MoMo's
Montrio/S
Moose's
Morton's of Chicago
Occidental Grill
One Market
Pacific
Pane e Vino
Park Grill
Pastis
Pisces/S
Postrio
Red Herring
Rist. Ecco
Rist. Umbria
Ritz-Carlton Din. Rm.
Rubicon
Sam's Grill
Scott's
Scott's/S
Shanghai 1930
Silks
South Park Cafe
Stars
Tadich Grill
Thirsty Bear
Tommy Toy's
Waterfront
Ya-Ya Cuisine
Zaré on Sacramento
Zibibbo/S

Caters

(Best of many)
Acquerello
Alegrias
Amber India/S
Aperto
Aqua
Aqui/S

Aram's
Arlequin Food to Go
Autumn Moon Cafe/E
Avenue 9
Azie
Barcelona
Betelnut Pejiu Wu
Bighorn Grill/E
Bistro Ralph/N
Bix
Bizou
Blackhawk Grille/E
Blowfish, Sushi
Bocca Rotis
Boonville Hotel/N
Brandy Ho's
Brannan's Grill/N
Brava Terrace/N
Buckeye Roadhse./N
butterfly
Cactus Taqueria/E
Cafe de la Paz/E
Cafe Lolo/N
Cafe Monk
Cafe Niebaum Coppola
Cafe Tiramisu
Caffe Delle Stelle
Caffe Macaroni
California Cafe/S
Camranh Bay/S
Carnelian Room
Cha Am Thai
Charcuterie/N
Chaya Brasserie
Chef Chu's/S
Chez Nous
Cielo/S
Cin Cin/N
Convivio Trattoria/S
Covey/S
Delancey Street
Deuce/N
Dragonfly Café/N
Dragon Well
El Palomar/S
Emile's/S
Emporio Rulli/N
Erna's Elderberry/S
Evvia/S
Farallon
Faz
Faz/E
Faz/S
Feast/N
Felix & Louie's/N

First Crush
Fountain Court
Frascati
Gayle's/S
Gaylord India/S
Gira Polli
Gira Polli/E
Gira Polli/N
Globe
Gordon's/N
Gordon's Hse.
Greens
Hana/N
Hungarian Sausage
Hyde St. Bistro
Iberia/S
Il Davide/N
Il Fornaio/S
Indian Oven
Insalata's/N
Iron Horse
Italian Colors/E
Jianna
Jimmy Bean's/E
Jocco's/S
John Ash/N
Julie's Supper Club
JZ Cool/S
Katia's
Kokkari Estiatorio
Kuleto's
Kuleto's Trattoria/S
Lalime's/E
La Mediterranée
La Mediterranée/E
La Note/E
Lapis
Las Camelias/N
Left Bank/N
Left Bank/S
Le Mouton Noir/S
Le Papillon/S
Livefire/N
London Wine Bar
Long Life Noodle
Lotus/N
LuLu
Macaroni Sciue Sciue
MacArthur Park
Mangiafuoco
Marinus/S
Mecca
Memphis Minnie's BBQ
Meritage/N
Mezze/E

Millennium
Mixx/N
Moishe's Pippic
Moosse Cafe/N
Mucca/N
Napa Valley Grille/N
North Bch. Pizza
North India
Obelisque/E
Osaka Grill
Palio d'Asti
Pane e Vino
Paolo's/S
Pearl/N
Piazza D'Angelo/N
Pinot Blanc/N
Postino/E
Postrio
Powell's Place
Primo Patio Cafe
Rasselas
Rest. at Meadowood/N
Rick & Ann's/E
Ricochet
Rio Grill/S
Robata/N
Rose's Cafe
Rouge
Royal Thai/N
San Benito House/S
Sanraku
Santa Barbara Grill/S
Shanghai 1930
Soizic/E
Spettro/E
Stokes Adobe/S
Straits Cafe/S
Sushi Ran/N
Swagat/S
Tachibana/E
Terra Brazilis
Uva/N
Uzen/E
Viaggio/S
Via Vai
Vic Stewart's/E
Vivande Porta Via
Voulez-Vous/E
Wente Vineyards/E
Wild Hare/S
Yank Sing
Ya-Ya Cuisine
Zao Noodle Bar
Zao Noodle Bar/S
Zibibbo/S
Zinzino

Dancing/Entertainment

(Check days, times and performers for entertainment; D=dancing; best of many)

Albion River Inn/N (piano)
Alegrias (flamenco/guitar)
Ana Mandara (jazz)
Angkor Wat (dancers)
AsiaSF (D/DJ/illusionists)
Azie (DJ)
Bacar (jazz)
Backflip (D/DJ)
Barcelona (D/flamenco)
Beach Chalet (jazz)
Big Four (piano)
Biscuits & Blues (D/blues/jazz)
Bittersweet Bistro/S (jazz)
Bix (jazz)
Black Cat (jazz)
Blowfish (Japanese cartoons)
Brasserie Savoy (piano)
Bruno's (jazz/varies)
Buffalo Grill/S (jazz)
butterfly (DJ/jazz/piano)
Cafe Bastille (jazz)
Cafe Borrone/S (jazz)
Café Claude (blues/jazz)
Cafe de Paris (D/world)
Cafe Niebaum Coppola (varies)
Carta (jazz/piano)
Cielo/S (jazz)
Circadia (music)
Clementine (jazz)
Cole's/N (jazz)
Compass Rose (D/swing)
Cosmopolitan Cafe (blues/jazz)
Crow's Nest/S (D/varies)
Cypress Club (jazz)
Deuce/N (one-man band)
Dragonfly Café/N (jazz)
Duck Club/S (piano)
E&O Trading (jazz)
Eastside West (jazz)
Enrico's (jazz)
Faz/E (jazz)
42° (jazz)
Fournou's Ovens (piano)
Ganges (Indian music)
Gordon Biersch/S (jazz/swing)
Gordon's Hse. (jazz)
Guaymas/N (mariachi)
Harris' (jazz/piano)
Harry Denton's (D/orchestra)
Hawthorne Lane (piano)
Hungarian Sausage (piano)

Infusion (rock/funk/jazz)
Iron Horse (D)
Jardinière (jazz)
John's Grill (jazz)
Jordan's/E (D/piano/swing)
Kan Zaman (belly dancer)
Kasbah/N (belly dancer)
Katia's (accordion/guitar)
Kelly's Mission Rock (bands)
La Note/E (jazz)
La Scene (jazz)
Le Colonial (jazz)
Leford House/N (jazz)
Left Bank/N (jazz)
Marinus/S (jazz)
Max's Opera Café (vocals)
Max's Opera Café/S (vocals)
Maye's Oyster Hse. (piano)
Mecca (jazz/R&B)
Moose's (jazz)
One Market (jazz/piano)
O'Reilly's (varies)
Ovation (piano)
Pacific (piano)
Pacific's Edge/S (jazz)
Palace/S (D/jazz)
Paolo's/S (piano/vocals)
Pauline's (cabaret/jazz)
Perlot (guitar/piano)
Piaf's (cabaret/piano)
Pier 23 Cafe (varies)
Plumed Horse/S (D/band/piano)
Prima/E (jazz/piano)
Rasselas (blues/jazz)
Rick's (blues/Hawaiian/jazz)
Ritz-Carlton Din. Rm. (harp)
Ritz-Carlton Terrace (jazz)
Rose Pistola (jazz)
Rue de Main/E (classical guitar)
Sand Dollar/N (jazz/piano/rock)
Santa Fe B&G/E (piano)
Saul's/E (varies)
Schroeder's (polka)
Scott's/E (jazz/piano)
Shanghai 1930 (D/jazz)
Station Hse. Cafe/N (jazz/varies)
Straits Cafe/S (jazz)
Tonga Room (D/bands)
Top of the Mark (D/jazz/swing)
Viaggio/S (piano)
Vic Stewart's/E (guitar/piano)
Voulez-Vous/E (D/jazz)
Wappo Bar/N (Brazilian/jazz)
Wild Hare/S (jazz)
Yoshi's/Jack London Sq./E (jazz)

Delivers*/Takeout

(Nearly all Asians, coffee shops, delis, diners and pasta/pizzerias deliver or do takeout; here are some interesting possibilities; D=delivery, T=takeout; *call to check range and charges, if any)

Absinthe (T)
Alamo Square (T)
Albion River Inn/N (T)
Alegrias (T)
Alioto's (T)
Amber India/S (T)
A.P. Stump's/S (T)
Aram's (T)
A. Sabella's (D,T)
Autumn Moon Cafe/E (T)
Avenue Grill/N (T)
Avenue 9 (T)
Bacchanal/S (T)
Backflip (T)
Baker St. Bistro (T)
Balboa Cafe (T)
Baldoria (T)
Barcelona (D,T)
Beach Chalet (T)
Bella Vista/S (T)
Big Four (T)
Bighorn Grill/E (T)
Bistro Aix (T)
Bistro Ralph/N (T)
Bistro Vida/S (T)
Bistro Viola/E (T)
Bistro Zaré (T)
Bizou (T)
Black Cat (T)
Blackhawk Grille/E (T)
Bocca Rotis (T)
Bontà Rist. (T)
Boonville Hotel/N (T)
Brannan's Grill/N (T)
Brasserie Savoy (T)
Brava Terrace/N (T)
Brazio/E (T)
Brother-in-Law's (T)
Buca Giovanni (T)
Buckeye Roadhse./N (T)
butterfly (T)
Cafe Bastille (T)
Cafe Beaujolais/N (T)
Cafe Borrone/S (T)
Café Claude (T)
Cafe de la Paz/E (T)

Café de la Presse (T)
Cafe de Paris (D,T)
Cafe Lolo/N (T)
Cafe Marcella/S (T)
Cafe Marimba (T)
Cafe Riggio (D,T)
Cafe Rouge/E (T)
Caffe Delle Stelle (T)
California Cafe/N (T)
Capellini/S (T)
Caprice/N (T)
Carta (T)
Casanova/S (T)
Casa Orinda/E (T)
Catahoula/N (T)
Cha Cha Cha (T)
Charanga (T)
Charcuterie/N (T)
Cheers (T)
Chloe's Cafe (T)
Christopher's/E (T)
Cin Cin/N (T)
Circadia (T)
Citizen Cake (D,T)
Convivio Trattoria/S (T)
Della Santina's/N (T)
Deuce/N (T)
Dragonfly Café/N (T)
E'Angelo (T)
Eastside West (T)
El Palomar/S (T)
Enrico's (T)
Evvia/S (D)
Fandango/S (T)
Faz (D,T)
Faz/E (T)
Feast/N (T)
Felix & Louie's/N (T)
First Crush (T)
Flea St. Cafe/S (T)
Florio (T)
Fly Trap (D,T)
Foothill Cafe/N (T)
Frantoio/N (T)
Frascati (T)
Fringale (T)
Garibaldis (T)
Gayle's/S (D,T)
General's Daughter/N (T)
Ginger Island/E (T)
girl & the fig/N (T)
Globe (T)
Gordon's/N (D,T)
Gordon's Hse. (T)
Greens (D,T)

Grill on the Alley/S (T)
Guaymas/N (T)
Guernica/N (T)
Herbivore (T)
Hotel Mac/E (T)
House of Prime Rib (T)
Hungarian Sausage (T)
Iberia/S (T)
Il Davide/N (T)
Il Porcellino/E (D)
Indigo (T)
Infusion (T)
Insalata's/N (T)
Iron Horse (D,T)
Izzy's (D,T)
Jocco's/S (T)
Joubert's (T)
JZ Cool/S (T)
Kan Zaman (T)
Kasbah/N (T)
Kate's Kitchen (T)
Katia's (D,T)
Kelly's Mission Rock (T)
Kuleto's Trattoria/S (D,T)
Laghi (T)
La Mediterranée (D,T)
La Mediterranée/E (D,T)
La Note/E (T)
Le Central Bistro (T)
Leford House/N (T)
Left Bank/N (T)
Liberty Café (T)
Livefire/N (T)
L'Olivier (T)
Lotus/N (D,T)
LuLu (T)
Luna Park (T)
Macaroni Sciue Sciue (T)
MacArthur Park (D,T)
MacArthur Park/S (T)
Magnolia Pub (T)
Mama's/Washington Sq. (T)
Mangiafuoco (T)
Massawa (T)
Matsuya (T)
Maya/N (T)
Maye's Oyster Hse. (T)
Maykedah (T)
Mazzini/E (T)
Meadowood Grill/N (T)
Mescolanza (T)
Mezze/E (T)
Mikayla/Casa Madrona/N (T)
Miss Millie's (T)
Mixx/N (T)

Model Bakery/N (T)
Mom is Cooking (D,T)
MoMo's (T)
Montrio/S (T)
Moosse Cafe/N (T)
Moss Beach/S (T)
Murasaki (T)
Nola/S (T)
Northstar (T)
Obelisque/E (T)
O'Reilly's (D,T)
Osteria (T)
Pacific (T)
Palace/S (T)
Palio d'Asti (T)
Palomino (T)
Pancho Villa (T)
Pane e Vino (T)
Paolo's/S (T)
Parma (T)
Pastis (T)
Pearl/N (T)
Perry's Downtown (T)
Piatti/N (T)
Piazza D'Angelo/N (T)
Picaro (D,T)
Pier 23 Cafe (T)
Pinot Blanc/N (T)
Pintxos (T)
PJ's Oyster Bed (T)
Plouf (T)
Pork Store Cafe (T)
Postino/E (T)
Powell's Place (D,T)
Prego (T)
Primo Patio Cafe (D,T)
Pyramid Alehouse/E (T)
Radicchio (T)
Rasselas (T)
Red Herring (T)
Red Tractor Cafe/E (D,T)
Red Tractor Cafe/S (D,T)
Rick & Ann's/E (T)
Rick's (T)
Ricochet (T)
Rio Grill/S (T)
Rist. Bacco (T)
Rist. Ecco (T)
Rist. Milano (T)
Rist. Umbria (T)
Rivoli/E (T)
Rose Pistola (T)
Rose's Cafe (T)
Roy's (T)

Rutherford Grill/N (T)
Sam's Grill (T)
Sand Dollar/N (T)
Santa Barbara Grill/S (T)
Savanna Grill/N (T)
Savor (T)
Scala's Bistro (T)
Scott's (D,T)
Scott's/E (T)
Scott's/S (T)
Sent Sovi/S (T)
71 Saint Peter/S (T)
Sierra Mar/S (T)
Skates on the Bay/E (T)
Slow Club (T)
Spettro/E (T)
Spiedini/E (T)
Splendido (T)
Station Hse. Cafe/N (T)
Stelline (T)
Stinking Rose (D,T)
Stokes Adobe/S (T)
Straits Cafe (T)
Suppenküche (T)
Swagat/S (D,T)
Swan Oyster Depot (D)
Tachibana/E (T)
Tadich Grill (T)
Tapestry/S (T)
Tarpy's Roadhse./S (D,T)
Taste Café/S (T)
Tavolino (T)
Ten-Ichi (D,T)
Thornhill Cafe/E (T)
Three Ring (T)
Tita's (T)
Town's End (T)
Tropix/E (T)
Valentine's Cafe (T)
Venezia/E (T)
Viaggio/S (T)
Vic Stewart's/E (T)
Viognier/S (T)
Wappo Bar/N (T)
Wild Hare/S (T)
Xyz (T)
Zin/N (T)

Dining Alone

(Other than hotels, coffee
shops, sushi bars and places
with counter service)
Absinthe
Bagdad Cafe
Bette's Oceanview/E

Bill's Place
Bistro Jeanty/N
Cafe Bastille
Café Claude
Café de la Presse
Cafe Rouge/E
Caffe Greco
Capp's Corner
Casa Aguila
César/E
Citizen Cake
Crescent City Cafe
Eos
FatApple's/E
Fog City Diner
Fringale
Gira Polli
Hahn's Hibachi
Hotei
House of Nanking
Iroha
JZ Cool/S
Le Cheval/E
Little City
Lovejoy's
Mario's Bohemian
Matterhorn Swiss
Mel's Drive-In
Mifune
Mustards Grill/N
Pasta Pomodoro
Pasta Pomodoro/E
PJ's Oyster Bed
Prima/E
Red Herring
Rose's Cafe
Swan Oyster Depot
Tavolino
Ti Couz
Tra Vigne/N
Tu Lan
Via Vai
Vivande Porta Via
Waterfront
Zazie

Expense Account

Acquerello
Aqua
Auberge du Soleil/N
Azie
Boulevard
Carnelian Room
Charles Nob Hill

Chateau Souverain/N
Chez Panisse/E
Club XIX/S
Cypress Club
dalla Torre
Elisabeth Daniel
Fifth Floor
French Laundry/N
Fresh Cream/S
Gary Danko
Gaylord India
Greens
Grill on the Alley/S
Harris'
John Ash/N
Julius' Castle
Kyo-Ya
La Folie
Lark Creek Inn/N
La Toque/N
Le Mouton Noir/S
Madrona Manor/N
Mandarin
Marinus/S
Masa's
McCormick & Kuleto's
mc²
Moose's
Morton's of Chicago
Napa Valley Wine Train/N
Pacific's Edge/S
Park Grill
Perlot
Plumed Horse/S
Ritz-Carlton Din. Rm.
Roy's at Pebble Beach/S
Sent Sovi/S
Silks
Stars
Tommy Toy's

Fireplace
Acre Café/N
Albion River Inn/N
Anton & Michel/S
A. Sabella's
Auberge du Soleil/N
Autumn Moon Cafe/E
Backflip
Bella Vista/S
Betelnut Pejiu Wu
Big Four
Bistro Don Giovanni/N
Bistro Jeanty/N
Bittersweet Bistro/S

Blue Chalk Cafe/S
Boonville Hotel/N
Brannan's Grill/N
Brava Terrace/N
Brazio/E
Brix/N
Cafe Citti/N
Cafe Mozart
Caprice/N
Casanova/S
Casa Orinda/E
Chateau Souverain/N
Chez Panisse Cafe/E
Chez T.J./S
Cielo/S
Cliff House
Club XIX/S
Covey/S
Crow's Nest/S
Dal Baffo/S
Della Santina's/N
Dipsea Cafe/N
Domaine Chandon/N
El Paseo/N
Erna's Elderberry/S
Evvia/S
Faz/E
Foreign Cinema
Fresh Cream/S
Gaylord India/S
Guaymas/N
Harris'
House of Prime Rib
Iberia/S
Il Fornaio/E
Il Fornaio/N
John Ash/N
Joubert's
Kenwood/N
Kokkari Estiatorio
Kuleto's
Lark Creek Inn/N
Leford House/N
Left Bank/N
Le Mouton Noir/S
Livefire
Livefire/N
Los Gatos Brewing/S
LuLu
MacArthur Park
MacArthur Park/S
MacCallum House/N
Manka's Inverness/N
Marinus/S
Mezza Luna/S

Mezze/E
Mikayla/Casa Madrona/N
Moosse Cafe/N
Mucca/N
Nepenthe/S
Nola/S
Oliveto/E
Ovation
Pacific
Park Chow
Piatti/N
Piatti/S
Piazza D'Angelo/N
Pinot Blanc/N
Plouf
Plumed Horse/S
Prima/E
Red Herring
Rest. at Meadowood/N
Ricochet
Rio Grill/S
Robert's Bistro/S
Rutherford Grill/N
Salute Ristorante/E
Sand Dollar/N
Scott's/S
Sierra Mar/S
Skates on the Bay/E
Sno-Drift
Spago Palo Alto/S
Stokes Adobe/S
Tapestry/S
Tarpy's Roadhse./S
Vic Stewart's/E
Viognier/S
Wild Hare/S
Wine Spectator/N

Health/Spa Menu

(Most places cook to order to
meet any dietary request;
call in advance to check;
almost all Chinese, Indian
and other ethnics have
health-conscious meals,
as do the following)
Club XIX/S
Delancey Street
Greens
Herbivore
Joubert's
Meadowood Grill/N
Millennium
Ritz-Carlton Terrace
Sonoma Mission Inn/N
Valentine's Cafe

Historic Interest

(Year opened; *building)
1830s Stokes Adobe/S*
1849 Tadich Grill
1862 General's Daughter/N*
1863 Cliff House
1864 Jack's
1864 John's Grill*
1867 Cafe de Paris*
1867 Maye's Oyster Hse.
1867 Sam's Grill
1868 Boonville Hotel/N
1876 Woodward's Garden*
1882 dalla Torre*
1882 MacCallum House/N*
1882 Wine Spectator/N*
1884 Terra/N*
1886 Cole's/N*
1886 Fior d'Italia
1890 Deuce/N*
1893 Schroeder's
1904 Compass Rose*
1905 San Benito House/S*
1907 Emma*
1909 Garden Court*
1912 Careme Room
1912 Swan Oyster Depot
1914 Balboa Cafe
1915 Bacchanal/S
1915 Jordan's/E*
1917 Manka's Inverness/N
1917 Napa Valley Wine Train/N*
1917 Tarpy's Roadhse./S*
1920 Sam's Anchor Cafe/N
1922 Julius' Castle
1922 Roosevelt Tamale
1925 Beach Chalet*
1925 John Bentley's/S*
1927 Harry Denton's Starlight
1927 Moss Beach/S
1928 Alfred's Steak Hse.
1930s Palace/S
1933 Sears Fine Food
1934 Duarte's Tavern/S
1935 Alioto's
1937 Buckeye Roadhse./N
1937 Original Joe's
1949 Nepenthe/S
1980 Spenger's/E

Hotel Dining

Abigail Hotel
  Millennium
Albion River Inn
  Albion River Inn/N

Alta Mira Hotel
  Alta Mira/N
Applewood Inn
  Applewood Inn/N
Auberge du Soleil Inn
  Auberge du Soleil/N
Benjamin Franklin Hotel
  Lark Creek/S
Bernardus Lodge
  Marinus/S
Blue Heron Inn
  Moosse Cafe/N
Bodega Bay Lodge
  Duck Club/N
Boonville Hotel
  Boonville Hotel/N
Campton Pl. Hotel
  Campton Place
Cardinal Hotel
  Osteria/S
Casa Madrona
  Mikayla/Casa Madrona/N
Claremont Resort
  Jordan's/E
El Dorado Hotel
  Piatti (Sonoma)/N
Fairmont Hotel
  Tonga Room
Fairmont Hotel (San Jose)
  Grill on the Alley/S
Galleria Park Hotel
  Perry's Downtown
Highlands Inn
  Pacific's Edge/S
Hotel De Anza
  La Pastaia/S
Hotel Griffon
  Red Herring
Hotel Mac
  Hotel Mac/E
Hotel Majestic
  Perlot
Hotel Metropolis
  Belon
Hotel Monaco
  Grand Cafe
Hotel Nikko
  Anzu
Hotel Palomar
  Fifth Floor
Hotel Vintage Court
  Masa's
Huntington Hotel
  Big Four

Hyatt Sainte Claire
  Il Fornaio/S
Inn at Southbridge
  Tomatina/N
Inn at Spanish Bay
  Roy's at Pebble Beach/S
Inn at the Opera
  Ovation
Juliana Hotel
  Oritalia
Lodge at Pebble Beach
  Club XIX/S
  Stillwater B&G/S
MacCallum House Inn
  MacCallum House/N
Madrona Manor Hotel
  Madrona Manor/N
Mandarin Oriental Hotel
  Silks
Manka's Inverness Lodge
  Manka's Inverness/N
Mark Hopkins Hotel
  Top of the Mark
Maxwell Hotel
  Max's on Square
Meadowood Resort
  Meadowood Grill/N
  Rest. at Meadowood/N
Monticello Inn
  Puccini & Pinetti
Mount View Hotel
  Catahoula/N
Olema Inn
  Olema Inn/N
Palace Hotel
  Garden Court
  Kyo-Ya
Palomar Hotel
  El Palomar/S
Pan Pacific Hotel
  Pacific
Park Hyatt Hotel
  Park Grill
Phoenix Hotel
  Backflip
Pine Inn
  Il Fornaio/S
PlumpJack Squaw Valley Inn
  PlumpJack Cafe/N
Post Ranch Inn
  Sierra Mar/S
Prescott Hotel
  Postrio
Quail Lodge Resort
  Covey/S
Radisson Miyako Hotel
  Dot

Renaissance Stanford Ct.
  Fournou's Ovens
Ritz-Carlton Hotel
  Ritz-Carlton Din. Rm.
  Ritz-Carlton Terrace
San Benito House
  San Benito House/S
San Remo Hotel
  Emma
Savoy Hotel
  Brasserie Savoy
Serrano Hotel
  Ponzu
Sir Francis Drake Hotel
  Harry Denton's Starlight
  Scala's Bistro
Sonoma Hotel
  Heirloom/N
Sonoma Mission Inn
  Sonoma Mission Inn/N
Stanford Park Hotel
  Duck Club/S
Ventana Inn & Spa
  Cielo/S
Villa Florence Hotel
  Kuleto's
Vintners Inn
  John Ash/N
Warwick Regis
  La Scene
Westin St. Francis
  Compass Rose
W Hotel
  XYZ

"In" Places

Ace Wasabi's
Alfy's/N
Ana Mandara
Anzu
A.P. Stump's/S
Aqua
Azie
Backflip
Balboa Cafe
Betelnut Pejiu Wu
B44
Bistro Jeanty/N
BIX
Black Cat
Bouchon/N
Boulevard
Bridges/E
Brix/N
Bruno's

Buckeye Roadhse./N
butterfly
Cafe Fanny/E
Cafe Marimba
Cafe Rouge/E
César/E
Charanga
Charles Nob Hill
Chaya Brasserie
Chez Nous
Chez Panisse/E
Chez Panisse Cafe/E
Cin Cin/N
Cucina Jackson Fillmore/N
Cypress Club
Delfina
DINE
Ebisu
Elisabeth Daniel
Emile's/S
EOS
Fifth Floor
Fleur de Lys
Florio
Foreign Cinema
42°
French Laundry/N
Fringale
Gary Danko
Globe
Gordon's Hse.
Harry Denton's Starlight
Hawthorne Lane
Il Davide/N
Jardinière
Jianna
Johnfrank
L'Amie Donia/S
Left Bank/N
Left Bank/S
LuLu
Luna Park
Mazzini/E
mc²
Mecca
Moose's
Mucca/N
Mustards Grill/N
Ne O
Oliveto/E
Oritalia
Palace/S
Piazza D'Angelo/N
Pisces/S
Plouf
PlumpJack Cafe
PlumpJack Cafe/N
Postrio

Ritz-Carlton Din. Rm.
Rose Pistola
Roy's
Santi/N
Slanted Door
Spago Palo Alto/S
Stars
Sushi Groove
Tokyo Go Go
Tra Vigne/N
Universal Cafe
Wild Hare/S
Xyz
Zibibbo/S
Zuni Cafe

Jacket Required

Acquerello
Barcelona
Carnelian Room
Club XIX/S
Dal Baffo/S
Flying Saucer
French Laundry/N
Harry Denton's Starlight
La Scene
Masa's
One Market
Ovation
Pacific's Edge/S
Rest. at Meadowood/N
Ritz-Carlton Din. Rm.
Rouge
Tommy Toy's

Late Late – After 12:30

(All hours are AM; *check
locations)
Absinthe (1)
Bacar (1)
Bagdad Cafe (24 hrs.)
Black Cat (2)
Bouchon/N (1)
Brazen Head (1)
Brother's (3)
butterfly (1)
Globe (1)
Great Eastern (1)
It's Tops (3)
King of Thai (1:30)
La Rondalla (3)
Mel's Drive-In (1)*
North Bch. Pizza (1)*
Taqueria Cancun (2:45)*
Tommy's Joynt (1:45)
Yuet Lee (3)

Meet for a Drink

(Most top hotels and the
following standouts)
Absinthe
Alegrias
Azie
Beach Chalet
Betelnut Pejiu Wu
Biscuits & Blues
Bistro Clovis
Bistro Don Giovanni/N
Bix
Black Cat
Boulevard
Bubble Lounge
Cafe Bastille
Café Claude
Cafe Flore
Cafe Niebaum Coppola
Cafe Rouge/E
Caffe Museo
César/E
Charles Nob Hill
Cliff House
Connecticut Yankee
Cypress Club
E&O Trading
Elite Cafe
Empire Grill/S
Eos
Farallon
First Crush
Fleur de Lys
Foreign Cinema
42°
Gordon Biersch
Gordon Biersch/S
Gordon's Hse.
Guaymas/N
Hayes & Vine
Infusion
Julie's Supper Club
Kelly's Mission Rock
La Rondalla
Left at Albuquerque
Left Bank/N
Linda's Seabreeze/S
Little City
Liverpool Lil's
Los Gatos Brewing/S
LuLu
Magnolia Pub
mc^2
Mecca
MoMo's

Moose's
Mustards Grill/N
Nepenthe/S
Nola/S
One Market
Perry's Downtown
Picaro
Plouf
Potrero Brewing
Prego
Rasselas
Rick's
Rocco's
Rose Pistola
Sam's Anchor Cafe/N
Santa Fe B&G/E
Scala's Bistro
Slow Club
Splendido
Stars
Tavolino
Thanya & Salee
Thirsty Bear
Timo's
Tokyo Go Go
Tra Vigne/N
Triple Rock Brewery/E
Zazie
Zibibbo/S
Zuni Cafe

Noteworthy Newcomers (51)
Alfy's/N
Ana Mandara
Azie
Bacar
Belon
B44
Bruno's
butterfly
Cafe Monk
Chaya Brasserie
Chaz
Chez Nous
Cin Cin/N
Cobalt Tavern
Cole's/N
Cosmopolitan Cafe
DINE
Doña Tomás/E
Dot
Elisabeth Daniel
Emma
Jianna

Johnfrank
Jojo/E
JZ Cool/S
Lapis
Livefire
Luna Park
Mariposa/N
Memphis Minnie's BBQ
Meritage/N
Mezze/E
Mojo/S
Mucca/N
Ne O
Nizza La Bella/E
Paragon
paul K
Perlot
Pisces/S
Pizzetta 211
Ponzu
Roy's
Santi/N
Sno-Drift
Three Ring
Tuscany/N
Twenty Four
Venture Frogs
Voulez-Vous/E
Walzwerk

Offbeat
Ace Wasabi's
Albona Rist.
Alegrias
Angkor Wat
AsiaSF
Backflip
Blue Nile/E
Caffe Sport
Carta
Catahoula/N
Cha Cha Cha
Cypress Club
Esperpento
Flying Saucer
Helmand
Hungarian Sausage
Isobune Sushi
Kan Zaman
Katia's
Khan Toke
La Palma
La Rondalla
Lhasa Moon
Lovejoy's

Maharani
Mario's Bohemian
Max's Diner
Max's Opera Café
Maykedah
Millennium
Mom is Cooking
Moss Beach/S
Rooster
Spettro/E
St. Orres/N
Straits Cafe
Tonga Room
Ya-Ya Cuisine

Outdoor Dining

(G=garden; P=patio;
S=sidewalk; T=terrace;
W=waterside; best of many)
Acre Café/N (G)
Albion River Inn/N (W)
Alfy's/N (P)
Alioto's (W)
Alta Mira/N (P,T)
Anton & Michel/S (G,P)
Applewood Inn/N (T)
A.P. Stump's/S (P,S)
Aqui/S (P)
Aram's (G,P)
Auberge du Soleil/N (T)
Autumn Moon Cafe/E (G)
Avenue 9 (P)
Backflip (P)
Baker St. Bistro (S)
Barney's (P)
Barney's/E (P)
Bay Wolf/E (T)
Beach Chalet (W)
Betelnut Pejiu Wu (S)
B44 (P,S)
Bighorn Grill/E (P)
Bill's Place (P)
Bistro Aix (G)
Bistro Don Giovanni/N (P,T)
Bistro Jeanty/N (P)
Bistro Ralph/N (S)
Bistro Viola/E (P)
Bistro Zaré (P)
Bittersweet Bistro/S (G,P)
Black Cat (T)
Blackhawk Grille/E (P,T,W)
Blowfish, Sushi (S)
Blue Plate (G,P)
Bouchon/N (P)
Brava Terrace/N (T)

Brazio/E (T,W)
Bridges/E (G,P)
Brix/N (P)
Bucci's/E (P)
Buckeye Roadhse./N (P)
Buffalo Grill/S (P)
Cafe Bastille (S,T)
Cafe Citti/N (P)
Café Claude (S,T)
Cafe de Paris (P,S,T)
Cafe 817/E (S)
Cafe Flore (P,S)
Cafe Niebaum Coppola (S)
Cafe Tiramisu (S)
Cafe Torre/S (P)
Caffe Centro (G,S)
Caffe Greco (S)
California Cafe/N (P)
Caprice/N (W)
Casanova/S (P)
Celadon/N (T,W)
Cha Am Thai/E (P)
Chateau Souverain/N (P)
Cheers (P)
Cheesecake Factory (T)
Chez T.J./S (T)
Chloe's Cafe (S)
Cielo/S (T,W)
Circadia (S)
Citron/E (P)
Club XIX/S (P,W)
Cole's/N (T,W)
Convivio Trattoria/S (P)
Cosmopolitan Cafe (P)
Covey/S (G,P,T,W)
Crow's Nest/S (P,W)
Delancey Street (S)
Della Santina's/N (P)
Deuce/N (G,P)
Dipsea Cafe/N (G,W)
Domaine Chandon/N (T,W)
Doña Tomás/E (G,P)
Duck Club/S (P)
Eastside West (S)
El Paseo/N (P)
Empire Grill/S (G,P)
Emporio Rulli/N (P,S)
Enrico's (P,S)
Erna's Elderberry/S (G,T)
Fandango/S (P)
Faz (T)
Faz/E (P)
Feast/N (P,S)
Felix & Louie's/N (P)
Flea St. Cafe/S (T)

Foreign Cinema (P)
42° (P)
Frantoio/N (G,P)
French Laundry/N (P)
Fresh Cream/S (W)
Gabriella Cafe/S (P)
Gaylord India (W)
General's Daughter/N (P)
Ginger Island/E (P)
Glen Ellen Inn/N (P,W)
Globe (S)
Gordon Biersch (P,W)
Gordon Biersch/S (P)
Gordon's/N (S)
Gordon's Hse. (P)
Greens (W)
Guaymas/N (P,W)
Heirloom/N (P)
Herbivore (P)
Hyde St. Bistro (S)
Iberia/S (G)
Il Davide/N (P,S)
Il Fornaio (P)
Il Fornaio/E (P)
Il Fornaio/N (P)
Il Fornaio/S (P)
Insalata's/N (P)
Jimtown Store/N (P)
John Ash/N (T)
John Bentley's/S (T)
Julius' Castle (T)
Kelly's Mission Rock (P)
Kenwood/N (G)
Kuleto's (S)
Kuleto's Trattoria/S (P)
La Fondue/S (P)
L'Amie Donia/S (P)
La Note/E (P)
Lapis (P)
Lark Creek/E (P)
Lark Creek Inn/N (G,P,W)
La Toque/N (P)
Le Charm (P)
Le Colonial (P,T)
Leford House/N (W)
Left at Albuquerque (P,S)
Left Bank/N (P)
Left Bank/S (S)
Le Mouton Noir/S (P)
Lion & Compass/S (P)
Livefire (P)
Livefire/N (P)
Liverpool Lil's (P,S)
MacArthur Park (P)
MacArthur Park/S (P)

Madrona Manor/N (T)
Marinus/S (P,T)
Mariposa/N (G)
McCormick & Kuleto's (W)
Meadowood Grill/N (T)
Meritage/N (G,P)
Mikayla/Casa Madrona/N (W)
Mio Vicino/S (S)
Miss Millie's (P)
Mojo/S (P)
Mom is Cooking (P)
MoMo's (P)
Montage (T)
Moosse Cafe/N (W)
Moss Beach/S (P,W)
Mucca/N (P,W)
Napa Valley Grille/N (P)
Nizza La Bella/E (S)
Nonna Rose (S,W)
O Chamé/E (P)
Olema Inn/N (G)
Ondine/N (W)
O'Reilly's (P)
Palomino (P,W)
Paolo's/S (P,T,W)
Paragon (P)
Park Chow (P,T)
Pastis (P)
Pazzia (P,S)
Pearl/N (P,S)
Piatti/N (G,P,W)
Piatti/S (P)
Piazza D'Angelo/N (P)
Picante Cocina/E (P)
Pier 23 Cafe (P,W)
Pinot Blanc/N (P)
Plouf (S,T)
Postino/E (P)
Prima/E (P,S)
Primo Patio Cafe (P)
Red Herring (S,W)
Rest. at Meadowood/N (P,T)
Rick & Ann's/E (G,P)
Rio Grill/S (P)
Rist. Fabrizio/N (P)
Ritz-Carlton Terrace (T)
Rooster (T)
Rose Pistola (S)
Rose's Cafe (S,T)
Roy's at Pebble Beach/S (P)
Rutherford Grill/N (P)
Salute Ristorante/E (W)
Sam's Anchor Cafe/N (T)
Sam's Grill (P)
Sand Dollar/N (P)

Santa Barbara Grill/S (P)
Santa Fe B&G/E (G,P)
Savanna Grill/N (P)
Savor (G,P)
Scoma's/N (P,W)
Sent Sovi/S (P)
71 Saint Peter/S (P)
Sierra Mar/S (T,W)
Skates on the Bay/E (W)
Sonoma Mission Inn/N (T)
South Park Cafe (S)
Spago Palo Alto/S (G,P,T)
Spiedini/E (P)
Splendido (T,W)
Station Hse. Cafe/N (G,P)
Stinking Rose (P)
Straits Cafe/S (P)
Sushi Ran/N (P)
Tapestry/S (P,T)
Tarpy's Roadhse./S (P)
Tavolino (S)
Tomatina/N (P)
Townhouse B&G/E (P)
Tra Vigne/N (T)
Triple Rock Brewery/E (P)
Tropix/E (P)
Truly Mediterranean (S)
Tuscany/N (P)
Twenty Four (P)
Valentine's Cafe (S)
Viaggio/S (P)
Via Vai (P)
Voulez-Vous/E (T)
Wappo Bar/N (G,P,T)
Waterfront (P,W)
Wente Vineyards/E (G,T)
Willow Wood Mkt. Café/N (P)
Wine Spectator/N (T)
Zazie (G,P,T)
Zibibbo/S (G,P)
Zinzino (G,P)
Zza's Trattoria/E (P)

Outstanding View

Albion River Inn/N
Alta Mira/N
A. Sabella's
Auberge du Soleil/N
Beach Chalet
Bella Vista/S
Bistro Don Giovanni/N
Blackhawk Grille/E
Brix/N
Caprice/N
Carnelian Room

Chateau Souverain/N
Cielo/S
Cliff House
Covey/S
Crow's Nest/S
dalla Torre
Domaine Chandon/N
Fresh Cream/S
Gaylord India
Gordon Biersch/S
Greens
Guaymas/N
Harbor Village
Harry Denton's Starlight
John Ash/N
Jordan's/E
Julius' Castle
Kelly's Mission Rock
Leford House/N
Linda's Seabreeze/S
Little City
Mandarin
Marinus/S
McCormick & Kuleto's
Meadowood Grill/N
Mikayla/Casa Madrona/N
Moss Beach/S
Napa Valley Wine Train/N
Nepenthe/S
Ondine/N
Pacific's Edge/S
Paolo's/S
Rest. at Meadowood/N
Roy's at Pebble Beach/S
Salute Ristorante/E
Salute Ristorante/N
Sam's Anchor Cafe/N
Scoma's
Sierra Mar/S
Skates on the Bay/E
Tarpy's Roadhse./S
Top of the Mark
Waterfront
Wente Vineyards/E
Wine Spectator/N

Parking/Valet
(L=parking lot;
V=valet parking;
*=validated parking)
Absinthe (V)
Acquerello (L)
Albion River Inn/N (L)
Albona Rist. (V)
Alfred's Steak Hse. (V)

Alioto's*
Allegro (V)
Amber India/S (L)
Ana Mandara (V)*
Antica Trattoria (V)
Anzu (V)*
Applewood Inn/N (L)
A.P. Stump's/S (V)*
Aqua (V)
Aqui/S (L)
A. Sabella's*
Auberge du Soleil/N (V)
Avanti/S (L)
Azie (V)
Backflip (V)
Balboa Cafe (V)
Baldoria (V)
Basque Cultural Ctr./S (L)
Beach Chalet (L)
Bella Vista/S (L)
Belon (L)
Betelnut Pejiu Wu (V)*
Big Four (V)
Bighorn Grill/E (L)
Bill's Place (L)
Bistro Don Giovanni/N (L)
Bistro Jeanty/N (L)
Bistro Viola/E (L)
Bistro Zaré*
Bittersweet Bistro/S (L)
BIX (V)
Black Cat (V)
Bocce Cafe (V)
Boonville Hotel/N (L)
Bouchon/N (L)
Boulevard (V)
Brannan's Grill/N (L)
Brasserie Savoy (V)
Brava Terrace/N (L)
Brazio/E (L)
Bridges/E (V)*
Brix/N (L)
Bruno's (L)
Bucci's/E (L)
Buckeye Roadhse./N (V)
Buck's/S (L)
butterfly (V)*
Cafe Borrone/S (L)
Cafe Citti/N (L)
Cafe de Paris (L,V)
Cafe 817/E (L)
Cafe Fanny/E (L)
Cafe Kati (V)*
Cafe Marcella/S (L)
Cafe Rouge/E (L)

California Cafe/E (L,V)
Campton Place (V)
Capellini/S (V)
Caprice/N (V)
Carnelian Room (L)
Carta (L)
Casa Orinda/E (L,V)*
Catahoula/N (L)
Celadon/N (L)
Cha Am Thai*
Charanga (L)
Charcuterie/N (L)
Charles Nob Hill (V)
Charlie Hong Kong/S (L)
Chateau Souverain/N (L)
Chaya Brasserie (V)
Christophe/N (L)
Cielo/S (L)
Clementine*
Club XIX/S (L,V)*
Cole's/N (L)
Compass Rose (V)
Convivio Trattoria/S (L)
Cosmopolitan Cafe (V)
Covey/S (L)
Crow's Nest/S (L)*
Cucina Jackson Fillmore/N (L)
Cypress Club (V)
Dal Baffo/S (L)
dalla Torre (V)
Deuce/N (L)
DINE (L)
Dipsea Cafe/N (L)
Domaine Chandon/N (L)
Dragonfly Café/N (L)
Duarte's Tavern/S (L)
Duck Club/S (L)
E&O Trading (L)
Eastside West (V)
Elisabeth Daniel*
El Palomar/S (L)
Emile's/S (V)
Enrico's (V)
Eos (L)
Erna's Elderberry/S (L)
Evvia/S (L,V)
Fandango/S (L)
Farallon (V)
FatApple's/E (L)
Faz/E (L)
Faz/S (L)
Feast/N (L)
Felix & Louie's/N (L)
Fifth Floor (V)
Fior d'Italia (V)

Flea St. Cafe/S (L)
Fleur de Lys (V)
Fly Trap (V)
Fook Yuen/S (L)
Foothill Cafe/N (L)
Foreign Cinema (V)
42° (L)
Fournou's Ovens (L,V)*
Frantoio/N (L,V)
Frascati (V)
French Laundry/N (L)
Fresh Cream/S (L)
Garden Court*
Garibaldis (V)
Gayle's/S (L)
Gaylord India*
General's Daughter/N (L)
Ginger Island/E (L)
Gira Polli/N (L)
girl & the fig/N (L)
Glen Ellen Inn/N (L)
Gordon Biersch*
Gordon's/N (L)
Gordon's Hse. (V)
Grand Cafe (V)*
Great Eastern (V)*
Greens (L)
Grill on the Alley/S (V)
Guaymas/N*
Guernica/N (L)
Hana/N (L)
Harbor Village (V)*
Hard Rock Cafe (V)
Harris' (V)
Harry Denton's Starlight*
Hawthorne Lane (V)
Helmand (L,V)*
House of Prime Rib (V)*
Hyde St. Bistro (L)*
Iberia/S (L)
I Fratelli (V)*
Il Davide/N (L)
Indigo (V)
Insalata's/N (L,V)
Iroha (L)
Italian Colors/E (L)
Izzy's*
Jack's (V)
Jardinière (V)
Jocco's/S (L)
John Ash/N (L)
John Bentley's/S (L)
Johnfrank (V)
Jordan's/E (L,V)*
Julie's Supper Club (L)

Julius' Castle (V)
JZ Cool/S (L)
Kasbah/N (L)
Katia's (L)
Kelly's Mission Rock (L,V)*
Kenwood/N (L)
Kirala/E (L)
Kokkari Estiatorio (V)
Kuleto's Trattoria/S (L,V)*
Kyo-Ya (V)
La Felce (V)
La Folie (V)
La Fondue/S (L,V)
Laghi (V)
La Mediterranée/E (L)
La Pastaia/S (L,V)
Lark Creek/E (L,V)*
La Scene (V)*
Le Cheval/E (L)
Le Colonial (V)
Leford House/N (L)
Left Bank/N (V)
Le Mouton Noir/S (L,V)
Le Papillon/S (L)
Lion & Compass/S (V)
Little Joe's (V)*
Livefire (V)
Livefire/N (L)
L'Olivier (V)
Los Gatos Brewing/S (L)
LuLu (L,V)
MacArthur Park (V)
MacArthur Park/S (V)*
Maharani*
Maki (L)
Mandarin (L)*
Manka's Inverness/N (L)
Marin Joe's/N (L,V)
Marinus/S (V)*
Mariposa/N (L)
Masa's (L)
Matterhorn Swiss (V)
Max's Opera Café/S (L)
Maye's Oyster Hse.*
Maykedah (V)
McCormick & Kuleto's*
mc² (V)
Meadowood Grill/N (L)
Meetinghouse (V)
Mel's Drive-In (L)
Mifune*
Mikayla/Casa Madrona/N (V)
Mixx/N (V)
Mojo/S (V)
MoMo's (V)

Moose's (V)*
Morton's of Chicago (V)
Moss Beach/S (L)
Mustards Grill/N (L)
Napa Valley Grille/N (L)
Narai*
Nepenthe/S (L)
New Pisa (V)
Nob Hill Cafe (V)
Nonna Rose (L,V)*
North India (L)
Oliveto/E (L)
Ondine/N (V)
One Market (V)
Original Joe's (L)*
Osaka Grill*
Ovation*
Pacific (V)*
Pacific's Edge/S (V)
Palace/S (V)*
Palio d'Asti (L)
Palomino (L)*
Paolo's/S (L)*
Paragon (V)
Pazzia (L)
Perlot (V)
Phuping/E (L)
Piatti/N (L,V)*
Piatti/S (L)
Piazza D'Angelo/N (L,V)
Picante Cocina/E (L)
Pinot Blanc/N (L)
Pintxos (V)
Pisces/S (L)
Plumed Horse/S (V)
PlumpJack Cafe (V)
PlumpJack Cafe/N (V)
Postino/E (L)
Postrio (V)
Prima/E (V)*
Pyramid Alehouse/E (L)
Red Herring (V)
Rest. at Meadowood/N (L)
Rick & Ann's/E (L)*
Rick's*
Rio Grill/S (L)
Rist. Fabrizio/N (L)
Rist. Milano (L)
Ritz-Carlton Din. Rm. (V)*
Ritz-Carlton Terrace (V)*
Robata/N (L)
Robert's Bistro/S (L)
Rooster (L)
Rose Pistola (V)
Roy's (V)

Roy's at Pebble Beach/S (L,V)
Rubicon (V)
Rue de Main/E (L)
Rutherford Grill/N (L)
Salute Ristorante/E (L)
Salute Ristorante/N (V)
Santa Barbara Grill/S (V)
Santa Fe B&G/E (L)*
Savanna Grill/N (L)
Scala's Bistro*
Scoma's/N (L)
Scott's (L)*
Scott's/E (V)*
Scott's/S (L)*
Sent Sovi/S (L)
71 Saint Peter/S*
Shanghai 1930 (V)
Sierra Mar/S (L,V)
Silks (V)
Skates on the Bay/E (L)
Slanted Door (V)
Sonoma Mission Inn/N (L,V)
Spago Palo Alto/S (V)
Spenger's/E*
Spiedini/E (L,V)
Splendido (V)*
Stars (V)
Station Hse. Cafe/N (L)
Stokes Adobe/S (L)
St. Orres/N (L)
Straits Cafe/S (L)
Sushi Groove (V)
Sushi Ran/N (L)
Swagat/S (L)*
Syrah/N (L)
Tapestry/S (L)
Tarpy's Roadhse./S (L)
Three Ring (L)*
Tomatina/N (L)
Tommy's Joynt (L)
Tommy Toy's (V)
Tonga Room (V)
Top of the Mark*
Tortola (L)
Townhouse B&G/E (L)
Trattoria Contadina*
Tuscany/N (L)
2223 Restaurant (L)
Venezia/E (L)
Venticello (V)
Viaggio/S (L,V)
Vic Stewart's/E (L)
Viognier/S (L)
Voulez-Vous/E (L)
Wappo Bar/N (L)
Waterfront (V)
Wente Vineyards/E (V)

Wild Hare/S (L,V)
Willowside Cafe/N (L)
Wine Spectator/N (L,V)
Xanadu/E (L)
XYZ (V)
Yabbies*
Yank Sing*
Yoshida-Ya (V)
Yoshi's/Jack London Sq./E (L)*
Zao Noodle Bar (L)
Zao Noodle Bar/S (L)
Zibibbo/S (V)
Zinzino*
Zuni Cafe (V)

Parties & Private Rooms

(Any nightclub or restaurant
charges less at off-times;
* indicates private rooms
available; best of many)
Academy Grill*
Acquerello*
Acre Café/N
Alamo Square*
Albion River Inn/N
Alegrias*
Alfred's Steak Hse.*
Ana Mandara*
Anton & Michel/S*
Anzu
Applewood Inn/N*
A.P. Stump's/S*
Aram's
A. Sabella's*
AsiaSF*
Auberge du Soleil/N*
Autumn Moon Cafe/E*
Avenue 9*
Azie
Bacchanal/S*
Backflip*
Balboa Cafe*
Baldoria*
Barcelona*
Basque Cultural Ctr./S*
Bay Wolf/E*
Beach Chalet
Bella Vista/S*
Betelnut Pejiu Wu*
Bette's Oceanview/E*
Big Four*
Bighorn Grill/E*
Biscuits & Blues
Bistro Aix*
Bistro Viola/E*
Bistro Zaré*

Bittersweet Bistro/S*
Bix
Blackhawk Grille/E*
Blue Plate*
Boulevard*
Brandy Ho's*
Brannan's Grill/N
Brasserie Savoy*
Brava Terrace/N*
Brazio/E*
Bridges/E*
Brix/N*
Bruno's
Bubba's Diner/N
Buca Giovanni*
Buckeye Roadhse./N*
Buck's/S*
Buffalo Grill/S*
butterfly
Cafe Bastille*
Cafe Citti/N*
Café Claude*
Cafe de Paris*
Cafe Kati*
Cafe Lolo/N*
Cafe Mozart
Cafe Niebaum Coppola
Cafe Riggio*
Cafe Tiramisu*
Caffe Delle Stelle*
California Cafe/E*
California Cafe/N
Campton Place
Camranh Bay/S*
Capellini/S*
Caprice/N
Careme Room*
Carnelian Room*
Carta*
Casanova/S*
Casa Orinda/E*
Catahoula/N*
Charcuterie/N
Charles Nob Hill*
Chaya Brasserie
Cheers
Chef Chu's/S*
Chez T.J./S*
Christophe/N*
Christopher's/E
Cielo/S*
Cin Cin/N*
Citizen Cake
Citron/E*
Clementine

Cliff House*
Club XIX/S*
Cole's/N
Convivio Trattoria/S
Covey/S
Crow's Nest/S*
Cypress Club*
Dal Baffo/S
dalla Torre*
Delancey Street*
Della Santina's/N*
Deuce/N*
DINE
Domaine Chandon/N
Dragonfly Café/N*
Dragon Well*
Duarte's Tavern/S*
Duck Club/S*
E&O Trading*
Eastside West*
El Palomar/S*
El Paseo/N*
Emile's/S
Empire Grill/S
Emporio Rulli/N
Enrico's*
Eos*
Erna's Elderberry/S*
Eulipia/S*
Evvia/S
Fandango/S*
Farallon*
Faz*
Faz/E*
Faz/S*
Felix & Louie's/N*
Fifth Floor*
Filou/N
Fior d'Italia*
First Crush*
Flea St. Cafe/S*
Fleur de Lys
Florio
Fly Trap*
Fog City Diner*
Fook Yuen/S*
Foreign Cinema*
Fountain Court*
Fournou's Ovens*
Frantoio/N*
Frascati*
French Laundry/N
Fresh Cream/S*
Gabriella Cafe/S*
Garibaldis*

Gaylord India*
Gaylord India/S*
General's Daughter/N*
Ginger Island/E*
Gira Polli/N*
Glen Ellen Inn/N*
Globe*
Gordon Biersch
Gordon Biersch/S*
Gordon's/N*
Gordon's Hse.*
Grand Cafe*
Grandview/S*
Great Eastern*
Grill on the Alley/S*
Guaymas/N*
Guernica/N*
Harbor Village*
Hard Rock Cafe
Harris'*
Harry Denton's Starlight*
Hawthorne Lane*
Heirloom/N
Herbivore
Hong Kong Flower/S
Hotel Mac/E*
House of Prime Rib*
Hunan Home's
Hungarian Sausage*
Hyde St. Bistro
Iberia/S
I Fratelli*
Il Davide/N
Il Fornaio
Il Fornaio/E
Il Fornaio/S*
Indian Oven
Indigo*
Insalata's/N*
Iron Horse*
Irrawaddy*
Italian Colors/E
Izzy's*
Jack's*
Jardinière*
John Ash/N*
John Bentley's/S*
Johnfrank
John's Grill*
Jordan's/E*
Julie's Supper Club*
Julius' Castle*
Kasbah/N*
Katia's
Kelly's Mission Rock

Kenwood/N
Khan Toke
Kokkari Estiatorio*
Kuleto's*
Kuleto's Trattoria/S*
La Folie*
Lark Creek/E*
Lark Creek/S
Lark Creek Inn/N*
Las Camelias/N
La Scene*
Le Central Bistro*
Le Colonial*
Leford House/N*
Left at Albuquerque*
Left at Albuquerque/S*
Left Bank/N*
Left Bank/S*
Le Mouton Noir/S*
Le Papillon/S*
Lion & Compass/S*
Livefire*
Livefire/N*
L'Olivier*
London Wine Bar*
Long Life Noodle*
Los Gatos Brewing/S*
Lotus/N
LuLu*
Macaroni Sciue Sciue*
MacArthur Park*
MacArthur Park/S*
MacCallum House/N*
Madrona Manor/N*
Mandarin*
Marinus/S*
Masa's*
Max's on Square*
Maya*
Maykedah
Mazzini/E*
McCormick & Kuleto's*
mc^2*
Meadowood Grill/N*
Mecca*
Mel's Drive-In*
Meritage/N*
Mezze/E
Mikayla/Casa Madrona/N*
Miss Millie's*
Mixx/N*
Mojo/S
Mom is Cooking*
MoMo's*
Montage*

Montrio/S*
Moose's*
Morton's of Chicago*
Moss Beach/S*
Nan Yang Rockridge/E*
Nob Hill Cafe*
Nola/S*
North India*
Obelisque/E*
Oliveto/E
Ondine/N
One Market*
O'Reilly's*
Oritalia*
Osaka Grill*
Osome*
Pacific's Edge/S*
Palace/S*
Palio d'Asti
Paolo's/S*
Paragon*
Pasta Moon/S*
Pauline's*
Perlot*
Piatti/N*
Piatti/S*
Piazza D'Angelo/N*
Picante Cocina/E*
Pier 23 Cafe*
Pinot Blanc/N*
Pizza Rustica/E*
PJ's Oyster Bed*
Plearn/E*
Plouf*
Plumed Horse/S*
PlumpJack Cafe*
PlumpJack Cafe/N*
Postino/E*
Postrio*
Prego*
Prima/E*
Rasselas
Red Herring*
Red Tractor Cafe/E
Red Tractor Cafe/S
Rest. at Meadowood/N*
Rest. Peony/E*
Rick & Ann's/E
Rick's*
Ricochet*
Rio Grill/S*
Ritz-Carlton Din. Rm.
Robata/N
Robert's Bistro/S*
Rooster*

Rose's Cafe
Rotunda*
Roy's
Rubicon*
Rue de Main/E*
Salute Ristorante/E
Salute Ristorante/N*
Sam's Grill*
San Benito House/S*
Sanraku*
Santa Barbara Grill/S*
Santa Fe B&G/E
Savanna Grill/N*
Scala's Bistro
Sent Sovi/S*
Shanghai 1930*
Silks*
Soizic/E*
Sonoma Mission Inn/N*
Spago Palo Alto/S*
Spenger's/E*
Spiedini/E*
Splendido*
Stars*
Station Hse. Cafe/N*
Stinking Rose*
Stokes Adobe/S*
Suppenküche*
Swagat/S*
Tarpy's Roadhse./S*
Taste Café/S
Terra/N*
Thanh Long*
Thirsty Bear*
Thornhill Cafe/E*
Three Ring
Ti Couz*
Tita's*
Tomatina/N*
Tommy Toy's*
Tonga Room
Top of the Mark*
Trattoria Contadina*
Triple Rock Brewery/E
Twenty Four*
2223 Restaurant*
Uzen/E*
Venticello*
Viaggio/S*
Via Vai
Vic Stewart's/E*
Viognier/S*
Voulez-Vous/E
Wa-Ha-Ka Oaxaca*
Wappo Bar/N*

Waterfront
We Be Sushi
Wente Vineyards/E*
Wild Hare/S*
Wine Spectator/N*
Xanadu/E*
Xyz
Yank Sing*
Yoshida-Ya*
Zaré on Sacramento
Zarzuela*
Zibibbo/S*
Zinzino*
Zza's Trattoria/E*

People-Watching
Ace Wasabi's
Ana Mandara
Avenue Grill/N
Backflip
Bagdad Cafe
Betelnut Pejiu Wu
Bix
Blowfish, Sushi
Bouchon/N
Cafe Bastille
Café Claude
Cafe Flore
Caffe Greco
Cha Cha Cha
Firewood Cafe
Foreign Cinema
Gordon Biersch
Gordon Biersch/S
Jardinière
Kabuto Sushi
Left at Albuquerque
Left Bank/N
Little City
LuLu
Mario's Bohemian
Max's Opera Café/S
Mecca
Michelangelo Cafe
Moose's
Mustards Grill/N
Palace/S
Pancho Villa
Pearl/N
Perry's Downtown
Postrio
Rose's Cafe
Sam's Anchor Cafe/N
Spago Palo Alto/S
Sushi Groove
Tavolino

Tokyo Go Go
Tra Vigne/N
2223 Restaurant
Wild Hare/S
Zibibbo/S
Zuni Cafe

Power Scene

Aqua
Big Four
Blackhawk Grille/E
Boulevard
Charles Nob Hill
Cypress Club
Evvia/S
Fifth Floor
Fleur de Lys
Fly Trap
Grill on the Alley/S
Hawthorne Lane
Jack's
Lark Creek Inn/N
Le Central Bistro
Le Colonial
Lion & Compass/S
mc²
Moose's
Occidental Grill
One Market
Park Grill
Pisces/S
Postrio
Ritz-Carlton Din. Rm.
Rubicon
Spago Palo Alto/S
Stars
Tommy Toy's
Waterfront

Pre-Theater Dining

(Call to check prices,
days and times)
Absinthe
Alamo Square
Anjou
Anzu
Brasserie Savoy
Caffe Delle Stelle
Campton Place
Farallon
First Crush
Grand Cafe
Hayes St. Grill
Indigo
Jardinière
La Scene
Millennium

Oritalia
paul K
Postrio
Scala's Bistro
Stars
Terra Brazilis

Prix Fixe Menu

(Call to check prices,
days and times)
Academy Grill
Ajanta/E
Alamo Square
Anzu
Aqua
Auberge du Soleil/N
Azie
Baker St. Bistro
Bistro Aix
Bistro Viola/E
Bocca Rotis
Brasserie Savoy
Brother's
Cafe Beaujolais/N
Cafe Jacqueline
Cafe Tiramisu
Campton Place
Capp's Corner
Careme Room
Carnelian Room
Carta
Cha Am Thai/E
Chapeau!
Christopher's/E
Citizen Cake
Citron/E
Clementine
Club XIX/S
Elisabeth Daniel
Emile's/S
Erna's Elderberry/S
First Crush
French Laundry/N
Gary Danko
Gaylord India/S
Gira Polli
Golden Turtle
Greens
Hunan Home's
Hyde St. Bistro
Indigo
Johnfrank
Jordan's/E
Juban/S
Kyo-Ya
La Folie
La Note/E
La Scene

La Toque/N
Le Charm
Le Mouton Noir/S
Le Soleil
L'Olivier
Los Gatos Brewing/S
Macaroni Sciue Sciue
Madrona Manor/N
Maharani
Mandarin
Manka's Inverness/N
Masa's
Moss Beach/S
Ondine/N
Pacific's Edge/S
Paolo's/S
Pastis
Pinot Blanc/N
Rest. at Meadowood/N
Rice Table/N
Ritz-Carlton Din. Rm.
Rubicon
Rue de Main/E
Sanraku
Scoma's/N
Sent Sovi/S
Sierra Mar/S
Sonoma Mission Inn/N
Splendido
Stelline
Viognier/S
Zaré on Sacramento

Pub/Bar/Microbrewery

Beach Chalet
Brazen Head
Clement St. B&G
Connecticut Yankee
Crow's Nest/S
E&O Trading
E&O Trading/S
First Crush
Gordon Biersch
Gordon Biersch/S
Hayes & Vine
Liverpool Lil's
London Wine Bar
Los Gatos Brewing/S
Magnolia Pub
Moss Beach/S
O'Reilly's
Perry's Downtown
Potrero Brewing
Pyramid Alehouse/E
Thirsty Bear
Tommy's Joynt
Triple Rock Brewery/E

Quiet Conversation

Acquerello
Auberge du Soleil/N
Baker St. Bistro
Bella Vista/S
Cafe Jacqueline
Cafe Mozart
Campton Place
Casanova/S
Charles Nob Hill
Chez Panisse/E
Clementine
dalla Torre
Elisabeth Daniel
El Paseo/N
Fifth Floor
Fournou's Ovens
Garibaldis
Gary Danko
Gaylord India
Julius' Castle
Khan Toke
Lalime's/E
La Toque/N
La Villa Poppi
Liberty Café
L'Olivier
Lovejoy's
Masa's
Napa Valley Wine Train/N
Pacific's Edge/S
Park Grill
PlumpJack Cafe/N
San Benito House/S
Sent Sovi/S
Silks
St. Orres/N
Zaré on Sacramento
Zax

Raw Bar

Absinthe
Alfy's/N
Bacar
Bacchanal/S
Belon
Black Cat
Blowfish, Sushi
Bouchon/N
Brannan's Grill/N
Brasserie Savoy
Cafe de Paris
Cafe Rouge/E
Chaya Brasserie
Eastside West

Elite Cafe
Emma
Faz/S
Fog City Diner
Foreign Cinema
Globe
Grandeho's Kamekyo
Hana/N
Harry Denton's Starlight
Jianna
Livefire
LuLu
Maye's Oyster Hse.
Meritage/N
MoMo's
Nonna Rose
Pisces/S
PJ's Oyster Bed
Red Herring
Ricochet
Spenger's/E
Station Hse. Cafe/N
Swan Oyster Depot
Ten-Ichi
Ti Couz
Xanadu/E
Yabbies
Zibibbo/S
Zuni Cafe

Reservations Essential

Acquerello
Albona Rist.
Alegrias
Ana Mandara
A.P. Stump's/S
Aqua
Auberge du Soleil/N
Baker St. Bistro
Barcelona
Basque Cultural Ctr./S
Bella Vista/S
Blackhawk Grille/E
Cafe Beaujolais/N
Cafe Lolo/N
Cafe Mozart
Camranh Bay/S
Casanova/S
Catahoula/N
Cha Am Thai
Chez Panisse/E
Chez Panisse Cafe/E
Christophe/N
Cielo/S
Cole's/N
Erna's Elderberry/S

Firefly
Fleur de Lys
Flying Saucer
Fook Yuen/S
French Laundry/N
Fresh Cream/S
Fringale
Gary Danko
Glen Ellen Inn/N
Globe
Harry Denton's Starlight
Helmand
Jocco's/S
John Bentley's/S
Jordan's/E
Kuleto's Trattoria/S
La Fondue/S
L'Amie Donia/S
Liverpool Lil's
L'Olivier
Los Gatos Brewing/S
Lotus/N
Madrona Manor/N
Mangiafuoco
Manka's Inverness/N
Marinus/S
Matterhorn Swiss
Mezza Luna/S
Mucca/N
Napa Valley Wine Train/N
Oliveto/E
Osteria
Ovation
Pacific's Edge/S
Pisces/S
PJ's Oyster Bed
Plouf
PlumpJack Cafe
Postino/E
Ritz-Carlton Terrace
Scott's (San Jose)/S
Sierra Mar/S
Sno-Drift
St. Orres/N
Taste Café/S
Trattoria Contadina
Venticello
Viognier/S
Wappo Bar Bistro/N
Wild Hare/S
Willowside Cafe/N
Yoshi's/Jack London Sq./E
Zaré on Sacramento
Zax
Zibibbo/S

Romantic

Acquerello
Alegrias
Anjou
Aram's
Auberge du Soleil/N
Baker St. Bistro
Bella Vista/S
Big Four
Bistro Clovis
Bruno's
Buca Giovanni
Cafe Jacqueline
Cafe Mozart
Carnelian Room
Casanova/S
Chapeau!
Charles Nob Hill
Chez Panisse/E
Chez T.J./S
Christophe/N
Citron/E
Compass Rose
Covey/S
Cypress Club
dalla Torre
Elisabeth Daniel
El Paseo/N
Emile's/S
Erna's Elderberry/S
Fifth Floor
Filou/N
Flea St. Cafe/S
Fleur de Lys
French Laundry/N
Fresh Cream/S
Gabriella Cafe/S
Ganges
Gary Danko
Gaylord India
Greens
Guernica/N
Il Davide/N
Jardinière
John Ash/N
John Bentley's/S
Julius' Castle
Kasbah/N
Katia's
Khan Toke
La Folie
La Fondue/S
Lark Creek Inn/N
La Toque/N
La Villa Poppi

Le Charm
Le Papillon/S
L'Olivier
Maharani
Manka's Inverness/N
Marinus/S
Masa's
Matterhorn Swiss
Meetinghouse
Napa Valley Wine Train/N
Obelisque/E
O Chamé/E
Olema Inn/N
Ondine/N
Ovation
Pacific's Edge/S
Palio d'Asti
Perlot
Plumed Horse/S
Rest. at Meadowood/N
Ritz-Carlton Din. Rm.
Rooster
Roy's at Pebble Beach/S
Salute Ristorante/E
Salute Ristorante/N
Sent Sovi/S
Sierra Mar/S
Silks
Soizic/E
St. Orres/N
Terra/N
Townhouse B&G/E
Venticello
Waterfront
Wente Vineyards/E
Woodward's Garden
Zaré on Sacramento
Zax

Senior Appeal

Acquerello
Alfred's Steak Hse.
Alioto's
A. Sabella's
Bella Vista/S
Big Four
Cafe For All Seasons
Charles Nob Hill
Clement St. B&G
Cole's/N
Covey/S
Dal Baffo/S
Emile's/S
FatApple's/E
Fior d'Italia

Fly Trap
Garden Court
Harris'
Hayes St. Grill
House of Prime Rib
Iron Horse
Izzy's
Jack's
John's Grill
La Felce
Marin Joe's/N
Masa's
Morton's of Chicago
Occidental Grill
Presidio Cafe
Rotunda
Scoma's
Sears Fine Food
Tadich Grill
Vic Stewart's/E

Singles Scene

Ace Wasabi's
Backflip
Balboa Cafe
Beach Chalet
Betelnut Pejiu Wu
Biscuits & Blues
Bitterroot
Bix
Black Cat
Blowfish, Sushi
Blue Chalk Cafe/S
Bruno's
Bubble Lounge
butterfly
Cafe Bastille
Café Claude
Cafe Flore
Cafe Marimba
Caffe Centro
Charanga
Crepevine
Elite Cafe
Foreign Cinema
42°
Godzila Sushi
Gordon Biersch
Gordon Biersch/S
Gordon's Hse.
Guaymas/N
Hamburger Mary's
Il Fornaio/S
Infusion
Kuleto's

Los Gatos Brewing/S
LuLu
Luna Park
Magnolia Pub
Massawa
Mecca
MoMo's
Nola/S
Palace/S
Palomino
Park Chow
Perry's Downtown
Pier 23 Cafe
Pluto's
Pork Store Cafe
Postrio
Potrero Brewing
Prego
Primo Patio Cafe
Pyramid Alehouse/E
Sam's Anchor Cafe/N
Slow Club
Suppenküche
Sushi Groove
Thirsty Bear
Ti Couz
Timo's
Tokyo Go Go
2223 Restaurant
Universal Cafe
We Be Sushi
Zibibbo/S
Zuni Cafe

Sleepers
(Good to excellent food,
but little known)
Angkor Borei
Anton & Michel/S
Anzu
Applewood Inn/N
Ara Wan/N
Avanti/S
Battambang/E
Bittersweet Bistro/S
Cafe 817/E
Camranh Bay/S
Charanga
Charcuterie/N
Charlie Hong Kong/S
Chloe's Cafe
Cielo/S
Cin Cin/N
Clouds Downtown/S
Convivio Trattoria/S

Duck Club/N
Dusit Thai
Feast/N
Flying Fish Grill/S
Gabriella Cafe/S
Grandview/S
Grasing's/S
Grill on the Alley/S
Hana/N
Heirloom/N
Irrawaddy
Jakarta
Jocco's/S
Koryo/E
La Felce
La Palma
Le Bistro Cafe/N
Leford House/N
Linda's Seabreeze/S
Lucy's Cafe/N
Macaroni Sciue Sciue
MacCallum House/N
Maki
Manuel's/S
Marinus/S
Massawa
Matsuya
Maykedah
Mei Long/S
Moosse Cafe/N
Murasaki
Narai
955 Ukiah/N
Omei/S
101 Main Bistro/N
Osaka Grill
Oswald's/S
Palace/S
Pazzia
Pearl/N
Primo Patio Cafe
Ramen Club/S
Rosamunde
San Benito House/S
Sierra Mar/S
Stillwater B&G/S
Syrah/N
Tarragon/S
Taste Café/S
Thornhill Cafe/E
Willow Wood Mkt. Café/N
Yukol Place

Tasting Menu

Acquerello
Anzu

Applewood Inn/N
Aqua
Auberge du Soleil/N
Azie
Barcelona
Blackhawk Grille/E
Blowfish, Sushi
Cafe Tiramisu
Campton Place
Catahoula/N
Chapeau!
Charles Nob Hill
Chez T.J./S
Cielo/S
Club XIX/S
Cypress Club
Domaine Chandon/N
Elisabeth Daniel
Erna's Elderberry/S
Fifth Floor
First Crush
Fleur de Lys
French Laundry/N
Gary Danko
Hyde St. Bistro
Jardinière
Kasbah/N
La Folie
Lark Creek Inn/N
La Toque/N
La Villa Poppi
Le Mouton Noir/S
Le Papillon/S
Le Soleil
Madrona Manor/N
Masa's
Mikayla/Casa Madrona/N
North India
Ondine/N
One Market
Pacific's Edge/S
Paolo's/S
Pinot Blanc/N
Postrio
Prima/E
Rest. at Meadowood/N
Ritz-Carlton Din. Rm.
Roy's
Rubicon
Sent Sovi/S
Silks
Sonoma Mission Inn/N
Spiedini/E
Terra/N
Tommy Toy's
Wine Spectator/N
Zaré on Sacramento

Tea Service

(See also *Hotel Dining*; the following are highly touted)
Citizen Cake
Compass Rose
Dragon Well
Garden Court
Katia's
Lovejoy's
O Chamé/E
Ritz-Carlton Din. Rm.
Rotunda
Watergate
Yank Sing

Teenagers & Other Youthful Spirits

Barney's
Cactus Cafe/N
FatApple's/E
Gira Polli/N
Hard Rock Cafe
Max's on Square
Max's Opera Café
Max's Opera Café/S
Mel's Drive-In
Mo's Burgers
Planet Hollywood
Rutherford Grill/N

Teflons

(Get lots of business, despite so-so food, i.e. they have other attractions that prevent criticism from sticking)
Beach Chalet
Bubble Lounge
Buca di Beppo/S
Café de la Presse
Cafe Flore
Capp's Corner
Cliff House
David's Deli
Fuzio
Gordon Biersch
Gordon Biersch/S
Hard Rock Cafe
Kelly's Mission Rock
Left at Albuquerque
Left at Albuquerque/S
Long Life Noodle
Long Life Noodle/E
Mel's Drive-In
Moss Beach/S
Pier 23 Cafe

Planet Hollywood
Sam's Anchor Cafe/N
Spenger's/E
Stinking Rose
Tommy's Joynt
Wa-Ha-Ka Oaxaca

Theme Restaurant

Hard Rock Cafe
Napa Valley Wine Train/N
Planet Hollywood
Stinking Rose

Wine/Beer Only

Ace Wasabi's
Acquerello
Ajanta/E
Alamo Square
Albona Rist.
Alegrias
Alfy's/N
Alice's
Angkor Wat
Antica Trattoria
Aperto
Applewood Inn/N
Aram's
Arlequin Food to Go
Aux Delices
Avanti/S
Avenue 9
Baker St. Bistro
Baldoria
Bay Wolf/E
Bella Trattoria
Bistro Aix
Bistro Clovis
Bistro Ralph/N
Bistro Vida/S
Bitterroot
Blue
Blue Nile/E
Blue Plate
Bocca Rotis
Bontà Rist.
Boonville Hotel/N
Brandy Ho's
Britt-Marie's/E
Brother's
Buca Giovanni
Butler & the Chef
Cactus Cafe/N
Cafe Borrone/S
Cafe Citti/N
Café Claude
Cafe 817/E

Cafe For All Seasons	Flying Saucer
Cafe Jacqueline	Fook Yuen/S
Cafe Kati	Foothill Cafe/N
Café La Haye/N	French Laundry/N
Cafe Lolo/N	girl & the fig/N
Cafe Marcella/S	Glen Ellen Inn/N
Cafe Niebaum Coppola	Godzila Sushi
Cafe Torre/S	Gordon Biersch/S
Caffe Centro	Gordon's/N
Caffe Delle Stelle	Grandeho's Kamekyo
Caffe Greco	Grandview/S
Caffe Macaroni	Greens
Caffe Proust	Green Valley Cafe/N
Cambodiana/E	Hamano Sushi
Carta	Hana/N
Casa Aguila	Hayes & Vine
Celadon/N	Herbivore
Cha Cha Cha	House
Chapeau!	House of Nanking
Charanga	Hunan
Charcuterie/N	Hungarian Sausage
Chaz	Hyde St. Bistro
Chez Nous	I Fratelli
Chez Panisse/E	Il Porcellino/E
Chez Panisse Cafe/E	Indian Oven
Chez T.J./S	Insalata's/N
Chow	Isobune Sushi
Christophe/N	Isobune Sushi/S
Christopher's/E	Jackson Fillmore
Cin Cin/N	Jimtown Store/N
Citizen Cake	Jocco's/S
Citron/E	John Bentley's/S
Convivio Trattoria/S	Jojo/E
Crescent City Cafe	Joubert's
Cucina Jackson Fillmore/N	Juban
Delancey Street	Juban/S
Delfina	JZ Cool/S
Della Santina's/N	Kabuto Sushi
Dipsea Cafe/N	Kasbah/N
Domaine Chandon/N	Katia's
Dottie's True Blue	La Fondue/S
Dragon Well	Lalime's/E
Dusit Thai	La Mediterranée
E'Angelo	La Mediterranée/E
Ebisu	L'Amie Donia/S
Elisabeth Daniel	La Note/E
Eliza's	La Toque/N
Ella's	Le Bistro Cafe/N
El Paseo/N	Le Charm
Eos	Liberty Café
Eric's	Little Italy
Esperpento	Little Joe's
Feast/N	London Wine Bar
Firefly	Long Life Noodle
Firewood Cafe	Long Life Vegi/E

Los Gatos Brewing/S
Lotus/N
Macaroni Sciue Sciue
Madrona Manor/N
Magnolia Pub
Maharani
Mama's/Washington Sq.
Mama's Royal Cafe/E
Mandalay
Mangiafuoco
Mario's Bohemian
Mariposa/N
Marnee Thai
Massawa
Ma Tante Sumi
Matsuya
Meetinghouse
Memphis Minnie's BBQ
Meritage/N
Mescolanza
Michelangelo Cafe
Mikayla/Casa Madrona/N
Millennium
Mio Vicino/S
Miss Millie's
Moosse Cafe/N
Nan Yang Rockridge/E
Neecha Thai
Ne O
Nob Hill Cafe
North Bch. Pizza
North India
Northstar
Oak Town Cafe/E
O Chamé/E
101 Main Bistro/N
Osteria/S
Pacific Cafe
Pane e Vino
Parma
Pearl/N
Picaro
Pintxos
Pizza Rustica/E
Pizzetta 211
Plearn/E
PlumpJack Cafe
PlumpJack Cafe/N
Primo Patio Cafe
Pyramid Alehouse/E
Radicchio
Ravenous/N
Rick & Ann's/E
Rist. Bacco
Rist. Milano

Rivoli/E
Roosevelt Tamale
Rooster
Rose's Cafe
Royal Thai/N
Rue de Main/E
Sanppo
Savor
Sent Sovi/S
71 Saint Peter/S
Slanted Door
Spettro/E
Stelline
Suppenküche
Sushi Groove
Sushi Ran/N
Swan Oyster Depot
Syrah/N
Tapestry/S
Taste Café/S
Ten-Ichi
Terra/N
Terra Brazilis
Thep Phanom
Thornhill Cafe/E
Three Ring
Tomatina/N
Tommaso's
Ton Kiang
Town's End
Trattoria Contadina
Tropix/E
Tuscany/N
Uva/N
Valentine's Cafe
Via Vai
Vivande Porta Via
Voulez-Vous/E
Wappo Bar/N
Wente Vineyards/E
Willowside Cafe/N
Woodward's Garden
Yabbies
Ya-Ya Cuisine
Zarzuela
Zax
Zazie
Zin/N
Zinzino
Zza's Trattoria/E

Winning Wine List
Absinthe
Acquerello
Albion River Inn/N

Alfy's/N
Alioto's
Ana Mandara
A.P. Stump's/S
Aqua
A. Sabella's
Auberge du Soleil/N
Avanti/S
Azie
Bacar
Bacchanal/S
Balboa Cafe
Bay Wolf/E
Bella Vista/S
Big Four
Bistro Clovis
Blackhawk Grille/E
Boulevard
Brannan's Grill/N
Brava Terrace/N
Brix/N
Bubble Lounge
Cafe Kati
Cafe Marcella/S
Campton Place
Carnelian Room
Casanova/S
Catahoula/N
César/E
Chapeau!
Chateau Souverain/N
Chez Panisse/E
Chez Panisse Cafe/E
Chez T.J./S
Cole's/N
Cosmopolitan Cafe
Covey/S
Cypress Club
Dal Baffo/S
dalla Torre
Domaine Chandon/N
El Paseo/N
Eos
Erna's Elderberry/S
Fandango/S
Farallon
Fifth Floor
First Crush
Flea St. Cafe/S
Fleur de Lys
Fournou's Ovens
French Laundry/N
Gary Danko
Gaylord India
girl & the fig/N

Glen Ellen Inn/N
Greens
Hawthorne Lane
Hayes & Vine
Jardinière
Jianna
John Ash/N
Julius' Castle
Kenwood/N
La Folie
La Pastaia/S
Lark Creek Inn/N
La Toque/N
Le Mouton Noir/S
London Wine Bar
LuLu
Madrona Manor/N
Marinus/S
Masa's
mc^2
Meadowood Grill/N
Mecca
Meetinghouse
Millennium
Moose's
Mucca/N
Mustards Grill/N
Napa Valley Wine Train/N
North Bch. Rest.
Ondine/N
One Market
Oritalia
Pacific's Edge/S
Park Grill
Pearl Alley Bistro/S
Pinot Blanc/N
Pisces/S
Plumed Horse/S
PlumpJack Cafe
PlumpJack Cafe/N
Postrio
Prima/E
Red Herring
Rest. at Meadowood/N
Rist. Ecco
Ritz-Carlton Din. Rm.
Rivoli/E
Rose Pistola
Rubicon
Santi/N
Sent Sovi/S
Silks
Sonoma Mission Inn/N
Splendido
Stars

St. Orres/N
Sushi Ran/N
Terra/N
Tra Vigne/N
Tuscany/N
Uva/N
Vic Stewart's/E
Viognier/S
Wappo Bar/N
Wente Vineyards/E
Willowside Cafe/N
Wine Spectator/N
Zuni Cafe

Worth a Trip

EAST
Berkeley
  César
  Chez Panisse
  Chez Panisse Cafe
  Jordan's
  Mazzini
  Rivoli
Livermore
  Wente Vineyards
Oakland
  Bay Wolf
  Oliveto
NORTH
Albion
  Albion River Inn
Boonville
  Boonville Hotel
Calistoga
  Catahoula
Gualala
  St. Orres
Healdsburg
  Bistro Ralph
  Ravenous
Inverness
  Manka's Inverness
Larkspur
  Emporio Rulli
  Lark Creek Inn
  Left Bank
Mendocino
  Cafe Beaujolais
Napa
  Celadon
  Mustards Grill
  Napa Valley Wine Train
Rutherford
  Auberge du Soleil
  La Toque

San Anselmo
  Alfy's
  Insalata's
Santa Rosa
  John Ash
Sausalito
  Ondine
Sonoma
  Café La Haye
St. Helena
  Rest. at Meadowood
  Terra
  Tra Vigne
  Wine Spectator
Windsor
  Mariposa
Yountville
  Bistro Jeanty
  Bouchon
  Domaine Chandon
  French Laundry
SOUTH
Big Sur
  Sierra Mar
Burlingame
  Pisces
Carmel
  Marinus
  Pacific's Edge
Half Moon Bay
  Pasta Moon
Menlo Park
  Wild Hare
Monterey
  Fresh Cream
  Tarpy's Roadhse.
Mountain View
  Amber India
  Chez T.J.
Oakhurst
  Erna's Elderberry
Palo Alto
  Spago Palo Alto
Pebble Beach
  Roy's at Pebble Beach
Pescadero
  Duarte's Tavern
San Jose
  A.P. Stump's
  Emile's
  Le Papillon
Saratoga
  Le Mouton Noir
  Sent Sovi
Woodside
  John Bentley's

Young Children
(Besides the normal fast-food places; * indicates children's menu available)

Alioto's*
Anzu*
Aqui/S*
A. Sabella's*
Autumn Moon Cafe/E
Avanti/S*
Barney's*
Beach Chalet*
Bette's Oceanview/E*
Bighorn Grill/E
Bill's Place*
Bistro Viola/E
Bittersweet Bistro/S*
Bocca Rotis
Brava Terrace/N*
Brazio/E
Bubba's Diner/N*
Buckeye Roadhse./N*
Buck's/S
Cactus Cafe/N*
Cactus Taqueria/E*
Cafe Marimba*
Cafe Riggio
Caffe Sport
California Cafe/N*
Capp's Corner*
Casanova/S*
Casa Orinda/E
Chez Panisse Cafe/E*
Chow*
Club XIX/S*
Convivio Trattoria/S
Coriya Hot Pot City
Covey's/S*
Crow's Nest/S*
Deuce/N*
Dipsea Cafe/N*
Duck Club/S*
E&O Trading
El Palomar/S*
FatApple's/E*
Faz/S
Felix & Louie's/N
Firewood Cafe*
First Crush*
Frascati
Garden Court*
Ginger Island/E*
Gordon Biersch*
Gordon Biersch/S

Harbor Village
Hard Rock Cafe*
House of Prime Rib
Hyde St. Bistro*
I Fratelli
Il Fornaio*
Il Fornaio/E
Il Fornaio/S*
Insalata's/N
Isobune Sushi
Italian Colors/E*
JoAnn's Cafe/S
Jordan's/E
JZ Cool/S*
Kuleto's Trattoria/S
La Ginestra/N*
Lark Creek/E
Lark Creek/S*
Lark Creek Inn/N*
Left at Albuquerque*
Left at Albuquerque/S*
Left Bank/S
Little Joe's*
Livefire/N*
LuLu*
MacArthur Park
MacArthur Park/S
Marin Joe's/N
Max's Diner
Max's on Square
Max's Opera Café
Max's Opera Café/S*
Mazzini/E*
Meadowood Grill/N*
Mel's Drive-In*
Mikayla/Casa Madrona/N*
Mixx/N*
Montrio/S*
Mo's Burgers
Moss Beach/S*
Napa Valley Grille/N*
New Pisa*
Nola/S*
Nonna Rose*
North India
One Market*
Pacific's Edge/S*
Palomino*
Park Chow*
Pazzia
Perry's Downtown
Piatti/N*
Piatti/S*
Picante Cocina/E
Planet Hollywood

Pluto's
Pluto's/S*
Puccini & Pinetti
Red Tractor Cafe/E*
Red Tractor Cafe/S*
Rick & Ann's/E*
Rick's
Ricochet
Rio Grill/S
Rutherford Grill/N*
Sam's Anchor Cafe/N*
Sand Dollar/N*
Santa Barbara Grill/S*
Saul's/E
Savanna Grill/N
Savor*
Schroeder's
Scoma's*
Scoma's/N*

Scott's/S*
Skates on the Bay/E*
Spettro/E*
Splendido*
Station Hse. Cafe/N
Stokes Adobe/S
Tapestry/S*
Tarpy's Roadhse./S*
Taste Café/S*
Tomatina/N
Tonga Room*
Tortola
Venezia/E*
Vic Stewart's/E*
Yoshida-Ya*
Zao Noodle Bar*
Zao Noodle Bar/S*
Zza's Trattoria/E

ALPHABETICAL PAGE INDEX*

---

* All restaurants are in the City of San Francisco unless otherwise
noted (E=East of San Francisco; N=North of San Francisco; and
S=South of San Francisco).

NOTES

NOTES

NOTES

Wine Vintage Chart 1985-1998

This chart is designed to help you select wine to go with your meal. It is based on the same 0 to 30 scale used throughout this *Survey*. The ratings (prepared by our friend **Howard Stravitz**, a law professor at the University of South Carolina) reflect both the quality of the vintage and the wine's readiness for present consumption. Thus, if a wine is not fully mature or is over the hill, its rating has been reduced. We do not include 1987, 1991 or 1993 vintages because, with the exception of cabernets, '91 Northern Rhônes and '93 red Burgundies and Southern Rhônes, those vintages are not especially recommended.

	'85	'86	'88	'89	'90	'92	'94	'95	'96	'97	'98
WHITES											
French:											
Alsace	25	20	23	28	28	24	28	26	24	25	24
Burgundy	24	25	19	27	22	23	22	27	28	25	24
Loire Valley	–	–	–	26	25	18	22	24	26	23	22
Champagne	28	25	24	26	28	–	–	24	26	24	–
Sauternes	22	28	29	25	26	–	18	22	23	24	–
California:											
Chardonnay	–	–	–	–	–	24	22	26	22	26	26
REDS											
French:											
Bordeaux	26	27	25	28	29	18	24	25	24	23	23
Burgundy	24	–	23	27	29	23	23	25	26	24	24
Rhône	26	20	26	28	27	15	23	24	22	24	26
Beaujolais	–	–	–	–	–	–	21	24	22	24	23
California:											
Cab./Merlot	26	26	–	21	28	26	27	25	24	25	26
Zinfandel	–	–	–	–	–	21	23	21	22	24	25
Italian:											
Tuscany	27	–	24	–	26	–	–	25	19	28	25
Piedmont	25	–	25	27	27	–	–	23	25	28	25

Bargain sippers take note: Some wines are reliable year in, year out, and are reasonably priced as well. They include: Alsatian Pinot Blancs, Côtes du Rhône, Muscadet, Bardolino, Valpolicella and inexpensive Spanish Rioja and California Zinfandel and are best bought in the most recent vintages.